OF THE SHEER DEPTH AN[...] ADVENTURES
[SU]RROUNDS. FROM THE IN[...] OF THE SLATE
[...]S, VIRTUALLY POSTCARDS[...], THE EDGE."

[R]EALLY DIDN'T SEEM TO AFFECT HIS PRODIGIOUS TALENT FOR
[M]OVEMENT, ADDED TO A DRIVE AND DETERMINATION COUPLED

[THROU]GH YEARS OF NEGOTIATING THE OLD ROCKS, AND THROUGH
[...] BURNING PASSION AND HOPE IN THE UNKNOWN … AND YET,
[SO]METHING ELSE THAN A DANCER THAT READ THE ROCK, MORE
[...]S AND CONCRETE. ANDY IS STILL IN AWE, STILL A PLAYFUL,
[LI]VE AND TO LOVE." ★ JOHN REDHEAD ★
[...] WHEN WAS THAT NOT ONLY WAS I MEETING A BRITISH 'ROCK
[RO]CK STAR', MICK JAGGER! YOU FITTED THE BILL PRETTY WELL
[JUS]T LIKE GOOD OLD MICK! THE MICK JAGGER OF ROCK CLIMBING

[A]ND ENDOWED WITH THE BOUNDLESS ENTHUSIASM OF YOUTH.
[...]ON – ANY GENERATION. NOW MY CLIMBING PHOTOGRAPHY
[THA]T ARE DICTATED BY THE ROUTE AND THE ROCK, NOT SOME
[...] LET ME TRY TO GET THE BEST BODY SHAPE AS IT HAPPENED.
[BE]AUTIFULLY AND NATURALLY – GOD'S GIFT TO CLIMBING

[DR]OPPED OFF AT PEN TRWYN THAT SUMMER AFTER HITCHING
[A]LL THE PEOPLE WHOSE PHOTOS I'D PINNED TO MY BEDROOM
[...] THAT I REALLY WAS WALKING UP THE MARINE DRIVE WITH
[...R]Y MOFFATT!" ★ BEN MOON ★

[ANT]ED VERDON GORGE. GLANCING AROUND WE SOAKED IT UP;
[L]EE, BASHER AND GORE ANIMATING THEIR PROJECTS AND
[...] RIGHT IN THE MIDDLE – GUITARS, LIE-INS, LYCRA, BEER AND
[...]NE HEROES AND FRONT-COVER STARS, FAR TOO BIG FOR US;
[...]D TO DRIFT INTO US. WE CLIMBED HARDER, BETTER, FASTER

[...]AND LLANDUDNO. FOR ME, IT'S NOT JUST THE ROUTES (SOME
[...]HE FUN INVOLVED … I REMEMBER THE FIRST TIME WE MET
[...], BUT YOU WERE BOTH SO SHY." ★ RON FAWCETT ★
[...]O DO IT OR WHAT?" ★ JERRY MOFFATT ★

Punk in the gym

4

Punk in the gym

ANDY POLLITT

Punk in the gym

Published by Vertebrate Publishing, Sheffield.
www.v-publishing.co.uk

First published in 2016 by Vertebrate Publishing.
Distributed in Australia and New Zealand by Andy Pollitt.

Vertebrate Publishing
Crescent House, 228 Psalter Lane, Sheffield S11 8UT, UK.
www.v-publishing.co.uk

Photography and illustrations Andy Pollitt Collection unless otherwise credited.

This book is a work of non-fiction based on the life of Andy Pollitt. The author has stated to
the publishers that, except in such minor respects not affecting the substantial accuracy
of the work, the contents of the book are true.

A CIP catalogue record for this book is available from the British Library.

ISBN: 978-1-910240-69-4 (Hardback)
ISBN: 978-1-910240-70-0 (Ebook)

10 9 8 7 6 5 4 3 2 1

Design and production by Nathan Ryder.
Vertebrate Publishing. www.v-publishing.co.uk

Vertebrate Publishing is committed to printing on paper from sustainable sources.

Printed and bound in the UK by T.J. International Ltd, Padstow, Cornwall.

CONTENTS

FOREWORD by MIKE OWEN

You know how it is.

You've been bumbling along for a couple of years, steadily working your way through the grades. You're quietly proud of your achievements and you feel like you're almost up there with the best, though you're not quite brave enough to try the hardest routes or take a look at those obvious blank spaces. Not yet: you've got loads of time and you'll do them sometime, maybe next year.

Then you start hearing rumours – there's a 'new kid on the block'. You've not met him, but your mates have. They tell you that he's really young (a spotty-faced youth still at school) and pushing himself really hard; so hard that he doesn't care much for traditions and grades and so on. It doesn't take him long to become the best. It actually takes you a few years to catch him up, but then only for a short while.

That's how it was with Andy Pollitt. We come from the same part of North Wales and both started to climb at Craig y Forwyn. Our paths soon crossed; we became good friends and climbed together several times during the next few years. By the summer of '82 Andy was climbing full-time, ticking off the big routes. I recall meeting him in the Vaynol Arms, just after he'd made a very early ascent of *The Cad* on North Stack Wall (a cliff that would become a very special place for us both). That route was a pretty audacious thing to do in those days – a fantastic effort. Secretly though, I was so envious!

Early the next year Andy came to live with us for three months, working with me at Blacks in Liverpool. Despite being such a dismal place to work it was a chance for him to earn some cash to keep him going awhile. We spent every evening talking about climbs or going to Pex Hill (where I could often sandbag him or burn him off!). Andy would often talk about The Brotherhood of the Bell and would burst out into fits of laughter when describing what you had to do in order to join.[1] Not surprisingly, there weren't many members.

---

1 The Brotherhood of the Bell … John Redhead recalls, July 2015: 'It was Paul "The Tick" who coined that phrase! I remember a few of us including "The Crook" in (homoerotic) Parisella's, thrusting and gurning like apes. Ah, imagine that now … impossible! What the hell went on with the '80s? The old Plas y Brenin climbing wall had a traverse and the problem finished in the corner by the doors where there was a pocket – the final move involved urinating into it. This was an initiation into the "Brotherhood" – fancy that these days … ! PC horror!'

Living with us enabled Andy to supplement his usual biscuit diet with Elaine's healthy cooking: dishes such as her legendary tuna bake, which she claims was the reason for his meteoric rise to fame! In April we went to Gogarth and Andy led a very early repeat of *Blackleg* in fine style – seconding that gave me the inspiration to go on to lead *The Cad* next weekend. Andy's enthusiasm and motivation were extremely contagious – soon we both started dreaming of leading *The Bells, The Bells!* We bounced ideas around and motivated each other – thought anything was possible with the right planning and psych. The rest is history: Andy showed the way and made the second ascent of this bold and difficult route in 1986. When I made the third in 1990, Andy phoned to congratulate me. Such a nice thing to do!

Andy moved to Sheffield where he became one of the first sponsored climbers, working closely with Berghaus and Scarpa. Who could forget that advert showing him on *Strawberries*, complete with pink Lycra, long greasy hair and several days' stubble? During that period he put up countless hard climbs in the Peak and also back on North Wales limestone and at Gogarth, always using his unique vision and creativity to produce something special. Andy's climbing career culminated in an ascent of that famous Arapiles testpiece *Punks in the Gym* in the early 1990s – soon afterwards he moved permanently to Australia to pursue a very successful career in vertical access work.

Those three intense months we spent together have had a very profound and everlasting effect on me. Thanks to the 'new kid on the block' I got so much closer towards realising my dreams. It's a great honour to have been asked to write a few words for Andy's autobiography.

Mike Owen, September 2015

EDITOR'S PREFACE

by

ANDY BOORMAN

Following an intensive period of climbing with Andy Pollitt in the late 1970s and early 1980s, first as his mentor then he as mine, Andy's performance rocketed stratospherically into a different universe – but we always kept in touch, even after he left the UK to live in Australia. My son Ian moved to Melbourne in 2010 where he married Sarah, a local girl, in 2011. Andy P was invited to the wedding – I even got him on a climbing wall and then used Pete Bailey as bait for Andy's first visit to a crag in nearly two decades. Pete and I hadn't met up with Andy since the early 1990s, but our visit triggered a flow of reminiscence about his years of climbing; hence this autobiography.

Andy always wore his heart on his sleeve – he still does and forever will. Throughout this book Andy recounts events with charm, humour and panache; he writes with clarity and real depth of feeling in his own unique and forthright style, all of which the editor has endeavoured to preserve (although in some cases words or even names have been omitted or changed to protect the innocent – or was it the guilty?). As a climber he had terrific raw talent, incredible enthusiasm and tremendous drive, using all these attributes to leave a brilliant legacy of high-quality routes, both trad and sport, in the UK and Australia. Despite his addictive personality, and at times somewhat outrageous lifestyle, the achievements of this truly gifted young lad from Dyserth, North Wales, rivalled those of his highly talented contemporaries.

Andy Boorman, September 2015

PROLOGUE:
A ROUTE TO
DIE FOR

No.

It *didn't* hurt.

In fact, there wasn't any pain at all. I guess my body had pumped out a flood of endorphins and other natural painkillers and I was gazing up rightwards through one bloodshot eye coz I'd landed face down, slap bang amongst the boulders beneath North Stack Wall. Geez, those barnacles are sharp – especially when you hit 'em from ninety feet. The little bastards had cleaved off the whole left side of my youthful face – *and* my left arm – and I saw my right leg flick over my right shoulder as I bounced on landing, only for it to splash down in a little rock pool and lie there twitching grotesquely in its cute rainbow tight.

And poor Mark, my housemate, friend, and climbing partner on that day, was left writhing around in his own agony having thrown out his arms in a brave but vain attempt to 'catch' me. Both limbs broken – as was his spirit – as he crouched there white as a ghost in floods of tears sobbing ... 'No, no, ahh fuck, no!'

And that was the last thing I ever saw – as the tide started running back in.

☆ ☆ ☆

Thankfully not all bad dreams come true. That tepid water washing over my broken and dying body was actually me wetting the bed in sheer terror.

This was many, many years later. Alone, terrified and immersed in a gnarly and uninvited recollection in my little flat here in Melbourne, Australia. Semi-comatose and now *seriously* pissed at four in the morning.

The dream was a flashback to 1986 ... I'd been bottling out of an on-sight due to a horribly burst fingertip pissing blood – making a desperate attempt to reverse the upper headwall of Britain's first E7 'chop' route: John Redhead's *The Bells, The Bells!*

Were it not for a complete and utter fluke – my left foot touched upon a little edge, about half the size of the narrow end of a matchbox, that I'd missed on the way up – my nightmare scenario would've been fact.

It was *that* close.

PART ONE:

THE POLLITT BUREAU

Welcome to ...

    ... The Pollitt Bureau. Being such a modest young man I've always called my book thus. I think the publisher renamed it for some reason or other.

    At last! You've found me – floundering here in the 'Reduced to clear' bin, so thanks for forking out the 35p (70c for Aus./NZ version), let's go ...

1.

THE POLLITT BUREAU

It had been nearly twenty years since I'd last uttered the 'C' word – in any of its tenses. Climb, climbed, climbing, climber – coz I'd 'cut my hair and got a real job' back in 1993 and emigrated to start a new life amongst the concrete and glass skyscrapers and huge tower cranes of Melbourne, Australia – as far away from any mountains as one could get.

Then a few years ago I arrived home from work to find an Australia Post 'Failed Delivery' note lurking in the mailbox.

So I took the little card down to the shops and signed for a neatly wrapped package – with *British* stamps on it. Back at my house, carefully prising open one end, out slid a copy of Jerry Moffatt's *Revelations*.

Ah, my old mate Jerry, he's written a book, how clever! He'd always maintained he was 'dystellic' and couldn't 'stell'.

Inside the cover was written: 'To Andy', then a lovely personal message, and 'Cheers, Jerry'.

I was truly touched and, though smiling broadly, a tear came to my eye (sentimental old fool Andy).

So I read it. Loved it. Laughed my head off at his tales of our early North Wales limestone and Tremadog adventures. I 'understood' and 'got' it; particularly seeing as this was one of my best-ever friends – got sweaty palms, the lot, egging him on up *Phoenix* in the USA, then back on home turf at the Leeds '89 competition final. Eventually, due to failing eyesight and starting work three hours later, I just had to put the book down at 3 a.m. – but finished the read on the following afternoon whilst shedding another tear, or two, and wallowing in a warm blanket of reminiscence; smiling and shaking my head in joy, mouthing, 'Jerry, Jerry, Jerry. You legend.'

I'd go on to reread *Revelations* many times.

For the first time in two decades I felt a connection to that long-forgotten climbing scene.

That last line took you a millisecond to absorb but please just think about it for a moment: Two decades ... is **twenty** ... ... **years!** *An extremely long time 'between drinks', but yes, I was disconnected – by my own, deliberate choosing – and it was only when murmurs of me writing my story did the rounds that clients, suppliers and 'industry folk' who I've dealt with for twenty years had even the slightest inkling that 'apparently' I once used to 'be someone' – 'someone else'.*

Transported back in time to a period in my life that I'd well and truly tucked away in the back of the sock drawer ... a period which started when Pete Livesey's *Right Wall* on Dinas Cromlech at E5 was one of the hardest climbs in Britain. Then E6, E7, E8 and E9 came along – all of this I was there to witness and play various bit-parts in. Not just brilliant times in the world of rock climbing but truly dynamic and historic. I was there when sewn-tape quickdraws first arrived, Rocks and Friends, RPs, boots other than EBs, female climbers en masse – and then sticky rubber, protection bolts and redpointing, home-made boards and climbing competitions – and there when the first-ever rudimentary bouldering mats began replacing folded jumpers and rucksacks.

There when Ron Fawcett was top dog, having dethroned Pete Livesey; around when 'The Ron and Jerry Show' was just unfolding – Jerry later to surpass Ron, only to suffer the same ignominious fate himself when young Ben Moon's talent came to fruition. There when *Crags* and *Mountain* magazines were at their best and during the brief life of the climbing newspaper we all called 'Mountain Worms' – a very South-West-biased effort.

Thus Jerry, as usual, had started a trend amongst his contemporaries: Johnny Dawes came out (should I rephrase that?) with his 'interesting' *Full of Myself* and I found it somewhat amusing how they put my ugly mug in both books. 'Leaning' on Jerry in his, and 'leaning' on Stevie Haston in Johnny's. Did I do that a lot – lean on people? I was always comfortably tactile in that way – with the few whose camaraderie and friendship I so trusted and cherished.

Ron soon published his historic memoirs and I guess the resurgence in retrospectives (and climbing books in general) kicked me into gear. Then I discovered *UKC, Chockstone, YouTube* and *Vimeo* – so could watch *actual footage* of the old stomping grounds. Bleedin' 'eck, even a few of my own routes! *And,* I got to read what all those people had written about me since the internet sites were started over a decade ago. It was just plain, fucking weird! 'Hang on,' I thought, 'they're talking about *me!*' And, as if I'd carked it years ago – and of course I was well too late to post any replies.

Generally speaking (well, reading), I was rather touched by the genuine fondness folks wrote with regarding 'Andy P the climber', and some of the glowing testimonies regarding various routes I'd put up or repeated were, well, simply heart-warming. I wasn't sure about the [paraphrased] 'Pollitt was a nut-job' quote from XXX, or YYY's reply to 'Whatever happened to … ?' being: 'He picked on a route he couldn't do, chipped it and quit!' (Even though it was qualified with an apology a bit further on.)

So I went out to the garage and fished out my box of old climbing diaries. Logbooks that my schoolteacher 'Mr Boorman' had suggested that I start … way, way back in 1978.

Reminiscence awakened, flashbacks of real clarity: I needed a personal project outside of Vertigo High Access – something for 'me'; so I nicked some pens and A4 pads from the stationery cupboard and …

It's all twaddle you say? … but it's *my* twaddle and I'm sticking by it. So even if you did only pay 35p (or 70c in Aus./NZ!) please press on and stay with me …

If nothing else I hope you have a giggle courtesy of a now-middle-aged-aholic, in both work and play, whose life these days is a never-ending merry-go-round of meetings with super-wealthy property developers and their architects, engineers and construction companies – a fairground ride which I thrive on. Most evenings after work are best enjoyed with a few beers, maybe a wine, and – until as recently as late 2014 – the nightly 'happy' pill.

And another crap night's sleep … 'G'night.'

Please don't expect too much though, the following pages aren't a Moffatt/ Grimes or Fawcett or Moon by Ed Douglas – I don't have their famous or world-class routes or achievements to write home about (I've saved thou-sands in stamps) and **these words**, almost without exception, are my own. You may just have to scratch your head a little later, going 'Yer what Andy?' when attempting to decipher my Dawes piece, although I do prefer to write in simpler terms than Johnny.

I most certainly don't have the word-smithery or artistic flair of John Redhead, coz all the rock climbs I ever did were simply that: rock climbs. They weren't 'fields of savagery' – I wasn't that imaginative; nor were they even close to dissecting say, the Bayeux tapestry and fingering its soft, delicate folds – a bit moist that undercut slot – whilst edging across some desperate traverse a hundred feet above the deck with only one poor runner at ten feet and nothing else (in Chouinard Canyons for heaven's sake).

'Bitch Slap' (or should I name it 'The Bleeding Slag'?). First ascents. Both oil on canvas and complete with prosthetic pink phallus.

I was a kid when JR and I first met; let's face it – he was my sort of hero and role model. Best climber on the North Wales coast and Jerry and I thought we had him measured – but we didn't, no way!

I wore the Ron Fawcett Union Jack woolly hat for a while, but it caused a fair bit of grief in deepest Welsh Wales and JR was always so cool in his Helly Hansens and black belt. Carried his gear on a bandolier, so, of course, would I.

Bitch Slap. A bitch of a slap for the sloper by the third bolt. Fair enough.

Bleeding Slag. That little, red, iron-rich stream running out of the Welsh slag heap on the back road out of Bethesda.

John loved toying with innuendo in his route names and many thought him sexist and a misogynist. Well, not being female myself I can't answer that, but from what I recall he most certainly wasn't and the women were drawn to his cool, 'sexual' persona. I rarely got a look in when we were together … and I was the single one!

The above is not a 'cheap shot' at John, definitely not. We're all aware of his masterful paintings (if not, how come?) and he writes brilliantly and has a unique charisma – always did – and I hold him in the highest possible regard – particularly now, twenty-five years 'after the fact', where we are back in contact via the interweb thingy – and the painting I commissioned, which he duly undertook and sent me in a hard tube from France, is a prized possession. A copy of his terrific book, *…and one for the crow*, too, complete with lovely personal message. Memories of the new routes we shared – *The Disillusioned Screw Machine, The Bloods,* same-day *Fingerlicker Direct* and *Sheer Resist,* then *Birth Trauma* and *Art Groupie* – all remain permanently etched in my mind, as are the welcomes received on numerous occasions into his and (then) Gretel's household back in the early eighties.

Stuck in the middle. With Dave and Sa at Walden Cottage.

2.
FLEEING PRIESTS
AND THE SWEEP'S BOY

Born at Chatsworth House Nursing Home in Prestatyn, North Wales, on 26 October 1963, I was raised at Walden Cottage on Upper Foel Road, Dyserth – the highest of the roads traversing the lower flanks of Moel Hiraddug. Spectacular northerly views drew the gaze beyond rolling rural greenery towards patchwork coastal plains, out across the resorts of Rhyl and Prestatyn, then onwards to the grey-green Irish Sea. The outlook way off west featured Llandudno's Ormes and the jagged heights of Snowdonia – two places where a large chunk of my future lay in wait.

Dyserth was a small village – but thriving. It had a large quarry with a quaint miniature train that took high-quality dynamited limestone via an iron bridge above the High Street to the crushers and kilns, there to be pulverised into gravel and baked into powdered lime to make cement products. Whilst I don't recall the quarry employing too many men, it was (apart from farming) a major local employer.

We had our primary school – Ysgol Hiraddug, a draper, ironmonger, baker, greengrocer, butcher, post office, chemist, barber, fish and chip shop, doctors' surgery and veterinary clinic. A library, police station, numerous pubs, a little cafe at the famous waterfall, two banks and an off-licence with a stainless-steel cigarette vending machine on the outside wall. Inside they sold tins of ale (all unrefrigerated of course), providing that your dad wanted either Guinness or Double Diamond, and wine for the ladies – two types, a red one and a white one, and Pomagne for special occasions. There was a petrol station, a few motor mechanics and a builder-cum-electrician/plumber, all dotted about amongst various little general stores, and – of course – the usual supply of churches and Welsh chapels.

The old piggery had been forced to close when foot-and-mouth-disease visited the district and all the animals had to be slaughtered and burned. Stank the village out for days, but before long the piggery was hosed out and back up and running – as a **food** depot! The proprietors were Jack 'The Cake' Dean and his business partner John Poole. Jack gave Justin Smart and me a few hours' work in the evenings, reloading the vans when they returned from daily deliveries. Payment was some broken bickies, or an out-of-date cake to take home for our families, no matter whether we worked two hours or six.

Justin was my classmate who lived at Tirion Cottage, a house just along the road – almost identical to our Walden. His father, an architect, had designed us both similar cottage extensions, but along with his wife he lost his life in the Stockport air disaster of 1967, leaving Justin and his brother Simon and sister Susan orphaned; the entire village was seized with shock and grief.

When school broke up for summer holidays we both ended up on the daily runs around the seaside towns or inland countryside; payment for the entire summer was twenty pence a day – one pound per week. I asked Jack if he'd please save it up for me and give it to me at the end of the season – lest I fritter it away – and so finally he owed me a fiver. He gave me six pounds, rumpled my hair with that friendly – I don't know what you call it – but that 'thing' where you open your hand and go 'wiggle, wiggle, wiggle' on a kid's head (you know the one) and then said I could grab some chocolates from the 'market shed' as well. Three Milky Ways for little sister Lizzie, some Fruit Gums for big brother Dave – he loved them – and a packet of McVitie's Jaffa Cakes and Jacob's Fig Rolls for the biscuit tin.

'Is this too much, Jack?' I asked, showing him.

'Nah, go on.'

'Ooooh, thanks Jack.'

Five weeks' work. Six quid and all these treats. Proud as punch me when I got home for tea!

Milk was delivered daily on an electric float, the bottles left at the doorstep where the birds would peck through the foil tops and pinch the cream. Coal was carted in by dust-black men hauling great sacks over their shoulders, and the round metal bins were all carried similarly then emptied into the open side of a cart by the dustmen. For several years my brother David was the 'upper' village paperboy. Once in a while a rag-and-bone man wheeled a rickety, timber cart around by hand, crying out, 'A … E … I … ' (any iron) as he trudged along. Most summers when the 'gyppos' and 'tinkers' and their caravans were passing they'd come knocking to sell you clothes pegs they'd whittled from sticks.[1]

Charming, innocent and unsophisticated times indeed. Crime was virtually unheard of in Dyserth and we kids would be out playing footy and climbing trees or whatever – often well after darkness had fallen, me only ever in my trusty wellington boots.

I don't think I was *ever* late for tea either. Mum had this 'call' you see. I always told her which general direction I was going – the playing fields, the old quarry we called Ghost Canyon (where in the future I'd go on to lead a bold new route I called *Genesis* having put in a home-made peg near the top), or to the woods, or down to the waterfall and the limestone cliffs and caves up the back.[2]

I'll never forget. I was eleven years old and went for a picnic with a tiny little schoolgirl friend of mine the same age. We sat by the stream underneath what is now the Dyserth Waterfall Crag. She told me something truly bizarre: if she went somewhere it was crucial to go back precisely the same way. Otherwise it's a 'bad way'. I felt exactly the same! Only in the back of my mind though, but how weird was that? Anyone?

Anyway, Mum's call. She'd simply put her open palms either side of her mouth, point herself in the right direction, take a deep breath and call 'Aaaaandrooooo' with a little upturn in the intonation for the 'oooooo' bit. Honestly, she had the audible accuracy of an Exocet missile! If I was playing goalie she'd land it right between the posts and the defenders wouldn't even have heard a thing. Bit like penguins returning to land I suppose?

Our mum wasn't a disciplinarian by any stretch of the imagination, but she did insist we all sit at the table together for our evening meal. No ducking off to watch telly, eating off our laps; no way. 'That's common,' Mum would say. She'd turn on our (highly collectible, I know now) Richards wireless, rotate it on its swivel base for best reception, and play BBC Radio 2 (though we were allowed *Pick of the Pops* on Radio 1 over our Sunday roast).

However, things were to 'head south' for Dyserth: on the morning of 11 February 1972, our school and immediate surrounds were deluged in stones when a quarry blast went awry. Rocks came crashing in through the classroom roofs and we all scrambled beneath our desks. It could have been carnage, but miraculously only a few children were affected by cuts and grazes.

---

1 *Editor's note*: It's more usually 'Romani' now Andy, although in British law the term 'Gypsy' is often still used.

2 *Editor's note*: Ghost Canyon is nowadays bolted up as Castle Quarry Slab, with *Genesis* – the best route on the crag by far – going at F6b+ (*North Wales Limestone*, 2014).

That incident was the catalyst for the quarry's later demise – though they did cart out the huge mounds of gravel to use for road building (the ones I used to scramble up) before laying off the workers and padlocking a meaty chain across the gates.

Walden, our place, was originally three quarrymen's cottages, later knocked through and extended. A hundred-odd years earlier the landowners would offer small plots on their estates to the labourers. Get four walls and a roof up and if there's smoke coming out of the chimney in the morning 'it's yours'. Apparently that was the arrangement. The walls were up to four feet thick, made from roughly hewn rocks stacked all higgledy-piggledy, but at least they'd been repointed sometime in the past. Great exposed timber roof beams with hundred-plus-year-old meat-hanging rails and wattle and daub ceiling beneath Welsh slate tiles. It still leaked terribly and was draughty as heck, but it was home. The title deed was on actual parchment and had a majestic red wax seal. We had what Mum told me (winding me up no doubt and feeding my youthful imagination) was most probably a priest hole – a throwback to the sixteenth century Protestant Reformation when Jesuit priests were persecuted! Dad had ripped out an old fireplace insert – one of those precast concrete fire-place-shaped things – and there it was: a concealed chamber between the walls. Enough for an adult to crouch in and iron rungs running all the way up the vast chimney above. Must be for the sweep's boy I figured, as I could never imagine how a fleeing priest would fit through the six-inch, T-shaped clay pot plonked on top. An arm out of each wing and head poking out the top – spluttering from the soot? How very Laurel and Hardy.

For some unknown reason I was a slightly 'troubled' child – Mum even took me to see the doctor once in an attempt to figure out my odd behaviour. Perhaps the telltale signs and the early onset of the 'condition' I'd go on to develop in the future? You see, I'd sometimes fly into a rage for no apparent or logical reason. I had a loving mother, two sisters and a big brother I looked up to (not that I'd ever really show it) – a totally stable family life, with Jack as a surrogate father figure (no connection to Mum!) and a big garden to play in. A few particular memories remain with me to this day, but doubtless there's at least as many I've forgotten where I lashed out, unprovoked, at David. We had a big ornamental copper kettle that sat on the 'tumpty' – a little brick ledge on one side of the lounge room fireplace. One day I grabbed that kettle and swung it with all my might; David's knee took the full brunt of the blow, which sent him crashing to the floor in agony, clutching his leg, the kettle dinted terribly. I fled and scrambled up the 'big' tree where he couldn't get me. Another time I threw an apple-sized rock at him – it hit him square in the guts. I was halfway up my tree by the time I heard his yelp: 'Ow! You're dead you little bastard!'

We had a five-foot snooker table in our bedroom, and one day Dave's friend Steve was over to play a round-robin tournament. I called Steve on a foul shot – he denied it, so I spun my cue around and whacked him with the thick end; dazed him enough for me to leg it and get back to the safety of the upper boughs of my tree – Dave and Steve screaming blue murder at the base of the trunk. 'Come on up then, ha!' I mocked, edging further out along a spindly limb. I figured (well, hoped) they'd simmer down, coz I couldn't stay up there all day but was surely in for a battering if I came down too soon.

Our Dad was always working away, but was earning ridiculous money for the time: it wasn't long before we had a 'new-fangled' electric immersion heater installed, so Mum didn't have to get a fire going in the mornings in order to heat the water for us to wash our hands and faces before wading through the snow to school ... luxury, and the local plumber even replaced the old lead pipes with copper ones. I still needed to traipse to the village regularly to get paraffin for the heaters though, as the immersion only fed the downstairs taps and we had no radiators. Always spent the 1d. (big old penny) change on a bag of Black Jacks, Fruit Salads or Golf Balls from the 'little' shop coming home though. Mum never minded.

One week Mum bought a new washing machine – a modern one complete with a wringer; the following week an electric upright Hoover and we could even warm and dry our clothes in the Flatley – a tin-clad dryer about the dimensions of a standard domestic fridge, with a row of thin timber slats about an inch apart which rested in little slots down both sides.

And that was when I lost my father. I was five years old. He'd survived active service during World War Two: North Africa, Egypt I think, but was cruelly taken from us in the prime of his life – dragged off down a disused London Underground tunnel ... by a yeti. Dead-set true the above, but somehow he'd managed to escape because he made it back home to North Wales on the train where we all awaited his arrival on the station platform in Prestatyn, dressed in our smartest clothes and brightly polished shoes. Daddy would have presents for us children in his suitcase, so his return was doubly exciting, but all I really wanted to know was how he'd escaped ...

A year or so later Daddy had returned to London: I was then six so had an inkling that my father's apparent brave escape wasn't quite all it was cracked up to be ... and sometime later I lost him for good: no, not on an expedition to some far-flung remote territory – he wasn't an explorer, it was, of all places, in a labyrinth of potholes deep beneath the nuclear research facility on Wenley Moor. Sent down there by 'The Brigadier' on night watch or something.

You see Mum had gathered us children together in front of our little black and white telly and twiddled the knob to BBC1 coz *Dr Who* was about to start, and Dad was going to be in this episode too. Baby sister Elizabeth cooing in her cot, sister Sarah and brother David old enough to know it was only acting, and me at that 'believe anything' age in-between. Totally scared, I urged him to go back, but to no avail and he was zapped by that pesky Silurian – a hideous creature best described as part man, part lizard and part fish – who spoke English FFS! The penny really should've dropped then …

I was mortified, Lizzie just made baby noises and Sa and Dave laughed their heads off.

Anyway, Dad was propping up the bar in the Rovers Return on *Coronation Street* a week later and shortly after was fleeing the 'rozzers' on *Z-Cars* then giving prophetic advice to 'The Cap'n' on *The Onedin Line* as 'Mr Pilgrim'. Amazingly, a plasterer mate of mine here in Melbourne told me recently that his dad was the 'wobbly' set carpenter for the BBC at that time!

Our Dad's problem was that he loathed and detested television acting – he was a highly accomplished RADA (Royal Academy of Dramatic Art) graduate; a stage actor (like his brother Clyde in the Royal Shakespeare Company) and only wanted to 'tread the boards' in theatre, so continually knocked back the lucrative TV work. Suffice it to say, within a short while his agent dropped him, so the offers stopped coming in and the strain – with a wife and four children to support – was obvious on my parents' marriage. He remained down in London, sharing his brother's flat in Wimbledon, out of acting work virtually throughout my entire teens, and one day I finally had to accept that he simply wasn't coming back.

I saw him twice, perhaps three times, over the following fifteen-odd years, but it was always awkward, plus he'd never call or write. Thankfully, my sisters lived near him by this time and were both extremely close to their father; and my brother, having taken on the 'man of the house' role until leaving for university in Aberystwyth, kept an eye out for him too. Derek Frank Pollitt slipped me fifty quid and wished me well the final time we ever met. It was the eve of my first flight to Oz (to anywhere actually) and I was staying at Sarah's place over in Kilburn. Parting ways and turning the first corner I hopped into a public phone box to let Sa know I'd be at her place in twenty minutes but ended up saying 'about two hours', as I'd plucked one of the 'business' cards – the ones the working girls left poked into the sides of the (not) scratchproof Perspex sheet across the area codes – and ended up getting **way laid**.

Thanks Old Man: ' …'stralia here I come.'

Day one at Craig y Forwyn, with Trevor Cotterill. **Photo:** Martyn Carr.

3.
RUGBY, A THIN RED LINE
and
RESPECT ONE'S TEACHERS

Yes. Rugby. That was what got me into *real*, proper rock climbing in the first place ...

'Rugger' – as we called it – was the sport reserved for the wealthy private school boys, wasn't it? Children whose parents dropped them off in Rolls-Royces and picked them up in Jaguars. Our school only had what I now fondly appreciate as an old 1930s art deco coach. All hand-crafted timber trim and beautifully upholstered interior and a massive diesel engine that was more 'in' the bus than under it. The engine cover was next to the driver's seat – yes, *inside* the vehicle – so it always smelled of burning oil, but the heat it generated was a godsend during our bleak Welsh winters.

But rugby was really out of place at Prestatyn High School (Ysgol Clawdd Offa at one time, but that name's now been adopted by a local primary school) – we were a soccer school, had a team in the county league an' all. We didn't 'do' rugby round here. *Na, nac oes* and *dim*: that was more **South** Wales and England. Our rugby-loving PE teacher for that day, Mr Hurst, was not our usual football one, and I wondered why he was in the gym dressed in full waterproofs, woolly gloves and a scarf: this didn't bode well and I needed a 'scheme'. Quick smart.

'Uniforms off, boys!' he bellowed in his best authoritative voice, so it was down to Marks and Spencer's string vest (much too small) and Everton footy shorts (much too big).

'Aww ... my mum's mixed up the washing again sir, sorry.' I had little sis

Elizabeth's top on and was scrunching up the waistband of older brother David's shorts so they wouldn't fall down. Somewhat embarrassing really: being such a very small skinny boy for my age, my sporting attire just accentuated my size – or lack thereof.

That day, like many during our Welsh springs, was bitingly cold – and outside it was worse: the goalposts had been enveloped by the blizzardly excuse for weather. Whilst running laps around the sports hall as a warm-up to the inevitable purgatory awaiting outside, I spied down the far end a recently arrived new teacher; he was a tall, thin man with thick, black-rimmed glasses: it was Mr Boorman.

I'd learn years later that he'd moved down from a private school position near Carlisle in the north-west of England. It was to be a return nearer to home for his wife Ann – one of a clutch of attractive Anglesey-born Welsh sisters he'd met during his teacher training degree days in Bangor – and an escape from the endless wet cliff faces of England's Lake District. They both were going to be happier in Prestatyn.

Mr Boorman was wearing a tracksuit and a pair of gym shoes like I'd never seen before – there he was, climbing back and forth across a funny brown brick wall. 'Funny' in the sense that it appeared to have some bricks pushed in and others sticking out and great big concrete ledges all over the place: Ah … ! For practising rock climbing on I realised, not that I'd ever seen anyone on it before.

Apart from not wanting to go outside and chase an odd-shaped pig's bladder around in the sleet, I had developed a bit of a thing for scrambling up the many limestone outcrops and disused quarries around Dyserth, Meliden and Prestatyn: it just felt like a perfectly natural and challenging thing for me to do.

Earlier, and in my child's mind – I would've been about ten years old at first – I pretended this was what 'proper' mountaineering must be like, except the real mountains were covered in snow. I'd seen the news on TV when Chris Bonington's expedition was going to scale Mount Everest, so I was being 'Chris' in my own happy, innocent little world.

Interestingly, looking back now from my fifties, it's obvious I preferred my own company as a young child and could occupy myself perfectly well with being outside – in all weather – and not in front of the telly watching *Jackanory* or *Blue Peter* like my classmates probably were. Maybe it was divine intervention, I don't know (we'll come to that), but I'd spend every summer evening after primary school and my depot duties wandering around the little rocks by myself – I had regular 'circuits' I'd do (in my wellies, mind) and would attempt virtually anything that looked even remotely possible.

When winter hit and the mountain we lived on was waist-deep in snow, I'd be 'Chris on Everest' … with a broken old wooden spade handle for an ice axe, numerous layers of pullovers, my brother's thick 'fishing socks' (he'll kill me), a woollen balaclava Mum had knitted for me and my cagoule on top to feel 'the part'. I'd trudge and struggle up the longest, steepest and most difficult slopes I knew; pick my route carefully and weave left and right between enormous swathes of shale bands to eventually break through the snow cornice at the summit ridge where my little red face was blasted with freezing snow, then struggle like all heck against the blizzard till I reached the summit and the little flag I'd placed there on my previous ascent.

Knowing Moel Hiraddug like the back of my hand, I knew there was a sheltered spot on the lee side of the summit (869 feet above sea level) and about two hundred yards from my flag, so I'd grip the shaft of my spade handle, kick my wellies into the soft snow and back myself down the steep slope until wind and snow were howling horizontally across above my head at a 'hundred' miles an hour. Mum had mentioned something about Bonington having to dig a snow cave to survive in, so being absolutely exhausted that's just what I did …

And promptly sat in it feeling really proud of myself …

For about three hours!

Till I got really bored …

'What day is it?' I pondered. 'Tuesday! Yes! It's mince on Tuesdays – my favourite.' So I exited my snow hole and slid, tumbled and ran back home in case I got into trouble for being late for tea.

You can't do that on Everest.

Climbing mountains and the local outcrops was so much more fun than the trees (which I'd virtually lived up as a kiddie), many of which had clusters of rusty old nails banged into their trunks – someone had been up there before …

Now all this was despite the many **Danger: no entry** signs around the quarries and warnings from parents, teachers and generally all around the village about such dangers – a schoolboy had recently fallen to his death trying to reach a bird's nest looking for eggs to blow. A young lad from down the road still wasn't perturbed – even after having witnessed the death plummet – and went back to try again, but returned home in floods of tears having found his little buddy's missing ear at the foot of the cliff.

Anyway, I digress.

We were in the sports hall so, jogging up to Mr Hurst, I inquired whether I could 'Please go and try that,' pointing towards the new teacher. 'I guess so Andriw,' emphasising the 'i' in his strong Welsh accent. 'If Mr Boorman allows it.'

And Mr Boorman *did* allow it, and the rest of the class were herded outside and I clambered left and right and right and left for the remainder of the hour on 'inny' holds and 'outy' holds.

'Not above the red line though, you could get hurt.'

'OK, sir.'

And my pumps were better than wellies and I got to dip my fingers into gymnasts' chalk, 'For a better grip, young master Pollitt'.

'Thanks, sir,' I squeaked.

Asked Mum if I could please have some chalk instead of pocket money next week.

'I need it Mum … I'm going to be a rock climber.'

It was April 1978 – I was fourteen and a half years old, and about seven and a half stone! (That's about 48 kilos in Oz money.)

☆ ☆ ☆

Oh, the 'divine intervention' I mentioned earlier – could the following even be questioned?

Being born and raised *where* I was and *when* I was:

Dyserth, North Wales, October 1963, growing up in the '60s and '70s on a steep mountainside surrounded by limestone crags that I was in my element scrambling over, and well before I even knew rock climbing existed.

Prestatyn High School, with quite possibly the first-ever indoor climbing wall in North Wales – how's that?

Mr Hurst, the stand-in teacher for that Single Fated Hour of a life-changing PE class, who simply smiled kindly at me amongst a hall full of jogging boys and said, 'yes Andriw, you *can* ask Mr Boorman'.

And, of course, Mr Boorman, the tall, skinny new teacher with the specs and funny white-powdery hands who said 'yes' too.

If my stars weren't aligned at *That Very Moment* on a filthy, wintery morning in 1978 inside a non-descript school hall in a non-descript town in North Wales, shivering in my siblings' ill-fitting clothing, I may never have gone on to …

… suggestions on the back of a fifty please.

Prestatyn High School Mountaineering Club. I'm back left, with (L–R) Trevor Cotterill, Chris Jones, Brian Connelly, Dave Prendergast, Ian Jones. Front (L–R): John Worsley, Andy Boorman, Martyn Carr. **Photo**: John Worsley.

A. SCHOOL'S OUT

Mr Boorman had collared support from on high in the form of Martyn Carr, a former missionary turned RE teacher; they managed to secure a modest slush fund from an interested school bursar, John Worsley, and set up the Prestatyn High School Mountaineering Club: classmate Dave 'Prendy' Prendergast (still around on the local climbing scene today), myself and perhaps five or six others put our hands up; but within weeks the numbers had swelled.

We took minibus trips out to Snowdonia – Tryfan, the Snowdon Horseshoe, the Glyderau, Cwm Idwal and Crafnant. Brilliant days and fantastic, strenuous walks; always with great packed lunches and flasks of hot tea or soup from Mum. One day, whilst descending alongside the Milestone Buttress in the Ogwen Valley, Mr B asked, 'Hands up who'd like to try rock climbing, like those people over there?', pointing at the bright red and orange helmets dotted about the rock face. And a few of us did, and he took us, and it was brilliant; I loved it, and couldn't wait to do it again. *Soon.*

Soon it was. Winter was long and dark and wet and cold as usual. 'Andy' (permission had been granted: 'But only outside school.') and his wife Ann now had young Chris, so Andy was loathe to venture out too far or too often with a new baby at home. Even so, we managed to climb virtually every line along the left-hand side of our nearest crag, Craig y Forwyn, plus grab an hour's traversing (I'd only just learnt the name for it) on a Tuesday or Wednesday during my PE lesson or after last class.

Most of the left-hand Forwyn routes were Very Difficult to HVS. With much encouragement and tuition – plus a fair amount of pleading on my behalf – Andy soon had me leading the VS routes and I could follow him up the HVS lines without falling off. One of Andy's great attributes was spotting nut placements or finding natural threads – particularly important on my belays at the top if he was seconding – and he taught me all about load-sharing and backing up. We both had one of those new 'Sticht plates' – the ones with a nine-millimetre and an eleven-millimetre slot and the big spring on the back. Our racks back then were basically MOACs and a range of clunky hexes on loops of kernmantle rope tied in a double fisherman's with the ends 'leccy-taped' up: a sort of colour and identity coding. We also had 'baby' MOACs on wire, a few Chouinard Stoppers, Clog karabiners from Joe Brown's and half a dozen Troll tape slings. This was just a year or so before the first Rocks appeared, a couple before the early rigid Friends made their commercial debut, and ages before decent rock shoes, RPs and (eventually) reliable protection bolts.

Little did I know that within a year I'd be leading regularly on the E1s and 'softer' E2s.

My final year at school was interminable. Hated it. It was 'option year' where we had a choice of preferred subjects. In the sciences it was either physics or chemistry; for craft skills it was wood or metalwork, and for languages German or French. I opted for French coz the teacher was a soft touch: thought I was a lost cause and disruptive to the other kids, so pretty much allowed me to read *Hard Rock* or *Climb!* or Gaston Rébuffat or Doug Scott down the back of the class, so long as I'd just shut up and stop throwing scrunched-up paper balls at him when he was writing on the blackboard, or stop tugging on Sara D's ponytail who sat in front of me. I looked forward to those three hours of French a week, marvelling at the words and pictures in my climbing books, desperate for my education to end.

Paradoxically, it was only a few years later I'd end up at Fontainebleau, Le Saussois, Buoux and the Verdon Gorge, and could barely recall more than bonjour, merci, and the hackneyed 'silver plate'!

Eventually the term passed. I didn't follow Sarah or David into the sixth form. Mum agreed I was no academic – never going to be. Thought I'd do something on the 'creative' side she said – whatever that implied?

'OK Andrew, you **can** leave but you **must** get a job and contribute towards your upkeep.'

'OK Mum, I will.'

Justin, from along the road, had an uncle who worked for the leisure company Trust House Forte in Rhyl and thanks to him we ended up as 'key boys' in the penny amusement arcade on the fairground, unjamming little old ladies' coppers from the one-armed bandits (I always slipped 'em a few extras back) and literally shovelling the pennies out of the 'penny falls' and 'wheel 'em ins' into wheelbarrows twice a week for counting. Had the keys to the safe, where the float was never less than twenty thousand pounds. Cash.

I was working on a new North Wales limestone guide for Dark Peak throughout this period, so going to the Ormes and Forwyn at every opportunity after work – at first with Andy B or Tim Freeman, but then mostly with Pete Bailey – repeating or soloing obscure routes and updating the descriptions when I got home. My publisher, Geoff Birtles, of Stoney Middleton and *Crags* fame, even popped over from Llanberis with his wife and child one day when they were down holidaying from Sheffield. Ooh, made my day that! 'Dead famous climber him,' I told the girl in the cashiers' cubicle as Geoff left. 'Chris Bonington?' ... 'Oh, never mind,' (shakes head).

This is how Geoff recalls the encounter, in a delightful email I received in April 2015:

> I first met Andy Pollitt in an amusement arcade in Rhyl in 1980 when he was a mere sixteen-year-old boy. I was publishing and editing *Crags* magazine at the time and this young man from North Wales was sending me material of new route activity on North Wales limestone, and asked me if I would consider producing a guidebook; this initiated me into a period of book publishing.

> Before I made this publishing leap I wanted to meet Andy in the flesh, so whilst my wife and baby sat in the car I met this affable young climber amongst the one-armed bandits. He was bursting with enthusiasm, which would do for me. He was like many other teenagers – a little puffy in the cheeks with a haircut that fell out of the sky – but I liked him and we became friends from that day on ...

It was high summer and I was a greenhorn, surrounded by gorgeous, tanned, holidaymaking girls – loads of 'em. From Liverpool last week, Stoke this week and Glasgow or wherever the next, for the entire twelve-week summer season.

Not only was I introduced to the delights of alcohol (more on that prickly subject later) but I misplaced my cherry somewhere in the previous paragraph (about where Geoff Birtles was talking just a minute ago, ha!) and now had powerful urges competing with my desire to climb. Was it out all night drinking and chasing the girlies, or early to bed and picked up by a bunch of big, hairy old blokes in a teeny-weeny car at seven? Miniskirt or Mini Clubman? I was a teenager (with a permanent hard on) for Chrissakes, what was I **expected** to do? Invariably it'd be both, but being shoe-horned into the back of Andy B's little car and driven rally-like over to the Pass, Gogarth or wherever – studiously flicking through the guidebook in anticipation as we all bounced and swayed about – was surely as exciting as life could get. Certainly more gripping than our funfair's roller coaster!

Andy Boorman puts quill to parchment:

We were proper keen in those early days but, what with my work and a young family, our climbing had to be limited to one day each weekend plus a couple of sessions on the school's 'brick wall' after work, or up at Forwyn once springtime evenings arrived. During my first year or so climbing with Andy P he became my main partner, game for just about anything and amazingly enthusiastic – I don't think I've ever met anyone, before or since, who tried so blinking hard – heart, soul and vocal chords into every difficult move! In some ways, being such a cautious climber myself, I probably held him back; but then again, this very fact may just have kept him alive …

Clutching our 1976 copy of *Climbs on North Wales Limestone* we set about checking out as many routes as we could, rapidly progressing through the grades at Craig y Forwyn, soon exploring the more exciting and less accessible crags on the Ormes, and escaping further afield whenever time and weather permitted. I too have kept detailed diaries and these serve well to catalogue just a few examples of Andy's remarkable journey from his first time on a 'real' rock climb when aged fourteen:

Sept '78 Bochlwyd Buttress, Ogwen – led AP up four routes including the superb *Wall Climb* Hard Severe.

Oct '78 Craig y Forwyn, led AP up *Pterodactyl* HVS and he led *Arian* HS. As soon as he turned fifteen it was an HVS trip to the Llanberis Pass for Carreg Wastad's *Cornix* and the Grochan's tough little *Wind*.

Feb '79 Three months later and it's AP's turn to lead me up *Pterodactyl*, then he seconds *Mojo* E1 and does first ascents of *Hairline* VS and *Arian Direct* HVS at Forwyn.

May '79 AP leads *Mojo* E1 and by autumn he's sixteen and we're swinging leads at Tremadog on E2s such as *Integral*, *Extraction* and *Grasper*; and at Gogarth it was *UFO* and *Nightride*.

March '80 AP hits the headlines with his foray on to *Mayfair* at Pen Trwyn, but back in the real world we're soon leading through on Lakeland's classic *Deer Bield Buttress* (years before it fell down!) and scaring ourselves on Pavey Ark's fine E2 *Astra*.

July '80 We swing leads on Castell y Gwynt's classic E4 *The New Dimension*, thinking (mistakenly) we'll be making the first free ascent! That afternoon Andy P effortlessly leads me up Forwyn's *Great Wall* … a second hard climb in a day proves a bridge too far for me: fell off on the traverse and used a point of aid higher up, couldn't bend my arms for a week!

Feb '81 Andy's seventeen and trying to lead *Right Wall* E5 on Dinas Cromlech whilst Pete Bailey and I shiver down below, but it's too cold and a bit damp so AP reverses back down. I'd now joined Pete and Andy on their Saturdays out because I'd got a little over-enthusiastic with the 45 bhp of my little red Clubman estate – picked up three endorsements and got a six-month ban.

Oct '81 We're ploughing excitedly through Pat Littlejohn's then-current Pembroke guidebook and also trying a bit of new routeing. Our most memorable effort was what Andy dubbed *The Candlestick Maker*, which unfortunately turned out to be a non-starter as – although a superb on-sight tour de force up a very steep part of St Govan's Head – it proved to be merely a hybrid of two Nipper Harrison E3/4s climbed a few months previously (and thus not in the guidebook!).

April '82 Andy accompanied us on the second of what were to become the legendary (in some quarters at least!) Bolton Tech Verdon Gorge minibus trips, most ably organised by Mick Quinn. On this occasion the team comprised Mick, Dave Hollows, Dennis Gleason, Mick Lovatt, John Monks, Joe and Gaz Healey, Pete Bailey, AP and me. It's maybe wise that much stays unrecorded, however one notable event of the trip (and excellent learning experience for AP and PB) was their ascent of the classic 400-metre boltless off-width jamming/bridging/squirming crack system known as *ULA* – unfortunately it was rather warm and they had the customary late start, a long traditional approach via Le Sentier Martel and its tunnels along the base of the Gorge, just one small bottle of water, no cams larger than two-inch and a dearth of chalk. Inevitably they were quite late back and looked somewhat parched!

By summer's end we'd done that superb Cyrn Las E4 *The Skull*, he'd shown me the way on Cromlech's *Right Wall* and then led me up *Barbarossa* on Gogarth (still had a pro peg back then, so 'only' E6, not the E6/7 it gets now). Thenceforward we didn't climb together much – Andy had left me in his wake; but thanks to him I'd begun to realise what was needed to succeed on hard-ish routes and, in the company of my new regular climbing partner Pete Bailey, managed my own lead of *Right Wall* in the brilliant summer of 1984 – that meant a great deal to me. Thanks Andy – thanks Pete! And thanks to Mrs P for understanding … I mean, a twenty-eight-year-old teacher and his fourteen-year-old pupil … could be tricky these days?

☆ ☆ ☆

School was now well out of the way but that mountaineering club Andy B had set up with the generous assistance of the bursar Mr Worsley had been one heck of a 'godsend'. We had met many other people over at Forwyn and some great friendships were developing. I know as I write this that these names may mean nothing (to either of you readers) but by the end I hope they'll all fall into place, perspective and context.

Tim Freeman. A year older than me, lived near Llandudno. Mousey fair hair, slim yet powerful as all-heck, but could rarely be bothered.

Pete Bailey. Hirsute in the neatly trimmed beard department and simply one of the most genuine, sweet men I've ever met. Denise Bailey too (err, as a woman I mean). Whilst Pete and I had occasionally bumped into one another when I was out with the school climbing club or with Tim, it wasn't until August 1980 whilst sharing the tree belay on *Vulcan/Falcon* at Tremadog that we'd actually introduced ourselves. It turned out Pete – originally from the Stoke area – lived only minutes from me in our little Welsh village and I'd unknowingly seen Denise, Pete's wife, walking their lovely three-legged dog many a time. Pete and Denny invited me around one evening and I don't think I've ever laughed so much, even to this day. A couple of bottles of Grolsch definitely helped.

Pete Bailey takes up the tale:

I first chatted properly to Andy at Tremadog and discovered we actually lived in the next road to each other … I'd been drifting along on easier routes, so teaming up with Andy opened my eyes to a much harder world of climbing.

Andy was keen to go out in any conditions – in December 1980 we abseiled into a crag on the Little Orme with the intention of freeing *Midnight Blues* of its aid points; it was very cold and very damp (ideal really!). The route was first done in '74 by Rowland Edwards with five points of aid – Andy managed to eliminate four of them, a brilliant effort considering the conditions. I still treasure the photo Andy shot of me prussiking out looking freezing cold and totally gripped.

Andy helped me to see what you could do with masses of drive and determination. These days I don't think many people are abseiling into the Little Orme in December to try and free aid points from routes. It was no use saying, 'slow the fuck down Andy', because this was the 'Dyserth Dipstick' – a man possessed! Over the next few years we did a lot of great routes together …

Moonwind Direct at Craig y Forwyn is a particularly brilliant route, it's a shame there are access issues there at the moment. And watching Andy climb *Great Wall* in his bare feet, and then soloing it, was really quite something in the early 1980s!

Andy became a force to be reckoned with in British climbing – single-minded and driven to be up with the best.

Then there were Pete's mates:

'Hot' Henry Clover. Henry left the scene after a while to study dentistry and he was a real loss to the local cragging community. His mum Frances typed the manuscript of my guidebook so I could send it to Mr Birtles all neat and tidy.

'Necky' Norman Clacher. All bulging biceps and big curly dark hair, and '80s 'porn mo'. In very short shorts. Norman worked night shifts, climbed all day and is still going strong as I write this.

Mike Owen and his mate *Huw Watkins.* Both regular E2 leaders (crikey!) and Chris Lyon who had the sports shop in Llandudno and whose mum was the mayor of the town (Dave, his brother, wasn't around so much back then, but would go on to great things a year or two later, and later, and later …), and a smashing chap called J*** who always had his teenage daughter T*** with him. Oh my God, Oh my God, Oh my God. I was totally smitten.

She was stunningly beautiful and I always tried to look cool when she was at the crag. I fumbled my words when trying to talk to her, so flexed my biceps and made sure I was leading something harder than her dad was – and where she could see me.

Pete and Andy used to tease me mercilessly (in jest of course) and suggest I strike up a conversation again next time they were there – doubtless all 'in the know' of 'Dad'. 'Psssst … Hey J***, you've noticed our Andy's smitten with your daughter?' Grown-up-speak kind of thing, but they must've moved or something coz they stopped coming.

I was crushed over a girl, truly – my first time; but then managed my first rest-free lead of the big roof on *Freedom*, and immediately got over the heart-break. Fickle, huh? She truly was a beauty though.

Yeah, there were lots of lovely people around that bustling local scene back then – before the crag got banned by the farmer; but within any crowd there's always *one* who stands out, isn't there – for whatever reason, and is simply …

Jerry and me outside the Tremadog barn in 1980. Look at the difference in our heights!

5.
SPECIAL

... *special*. To me it was that Jeremy Moffatt boy, so I suppose he deserves a mention ☺. Same age, boarding at St David's College in Llandudno. Taller than me, but most of that was his mop of curly hair. St David's and our school's climbing club outings often coincided at Forwyn, so Jerry and I saw each other quite regularly. We soon agreed to climb together. We'd hitch-hike or cycle to Forwyn (where the farmer still kindly allowed us two entry to the main cliff) and also to the Ormes – to Pen Trwyn, where we made our joint first-mark on the scene and got our names in the magazines by 'freeing' (in our own way) the old A2 aid route *Mayfair*, me the first pitch and Jerry the next.

In retrospect that route was pivotal to both our progressions and our desires to tackle things seemingly miles beyond us – there were hundreds of better climbers around, but they obviously hadn't *seen* the line or felt its magnetism. I had though. Jerry had been miffed with me on arriving at Pen Trwyn that cold day on 16 March 1980, a week before his seventeenth birthday, to stand beneath what he thought from my phone call would be an easy romp. Four hours later we were both grinning and ranting as we walked back down the Marine Drive.

'That line of old bolts to the left next time Jez?'

I very nearly freed that line to the left sometime later, but was beaten to the first free ascent by Mel Griffiths and Leigh McGinley when they nipped over from Llanberis to produce their excellent *Axle Attack*. Another old Rowland

Edwards aid route *Oyster* deserved a look, but I needed a point of aid crossing the bulging roof with Tim, although I'd freed ninety-nine per cent of it.

Over the next year or so Jerry and I'd camp or doss (in some godawful places, believe me) and climb till dark. Heat up a pan of baked beans on my Camping Gaz stove and throw in some cheese. Dessert was out-of-date cakes or biscuits from the depot in Dyserth – earned in lieu of wages.

One morning we awoke bitterly cold in the old concrete look-out post on the tip of the Great Orme, having the previous evening walked the whole way around carrying massive packs, ropes and two carrier bags of stale cakes and crisps. Jerry decided we should hitch south to the Avon Gorge in Bristol – we'd seen a recent article in *Crags* and a route called *Think Pink* which looked desperate. Reckoned the weather would be better down south, plus his older brother Simon was at uni there and he wanted to catch up. We arrived that evening within an hour or two of each other, stashed our packs in a little stone hut and made the strenuous stroll up to Clifton town for fish 'n' chips and pizza – our first proper meals in ages.

Simon met us and showed us around a bit, but I felt I should do the right thing so left the brothers to their own devices and went for a wander. Sitting outside a cafe having a brew and a ciggie, a rucksack was suddenly dumped on the footpath next to me with that all-too-familiar sound of karabiners clanking – out the corner of my eye I caught sight of ropes strapped to the pack. Looking around, its owner and I immediately recognised each other.

'Oh! You're Andy Pollitt aren't you?'

'Yeah, and you're Chris, err … Brear, right?'

We'd met a year or so earlier. Maybe Forwyn or Tremadog, and it was particularly nice to see him again.

'A few of us meet at the pub every Tuesday [or whatever the evening was] – come along around seven, it's just down that street and around the corner.'

So while Jerry was out with Simon I got to meet many from 'The Bristol Scene'. I cannot be 100 per cent sure that it was all that evening coz Chris had told me of a cafe climbers used to frequent too, which Jerry and I subsequently visited. Either way, I met Arnis Strapcans – delightful chap, Steve Findlay (the *Think Pink* cover shot star) and Steve Monks, their hardest climbers, plus several others, and had a terrific night. Steve Monks was actually compiling the new Avon guide for Dark Peak at the same time as I was doing North Wales limestone, so we chatted and compared ideas – both wondering whether Mr Birtles would come good with our commissions (he did!).

Jerry and I did a few routes during our brief visit, including *Think Pink* (which he led) and we both free-climbed (on a top rope and with rests of course) the partially-aided *Pink Ginsane* to its left, then hitched off – he to Leicester, me to North Wales – for our first baths and shaves in weeks and some decent home cooking from our mums.

We both really were climbers now and making our first inroads into the harder stuff.

Jerry following the first pitch of *Mayfair* on our first free ascent.

6.
TWO OF THE GREATS

The Great Zawn on the Little Orme is undoubtedly one of the most atmospheric amphitheatres along the entire North Wales coast – I always felt a heightened sense of trepidation when half scrambling, half sliding down the steep grassy approach to the sanctuary of The Meadow where we'd dump our sacs and gear up. The earlier routes were mainly the work of Rowland Edwards, as were pretty much most climbs on the Ormes, but it was such a pity how quickly the sea grass would reclaim the top pitches of the lines once they'd been manicured and climbed (these pitches are now left in peace as it turns out this 'sea grass' is pretty rare and is now protected).

If one could assign gender to a piece of rock I'm not too sure which way I'd go with this place. While the cliff is smooth and delicate in the nether regions – as if freshly waxed, the aura is somewhat more masculine and 'blokey' above 100 feet, and after only days of regrowth you'd often as not be scratching your way up through the stubble. 'Hairy' – in more ways than one – is perhaps the best description for this face. It really needed traffic, and plenty of it, but climbers stayed away in droves.

I recall one keen local spending five long days on abseil unearthing, pruning and mowing the 'lawn' that had consumed the near 600-foot *Rabble Rouser*. Unfurling great thick mats of turf only to discover Edwards' rotten old pitons which hadn't seen the light of day for over a decade. But these easier and more vegetated routes were not on my list, I was after the steeper Extremes – the easier 'veg fests' would need a good dose of Napalm or a weekend working-bee with a few dozen navvies all abseiling in unison from new stainless steel anchors, peeling back the vegetation and trowelling off the earth. Give me the clean, bare rock (and eventually the queues!) on the lower pitches of *Quietus*, *The Glass Wall* and *Old Sam* – three sensational low- to mid-grade Extremes in that fabulous and atmospheric setting.

One evening, after a monster day at Forwyn, Pete Bailey and I abseiled into the Great Zawn, pulling our ropes down after us – only to immediately realise the error of our ways. It simply wasn't possible to squeeze a four-hour route into one hour of rapidly diminishing light. This was clearly an epic in the making – the watery sun was fast dipping beyond the horizon and the light was fading. Someone, a while later (we never found out who), had called the Llandudno Coastguard who'd promptly rallied the troops and sent out a rescue boat, which duly sped into the zawn 200 feet below us. Perhaps they'd spied the flickering of my lighter as I tried to spark up a fag at half height? The mountain rescue chaps had also been scrambled and were presently making their way over the headland to offer assistance and a rope from above – we gleaned all this via the loudhailer from below …

It would've made sense to simply abseil from the stance directly into the little dinghy bobbing around beneath us, except the belay was my left hand jammed in a crack, plus the pathetic, rusted-out remnants of an old peg and a wild cabbage stalk out to one side. Taking in Pete's ropes one-handed was problematic to say the least – thankfully he needed no tight or we would've been screwed. Yet it was thanks to those cabbages (and my lighter) that we managed to get ourselves out of there in one piece.

'Whaddya think grade-wise?' I asked a most-relieved Pete at the top.

'E Veg 5c,' Pete reckoned.

One lovely evening at Craig y Forwyn – around that time – I wandered off from Pete and the others (I really didn't fancy being third up a route I'd down-soloed many times) and went to look for mine and Jerry's old boulder problems beneath *Scalar* wall – and also the one we'd seen John Redhead do but I still hadn't (Jerry and Tim had, naturally). John's problem was a direct start to *Quickstep* pulling over the first roof – but on the little holds not the big ones. *Quickstep* itself was (Still **is**, I keep thinking **was** as if it's evaporated! It hasn't, nor has it fallen down. The landowner's just not very keen for you to enjoy it, that's all.) … where was I – oh yes, *Quickstep*; a Pete Livesey-freed route that took (**takes**, grr!) the prominent, overhanging ninety-foot arête that separates the classic corner and roofs of *Freedom* and *Mojo* from his other stunning Welsh free route, *Great Wall*, which rears up just around the corner. Unfathomably, neither of these superb Welsh classics –

GW in particular – were mentioned in his posthumous biography.

I got John's problem first try and was dead chuffed, so, rather than stepping left and reversing the polished and slip-offable layback start to *Mojo*, I swung around the arête to traverse downwards across the bottom of *Great Wall* to get off. Before I knew it I was forty feet up the route. This was the climb that barely eighteen months earlier myself, Tim, Mike Owen and Huw Watkins had all failed (appallingly low down) to top-rope, though of course I had led it many times by this point and mostly without falling off. I think my 'flash rate' was about 6:1, so this was most certainly not a 'given'. Nevertheless, this time I was at the shake-out at the big, long pocket at half height – the one with the sinking hand jams and good footholds and the obvious thread and 'Friend'-ly crack – when another local, Keith Simpson, wandered past below.

'Shit, Andy, what are you doing boy, can you hang on? I'll just run round the top.' Figuring a rescue rope mightn't be a bad thing in case I got much more pumped or chickened out, I stayed there shaking out for what felt like an age … when Keith *finally* arrived, thirty feet away and up over my right shoulder in the bushes at the top of *Demolition*, he just pulled out his camera, twiddled his focus and called across, 'OK, I'm ready'.

'Well bugger me!' I thought. 'Thanks for nothing Keith!'

I'd lost my rhythm and he'd pricked that little bubble we all get into when we're on form and in the zone – so it became a case of, 'Shit – I've got to start *thinking* now,' as autopilot had been very much switched off.

There are a few pretty dynamic moves on the upper half of *Great Wall* so I decided just to go with what my young head knew: that move above the bolt ten feet from the top in particular – I never liked that one. Being a short-ish young kid I'd only ever done it in a barn-doory 'catch the flake on the way past' kind of way, and with the bolt below it never really mattered if I caught it or not. Now solo, I considered the more static though harder sequence Jerry had shown me, but scared myself when something in my head refused to allow me to commit. Unroped, eighty feet above the ground, telling myself **out loud**, 'pull yourself together!', I reverted to the tried and trusted barn-door move. And know what? It was one of the worst executions of that move I'd made in a long time (bar the falls obviously). Dreadful! Barely caught the layaway you swing into, which in turn made the reach for the finishing holds that little bit trickier.

So, considering this little escapade started when I'd managed Redhead's boulder problem ninety feet down below and needed to get off and back down to rejoin Pete and crew, I suppose – for the soloing to the shake-out where Keith discovered me – I very much *was* 'getting off'! As for the upper half?

I can only suggest I 'got off' once more, but perhaps somewhat lightly – given the delay and untimely break in concentration. I can't recall whether Keith actually took a rope up as I never called for one, so who knows?

Pete turned quite pale (and went very quiet) when I raced down the descent gully and told him – still pumped-up and thrilled – that I'd just soloed *Great Wall*. I thought he'd be impressed – I'd just turned eighteen after all so was 'technically' no longer in his charge. He didn't talk much in the car on the way home either, he probably still felt responsible for me – he'd always call back, 'course Mrs P,' when Mum waved us off with her usual, 'bring him back in one piece, Peter, ha ha … '

Bounding up the drive, through the sunroom and hall, and into the kitchen, I panted, proud as punch, 'I free-soloed *Great Wall* this evening Mum, it's a really pumpy E3'.

'Ooh, did you darling? How nice!'

And two weeks later I'd gone one further on an evening out with Andy B. 'Soloed *Quickstep* today Mum, that's E4.'

'Well done dear, they go up to number five don't they? Remind me what free-soloing is again?'

Oops!

Soloing hard stuff could perhaps be regarded as a most selfish act, especially if you're around others – particularly friends who feel responsible for you; but irrespective of any external influences, when it just 'happens' that way, nothing can beat it. I'll admit, I did feel dreadful for Pete and Andy's sakes much later, and I do still reckon soloing's a dodgy game: take Dave Thomas's unroped ascent of *Lord of the Flies* for example, on a day when the Cromlech was apparently chock-a-block and people were queuing for routes – I thought this was an absolutely deplorable act when I read about it many years later. But, that's just *my* opinion … it's an individual's choice … just pity the poor buggers who have to witness and clean up after the ones that go wrong, that's all.

I'll add though that I'm happy about, and have complete respect for, Alex Honnold, though must add; I met the young fellow here in Oz a year ago – *absolutely charming* to a tee – didn't know he'd led my *Knockin'* 'up there' on the grit … but I've digressed again …

Our dear Craig y Forwyn – what a fine, fine crag it was, *still is*: its sunny aspect, generally immaculate limestone and complete spread of high-quality routes of every imaginable style and grade. Of course, Craig y Forwyn was the scene of many of my 'firsts'. *First* limestone climb. *First* trad lead. *First* time meeting Timothy Freeman, Jeremy Moffatt, Michael Owen, Huw Watkins, and T***, the young goddess who'd turn me to jelly just by being there.

My *first* leader fall too – from the roof of *Scalar*, a Very Severe, where both my hex 5 and Andy B held the plummet. I was leading the pitch in my Troll waist-only belt, which even at size small still ended up under my armpits and left nasty burns up my sides.

Unbeknown to anyone at the time, I'd go on to climb the super-stunning wall just to its left many years later – as well as an even tougher one nearby, and name them both along lunar themes (but for totally different reasons – the first, *Moonwind*, being after an Avon cosmetic product would you believe? Ha! The second after a friend gone 'off the rails'.). Those future routes may as well have been on another planet on that day, when I dropped my 4c crux and went for a flyer.

Jerry Moffatt opines in the hilarious *Peak Rock* book launch video on *UKC* that his own worst fear was to have put up a fantastic new route and the cliff got banned so no one could do it anymore ... Maybe Jez had Forwyn in his mind when he said that?

Unfortunately, there's an awfully sad postscript to those beloved early Forwyn days.

On about my second or third ever day on rock, Huw Watkins had just led *Mojo* – an Extremely Severe. 'Crumbs! Even Mr Boorman hasn't done that one,' I thought, as I followed my teacher up the VDiff *Left Hand Y-Chimney*. And on a later occasion Tim and I sat and gawped as Huw led the even harder roof on *Freedom* with his regular climbing partners Brian Jones and John Roberts.

Huw was the local 'hard man', along with Mike Owen at the time, and they'd often be at the crag when we were. However, a few years later he'd sadly gone very off-track and mucked up his head something shocking with far too many recreational drugs – and then, unfortunately, he tried acid. Huwie's behaviour and general demeanour had become stranger and more questionable as his ill-chosen lifestyle took hold; he seemed more and more distant and vague. Always really pleasant and friendly to me though, and although I'd held him in high regard earlier he was now merely a shadow of the man Tim and I had once so looked up to. I was by that time climbing much harder than Huw – looking back it's uncomfortable to recall how our trajectories crossed mid-point. Not just in climbing but in life itself. One on the upward incline, the other in almost free fall.

Norm told me Huw had abb'd and cleaned a new route over on Forwyn Left Hand, but had used some aid. I rang Huw in Abergele to ask if he was going back, or could I please try to free it – he offered it up without hesitation. It was a perfectly pleasant line – typical Forwyn and went free nicely –

but inadvertently I named it Hugh's Groove in his honour, knowing full well he wasn't in a good place; unfortunately his name was spelt 'Huw'.

Pete B recounted to me, over twenty years later, how he'd once swung leads with Huw on a 130-foot route called *The Snake* at Forwyn – which hosted possibly the most fallen-off top pitch of its Extreme grade on the entire cliff. Fighting hard following this pitch, Pete – barely making the finishing holds – pulled over to discover Huw just sitting there in a daze, taking in the slack hand over hand, not even tied in and with no belay device. Pete and his wife Denise had only just had their baby daughter, so he was justifiably beside himself – totally unlike Pete – no doubt a combination of anger and terror at the consequences had he slipped or broken a hold.

Along the way and a couple of years later, I did a big new route between *Quickstep* and *Great Wall* with Norman (I'd placed a bolt runner about seventy feet up). Huwie's health had continued to decline and he'd become more and more erratic – the 'beris lads in Pete's Eats had nicknamed him Space Case, so that's what I called my new 'hardest on the crag' – not exactly *after* him this time, more at his expense I'll admit.

It was a few years later, when I was living in Sheffield, that Huw suddenly appeared in Hunters Bar – one thing on his mind. One evening, when all the lads were away competing, he arrived at our no. 84 unannounced. I hadn't seen him for ages … he had a skinhead haircut, crazy look in his eyes and was totally scattered and burbling manically … kept going on about 'Ali', a member of the local 'climbing society', and how he was madly in love so had come to 'claim her' from her long-term partner 'Chip'.

He had two numbers in his jumbled-up head, 84 and 124 (mine and Tim's addresses on Hunter House Road respectively – 124 was where 'Ali' hung out). Having no luck finding his damsel at mine, Huw staggered off; I dead-bolted the doors and turned out the lights in case he came back. I honestly can't remember whether I rang ahead to warn 'em Huwie was at large, but I'm sure I would've done, though their phone would've doubtless been cut off anyway. From what I gathered next day, Huw had turned nasty and violent when he got the inevitable rejection. Violent to the point that he had to be forcibly restrained and hog-tied with ropes until he'd calmed down sufficiently to be released and sent off on his (not so merry) way.

Not long after that ignominious ejection – barely a week – someone rang me from back home in North Wales: Huw's body had just been discovered at Forwyn – hanging from my bolt!

Suicide.

I cried my eyes out and said loads of prayers for Huw and his family. I really wanted to acknowledge his influence on my early climbing progression and to pay my respects in this book, but neither Pete nor Andy could confirm the exact circumstances surrounding poor Huw's death. I emailed Dave Lyon in Llandudno a few times but got no response; thankfully Mike Owen passed on my details to their old climbing partner Brian Jones in Old Colwyn. Brian kindly took the trouble and clarified things:

Yes, Huw was discovered hanging at Craig y Forwyn – his father had called the police when Huw hadn't come home one day. His rope was tied to a tree, not to my bolt (I'd carried a most uncomfortable sense of guilt for over twenty years) and according to the mountain rescue fellow from Rhyd-y-Foel who had to retrieve his body, it was obvious the knot around his neck was deliberately tied. 'Bri' added that he'd recently jumped the fence (Forwyn's still banned, remember) and gone for a nostalgic walk along the clifftop, and there, laid against the base of that tree were some flowers wrapped in cellophane. No note or anything, just a lovely bouquet of white roses.

Silly Arête, Tremadog. **Photo**: Andrew Brazier.

7.
TREE, MUD, ROCK
and 'THE DYNAMO KID'

If you have access to Jerry's excellent book *Revelations* please take twenty minutes to reread his Crag Rat chapter as what I have to say below is really in context and refers to Jez's take on things – I'll make a bit more sense if you read him first, honestly; but if not, the following notes may still provide some amusement.

☆ ☆ ☆

I'd fallen in love with Tremadog on first acquaintance – I mean, who doesn't really? I followed Andy B up *Valor*, a classic HVS on Bwlch y Moch[1], and later he manually hauled me up the severely overhanging ramp-line of *Geireagle* – one of the best-looking routes on the crag (from ten feet out in space) – whilst I thought, 'I'll come back and lead you one day, just you wait!' (Not that it was going anywhere.)

Spent five days there in February 1980, camping in the water-logged field next to Eric Jones's cafe with Tim – swinging shifts to spoon out the water. Guess we were climbing HVS/E1 at the time and Tremadog was the ideal spot for climbers of that standard. We made friends with the climbers in the other tents too: Johnny Tout and Con Carey (who were from the Peak District) and

---

1 *Editor's note*: The team climbed the route free, definitely not the first party to do so – it's now given E2 5c.

Fred Curry and Alan Moist (who weren't). Incredibly I still remember them – and their names – from 1980.

And Eric bestowed me with a nickname – 'The Dynamo Kid' (how cute). I liked that, kind of a mark of recognition, and coming from such a legendary local climber and alpinist it felt even more special. I discovered recently that the 'baton' has been passed on to a young kid from Bethesda (I think) when Eric responded kindly to a research email I'd sent him a year or so ago. I replied, wholeheartedly relinquishing the moniker and asking Eric to pass on a personal message: 'Use the nickname wisely and be safe young lad. Best wishes, Andy P.'

Come the brilliant, long summer holidays, Tremadog was both Jerry's and my first choice, and this time Eric allowed us to doss in the derelict (old) hay barn which was a vast improvement on camping – as long as you could handle the nocturnal scurryings. Rats – lots of them, but it was definitely five-star accommodation (I could count them through the gaping holes in the roof. Boom boom! Thanks to my late father for that gem.).

There was another lad around our age knocking about too: 'Veerry, veerry' Welsh he was, maybe Eric introduced us? 'Hi, I'm Chang.' He seemed even keener than Jerry and me, if that was possible.

Jez and I knocked off the E2s, struggled on the E3s and sieged our way up the E4s.

Now then: Jerry's Crag Rat chapter from *Revelations* recounts **his** memories of our summer climbing there, but let's have a bit of fun – please allow me to fill in a few of the blanks:

We'd agreed to live on 50p a day – yes, fifty pence. That was enough to cover Eric's morning cup of tea (dutifully delivered on a tray by The Great Man himself at 9 a.m.) and the barn fee, leaving us 30p each, or 60p combined, for food.

'No Andy,' Jerry would insist, 'only one spoonful each; this piece of cheese will last us three days if I melt it in with the curry sauce.'

'But I'm starving, Jez,' I'd whimper.

Where the heck two teenagers got the energy to climb, or attempt what we did, day in day out (rest days hadn't been invented then) astounds me – oh to be a late teen again! But the smile on my face suddenly turned sour on reading, in Jerry's own words, 'I was living on 70p a day'. Hang on a minute, we'd agreed fifty, that's all I allowed myself. Had he gipped me? His extra 20p could buy a whole family-size block of chocolate or a bag of apples or something. No wonder he always had so much more energy and was stronger than me.

But Jez's memory is spot on regarding our hang-dogged ascents of the routes we did, and confirms my words from *Extreme Rock* re Douggie Hall's 'tut-tutting' on the stance of *Void*. And the grey Ford Cortina with the guy who spat in my hat. Abusing us for being 'Sais' (English). Yes, it *was* a Cortina *and* grey. I can see it now as if it were yesterday. We were approaching the big sweeping right-hander that marked the halfway point on our nightly hour-long walk home from bouldering at Hyll Drem and the half pint of still orange at The Ring. That episode really upset me and I did grumble, 'but I'm **Welsh** Jez, I'm **Welsh**,' all the way back.

And the other time, running out to one of our climbing heroes, Pete Livesey, on the garage forecourt and asking him how to climb *Zukator* – Jerry's wide-eyed young face pressed up against a little porthole he'd wiped in the steamed-up window, too intimidated to come outside.

A couple of years later there was another memorable event in the cafe. I was there with Paul Williams and he'd just nipped outside when another 'older' climber, Stuart Cathcart, chose his golden opportunity to stride across and stand glaring above me – threatening to bash me up if I ever nicked a new route off him again:

'Ya cocky little ... '

In truth, I'd gone very off-route on *The Moon* on Craig y Llyn with Pete Bailey and inadvertently led the freshly brushed line that Stuart had just prepared. Thought it was a bit stiff for E2! Called it *Death can be Fatal* – a seriously run-out E5.

☆ ☆ ☆

Back to Jerry's book:

My girlfriend 'Bronwen' (not her real name – it was 'Myfanwy' (not her real name either)) and I *did* sing Sheena Easton and Leo Sayer songs to each other before her school bus arrived, 'cept some of the 'woahs' and 'yeahs' were coz she would straddle me, little skirt pulled up and ...

I really should've explained to Jerry it wasn't just for pissing out of. I was ahead of him in that department. Way ahead. Sadly the bus always tooted at the most inappropriate moment and she had to flee, so that became Jerry's cue to take off the weird little blindfold he slept in and get up and dressed. He'd put the pan on the stove.

'Get up Andy, we've got to go cragging.'

'In a minute Jez, why don't I meet you over at the cafe?' (Something else on my mind.)

Finally, Jez's account of *Zukator* – that classic, desperate, overhanging groove – and me feeling utterly dejected having failed on Livesey's sandbag 'secret way' of climbing the left arête, taking a whipper when the holds 'Petered' out.

Tim had joined us for a few days and was second up. Jerry had cruised it, Tim following in similar fashion but taking out all the runners. Being third up (and very outwards), Tim, egged on by Jerry, refused to take in the slack and I had a huge loop of top-rope swaying in the breeze down between my legs – pretty much soloing the entire pitch – as I fought in extremis to bridge up and outwards towards the daylight with no runners to grab.

I'll never forget their adolescent faces peering inwards from the top, tears of laughter welling in their eyes:

'Come on Dynamo Kid, show us what you've got.'

I did, and, with a 'bastards!', untied and stormed off in a right old huff!

☆ ☆ ☆

Let's face it, Jez and I were only young lads really – just hovering around the sixteen to seventeen mark, up for trying anything, nothing fazed us – climbing grades above most others our age at that time, and motivated only to keep working at getting better.

Perhaps (semi-seriously) the true measure of our ambition and eventual improvement was that we had both 'led' what we knew as 'Peaches'. Jerry with two falls, me with four (neither lowering back down of course). Everyone knew the 'route' – it was the great unclimbed line on the cover of the guidebook and took the tenuous crack-line up the overhanging wall left of *Cream* on the spectacular Vector headwall.

But then the grown-ups arrived …

Ron Fawcett (Jerry's No.1 hero) and John Redhead (I'd seen him around a bit up on the coast – he was mine) were alternately attempting to lead Peaches and some local wag had superglued three bolt hangers on to the route – you could see them from down on the road below, twinkling in the sun. John was beside himself with rage but got the joke having abseiled down and prised them off.

He looked so smooth on his lead attempts too. I really thought (and privately hoped) he'd do it before Ron – the Peak Raider as he was referred to – but credit where it's due, Ron topped out first (albeit in the yo-yo style of the day).

And called it *Strawberries* – catching everyone by surprise.

Nice one Ron!

And guess what? Ron Fawcett still recalls meeting us two little lads. In a lovely email, from February 2015, he writes:

> Great memories of those early days down at Tremadog and Llandudno.
> For me, it's not just the routes (some of which were mega for sure) but the

characters and the fun involved … I remember the first time we met in Eric's barn, you and Jerry; I know it's hard to believe, but you were both so shy … and yes, I suppose some of my first ascents were a tad rushed in those days because I was always thinking about the next 'first ascent'. I remember writing something about *Strawberries* and mentioning Jerry's 'ascent' – he wrote me a really funny letter (it wasn't supposed to be humorous) – he said the only reason he rested on all the pro' was 'cos he was tired!

I spent my final night of that Tremadog holiday (and what a holiday it'd been) curled up in a warm, clean bed with my beautiful little Welsh girl, singing Sheena and Leo to each other, talking about our respective futures, giggling, breathing heavily and fumbling nervously like the innocents we were and taking it in turns to cuddle and spoon one another. As she slept peacefully early next morning, I planted a loving last kiss on her forehead and cheek and slipped quietly out the door with a hushed 'God bless, Cariad,' (Welsh for 'darling') to make the long, pre-dawn trek back to the barn.

Jerry was just up and boiling a pan of water. As the tea was brewing I started packing up my stuff.

'Where've you been all night, I was worried? … What are you doing Andy?'

'Gotta go Jez, out of dough and there's six weeks' work with Jack back on the coast; two quid a day Jez.'

'But Strawbs?'

'I know, I'm sorry Jerry. You'll repeat it; I'm not good enough yet. Ring us as soon as you've done it Jez, T'ra,' and stuck my thumb out.

He did do it, 'à la' Ron, about three weeks later – and I was chuffed beyond belief when the call came and Mum handed me the old Bakelite handset at Walden Cottage saying, 'Hurry, it's Jerry, he's got some news!'

He went on to say he thought the Peak District was where the 'real hard stuff' was and that he'd let me know when he'd got there. Tim was well ensconced in Sheffield having dropped out of Bradford uni, and a whole new scene was kicking off.

I'd join them in due course, but needed the money from work and had a few routes I wanted to do in Wales first.

Little did the Peak lads know what was about to hit them.

The climbing **world** would soon find out too, courtesy of a young Jerry Moffatt.

A year or so later I was back at Tremadog when John Redhead's little white Renault van swung into the car park with a gravelly screech. His climbing partner had pulled out and I'd hitched there on the off-chance of finding someone to climb with. He was flipping through the new-route book in the cafe so (never one to be backwards in coming forwards) I approached him and nervously asked what he was down to do:

'Back on *Strawberries*, John?'

'Maybe youth, maybe.'

'Well I'm trying a new route,' pointing out the striking right-leaning slash mark up the steep wall above the first pitch of *Fingerlicker*. 'Shall we go and try it?'

'Sure, why not, come on then youth.'

I'd only a few days prior abseiled down and placed two pegs for protection – regrettably the second one reachable from *Silly Arête* (don't, you'll cut your ropes if you fall off above). I was in the presence of climbing royalty and John Redhead was going to hold my ropes!

And crumbs, I so nearly got it first try. John really hadn't been paying much attention though and had fed out far too much slack, so my fall approaching the top peg was an absolute monster. Tossing me a loop of rope and pulling me back into the stance from mid-air, John nodded his head towards the rocks below.

'Sorry youth, but look … ' and we spent the next several minutes ogling some lass who'd stripped down to her undies and was sunbathing topless on a big flat boulder right beneath us.

John too almost succeeded first go, as I rested and admired the view – till his body came hurtling past and broke my reverie. I got a couple of inches higher next try but was spent. Damn! I'd blown my chance to shine. John ran up it beautifully next go and, though exhausted, I fought my way to the top without falling off.

Though to all intents and purposes it was my route, it really didn't matter who'd led it; I was just happy to share the experience – with one of the most talented climbers ever to lace on a pair of boots.

I gave it the ridiculously imaginative name of *Fingerlicker* **Direct**!

☆ ☆ ☆

In 1984, Martin 'Basher' Atkinson and I fancied Tremadog as a break from Pen Trwyn – both on the same specific mission – so hitched off together towards Snowdonia, heading for 'the route'. We got separated when a car in

Caernarfon could only take one of us, but ran into each other again a few hours later in a quaint little village.

Warws Beddgelert (Beddgelert Warehouse) was a huge outdoor equipment barn that had opened up recently and was being heavily promoted on Welsh radio stations and in the local press: 'Warws Beddgelert – where the best costs less!' they spruiked.

Truth is it cost fuck all and some of us would sing that jingle over the car radio advertisements as we gassed it down the slippery road heading for Tremadog, pissing ourselves laughing. They had absolutely no security and the dear old lady on the till must've been in her nineties and was usually asleep, God bless her.

Basher and I wandered in and bought a block of chalk each (I had to prod her on the shoulder to pay our 20p's coz she was dozing again). We never nicked anything, but there were at least two Sheffield 'raiding parties' dispatched (no names) – one of which I witnessed – where a couple of lads grabbed brand-new rucksacks off the rack, pulled out all the stuffing, filled them full of gear, completely changed their clothes to new ones and casually strolled out. Hilarious I thought at the time, albeit very wrong!

Shortly after arriving at our destination and happy seeing Eric again (even though the barn fee wasn't 10p anymore and nor was the morning brew, but there weren't any rats and he'd fixed up the leaking roof), Basher dispatched *Strawberries* in quick fashion, myself the following day.

Undoubtedly the most fortuitous moment of that brief visit was when I was approached in the car park by a slightly portly chap – non-climber-looking he was – who introduced himself with outstretched hand and an Australian accent: 'Andy Pollitt isn't it? Glenn Robbins from 'stralia, G'day.' Unbeknown to us at that time, Glenn would become not only my regular photographer – commencing the very next day by shooting the classic pink tights and greasy hair sequence of me making the ninth ascent of *Strawberries* – but a dear, dear friend to this very day.

I'd read about Glenn and seen photos of him in wild situations hanging amid no end of complex rigging, pointing his lens at the Aussies on Arapiles, 'cept he was clad in full 'joy boy' attire – leather chaps and waistcoat, cap and various buckles and straps – the use of which I could only imagine! But Glenn was anything but the effeminate 'mincer', rather a genuine 'blokes' bloke' who, quite openly, had an admiration for **bears**!

'Bears, Glenn?'

'Yeah. Big, weighty men, preferably older. You lads are safe, you anorexic young fuckers.' Glenn was – is – a total hoot, as well as a superlative lensman and wordsmith.

Here's just one of a million examples of hilarity (remember – we're talking 1980s climber chat now) – we'd just left the barn for the dark, rainy walk to seek beer in Porthmadog when I let rip a voluminous, high-pitched fart.

'Virgin.' That's all he said. Just one word – bang – quick as a flash, and I cried with laughter the whole way to the pub – no other words were exchanged, I couldn't draw enough breath to get them out!

Glenn Robbins by email, September 2015:

> While sorting slides for Andy's book, I am reminded of the sheer depth and breadth of our adventures together; of our perilous pursuits in breath-taking surrounds. From the industrial wastes of the slate quarries to the most remote sea cliff zawn. The images, virtually postcards from the fringes, the edge.

> We'd first met at Tremadog. I'd been cruising the crags for muscular types, in tights and extremis; people that I'd been reading about in *Mountain* and *High* magazines. Big game (name) hunting, with a camera, their images (not their heads) intended for people's walls. Or, as the butterfly collector, marvelling at their colour and movement, at times startling as they take flight. On occasion, and in certain company, regretting the lack of a 'killing jar'.

Glenn made up 'my' regular photographic 'team', alongside Bernard Newman and Richie Brooks – though I'd occasionally pose for David B.A. Jones or Neil Foster or 'Piggy' Johnstone who were all great behind the camera too.

Despite our successes on *Strawberries* the real plum of this visit was the continuation of the initial crack – the straight-up finish. I'd practised it twice on abseil and was dead keen to try and lead it. I really wanted that route and it was my original intention to do it placing and clipping all the runners on the lead and thus, egotistically, surpassing Ron and Jerry from 1980. But I had a few bolted-up, ready-to-go projects back on the Ormes, so was torn …

Martin had a wealth of routes to do at Tremadog – all the classic Extremes like *Silly Arête, Fingerlicker, Vector, Void, Cream, Marathon Man* and *Zukator* etc., as I think he'd only ever been there once or twice, back when he was an HVS leader; so he decided to stay on for a fortnight.

'Andy, let me try it … Pleeeease!' (You could lay claim to new routes back then if you'd abbed, brushed and tried them – as I had with this one.)

Now Martin was my very best friend on the entire planet and he *really* wanted that route. If you ask him today his recollection should be similar. Mine has never left me. It's even noted in my diary: 'You have it Biff, it obviously means more to you.'

Isn't that what 'besties' do?

Apart from producing a tremendous and stunning climb, he came up with probably the most apt route name ever – *Dream Topping*, and some anonymous wag scribed in the new routes book next to the description: 'I thought *Dream Topping* was instant, I didn't know it took eight days to prepare!' Priceless.

There were many subsequent visits to Tremadog, each one memorable in its own right, as much for the climbing partners as the routes themselves:

An early ascent of Jerry's *Psyche 'n' Burn* with friendly Welsh lad Mel Roberts. Repeats of *Surreal* – and adding a harder finish with Martin Wilson – a Llandudno 'local'. Swinging leads on *Sultans of Swing* with Steve – one of the Bristol gang I'd met at Avon: 'Chalk free, lad, or I'm not climbing with you … ' Steve Findlay (amazing young Hazel's dad) had the hard pitch and recalls he was ' … followed by some tiny little schoolboy … '!

Next up were *Sexual Salami*, *Hitler's Buttock* and *Cardiac Arête* with Pete Bailey, then *Mongoose* – the 'hard' way (Crikey! The 'easy' way must be piss!); *Atomic Finger Flake* about six times, a brilliant route – I recall standing in the bushes above *Boo Boo* half witnessing John's first ascent – 'half' because at the time 'Myfanwy' was knelt below me, doing what she did … and did so very well! Then it was *Bananas* when Mel Griffiths won a mug of tea off Paul Williams, coz whilst watching from the road Mel says to Paul, 'Andy-boyo's pumping out, been aangin' there for ages, gonna fall off any seecond,' and Paul (as he recounted later) confidently took a deep breath, folded his arms across his enormous chest, shook his head and winking at Mel confidently replied, 'no he won't, he's my lad – The Human Clamp.'

Later in the cafe it was, 'but only once Paul.'

'That's not the point, kid, I bet him you wouldn't!'

'Sorry Dad, I'll pull harder next time I promise.'[2]

In his March 2015 email, Elfyn 'Chang' Jones shows great recall of some exciting escapades from that period:

Those Tremadog days now seem a long time ago – halcyon days of youth, eh! I still climb there a lot and still get great delight from the place (I was

---

2 Fifth ascent, *Bananas*, with Dominic Lee on the BMC American meet; I think the second route 'given' British 7a (now E5 6b). Immediately to my right Johnny Woodward was making an impressive early ascent of *Strawberries*, so most eyes were on him.

shivering away on *Weaver* just over a week ago!). It's quite scary that some of the pegs we thought old and dodgy back then have actually survived and are still being clipped.

I recall that soloing was always a big thing back in the early eighties and have memories (and nightmares?!) of soloing with you and Jerry. Tremadog was the 'in' place to be back then – lots going on such as the race for the first ascent of *Strawberries* between Fawcett and Redhead, etc. Eric had not long taken over the cafe and barn, and young upstarts such as Jerry and you (and, I guess, myself!) were hanging about. Normally we'd get a few good routes done in the daytime, then often finish off by soloing a few more in the evening sunshine. As with all such youngsters, we wanted to try new or different things and you had a great idea to try barefoot soloing – very bizarre and very scary, soloing routes in bare feet and trying to get some chalk on to sweaty toes to get a better grip! Another time I recall soloing a route (*G-String* or *Merlin Direct* maybe – anyway some HVS) as a warm down after a long hard day during which we'd probably climbed a few E3s or E4s – I got really bad cramp in my hands – I could barely open them and was getting quite scared and could literally not grip any of the holds: it was you who coaxed me to continue, bubbling as always with your infectious enthusiasm!

I also remember you making an early ascent of *Marathon Man* (possibly the fourth ascent?) around the same time – a scary lead in those days with only a limited number of cams. You were struggling on a really hot day and had placed the only (and crucial) cam in a poor undercut, but it was the wrong size. Above you and not far from the top was a poor spike just out of reach, but you didn't have a spare sling to flick over it for a runner.

I was on top of the crag but didn't have any gear or a rope or harness (I'd probably been soloing again!). You were in real difficulty and a fall would have been very serious, so I was volunteered to be hung by the ankles over the edge of the buttress by someone (can't remember who it was, but he also didn't have any gear or rope) to lower a sling for you to put over the poor spike. You completed the route – the sling fell off!

By the way, the 'Chang' nickname exists to this day and is still used by many from the '80s (it took Leigh McGinley quite a while to realise that Elfyn and Chang were the same person – for years he only knew me as Chang and he was convinced for ages that the Elfyn character was a fictitious person – he even asked me once who that Elfyn person was and had he really done all those routes, as he'd never met the lad!). Cheers, Chang (or am I Elfyn?).

Oh, and yes …

I did go back eventually and settle my old score with *Geireagle* – got up close and personal on the pointy end and even though I'd waltzed up three E5s before breakfast, still found that E2 bloody desperate!

If I ever see Jerry again I'll slap him for soloing that!

Central Pillar, Castell y Gwynt. Second ascent and first redpoint ascent.

8a

'83 – '89 @ 84

AKA Sex and Drugs and Rock 'n' Dole (which I thought was pretty bloody clever coming from Plantpot – considering he didn't do drugs, never had a girlfriend in all the years I knew him and preferred Radio 3 Classic. 'Classic' indeed Chris P!)

So Jerry had rung … letting me know he'd 'done' *Strawberries* … and I was back on the coast delivering bickies and cakes and crisps and pop with Jack and working in the amusement arcade – and missing my climbing.

A few years earlier John Redhead had put up *Plas Berw* and *The Bittersweet Connection* on Castell y Gwynt, just about the hardest things around so most reckoned – till 1982 when Ron Fawcett came down from Derbyshire one day and led *Imminent Crisis* at Forwyn … the line that both young Trevor Hodgson (Andy B's new protégé) and I had failed on. In autumn '82, Bill Wayman and Fred Crook showed Pen Trwyn's potential with the bold and desperate *Gold Rush*. All on 'my patch' and tougher propositions than any of my offerings. I needed to lift my game …

With Pete Bailey I'd repeated *Plas Berw* – no falls, was chuffed with that – a brilliant route by John. Then a while later I got the second ascents of *Imminent Crisis* and *Gold Rush* and then Pen Trwyn just took off – by 1983 it was *the* place to be!

We went to Pen Trwyn almost every day.

PAUL WILLIAMS – WHEN 50% IS NOT ALWAYS HALF!

Paul lived in a lovely old house called Tal y Waenydd in a hamlet just outside 'beris called Penisarwaen – pronounced 'Pen-isar-wine' for those who struggle with our Welsh sounds. Paul would always try to embarrass the girls in the petrol station at Llandudno Junction (pronounced 'Thlandidno' if you can't pronounce 'Ll') when the girls would go, 'How do you spell that?', whilst writing his address on the back of the petrol cheques (yes, we used to do that!).

'P.E.N.I.S ... ' he'd spell slowly, then pause till they went all red in the face. Got 'em every time he did! Oh how he giggled! Toilet humour, fart jokes and sexist and racist quips were common from Paul, and I often cringed. I figured he was bitter about previous failed relationship/s, but thought he was better than that and didn't need to sink to such depths to get a laugh. Not that I didn't chortle too, albeit sometimes in genuine embarrassment. Notwithstanding, I adored that man. I once overheard Paul play a most beautiful and moving piece of classical piano; he'd never mentioned he could do that and seemed quite sheepish about it. Almost embarrassed. Nonsense, it was breathtaking.

I did countless climbs with Paul in '83, not only at Pen Trwyn though, as he knew and loved all the mountain and sea cliff crags and would, over that summer, guide me to pretty much all of them.

Paul was 'me Dad'. Referred to me as 'me lad' or 'Son', even though he spoke, just occasionally – although only ever fondly – about his natural boy Chris. I hung off every word Paul said and was totally absorbed with his tales of finding classic unclimbed lines, and of knowing and climbing with all the 'big names'. Ron Fawcett recalls a 'Welsh scene where Paul was such a pivotal part: supporting, prodding and entertaining us in so many ways. Right place, right time, Andy.'

I freed Pen Trwyn's *The Disillusioned Screw Machine* with Paul – JR had given me 'tight' on it the previous year and wasn't bothered about coming back to it, said he had some 'amazing, scary madness up on Cloggy, youth.' In fairness, it was Liverpudlian climber Tom Jones who passed the aid point first, but he couldn't do the rest of it.

Again with Paul, the second ascent of Pete Livesey's *Zero* – a genuine frightener on Idwal's Suicide Wall. On my first attempt, facing a ground fall from about seventy feet, my left index finger ended up in the pocket that my hex 3 needed to be in. Committing to the 'dead-point' principle, I pulled my finger out with a 'pop' and hurriedly stacked the little nut upright to cam it in the pocket, then grabbed it and clipped my rope in. On reaching the ground after a rapid but gentle lower-off, the nut must've come out of tension so slid all the way back down to the bottom ... along with my rope a second or two later!

Thankfully the next day went better ...

Sometime later I belayed Jerry as he boldly flashed *Zero*'s third ascent, then we both led Ron's *Mur y Meirwon* – aka *Wall of the Dead*. Chris Gore also went up and led *Zero* – probably (and not surprisingly) one of the last trad routes he ever did. It was wonderful to be back out in the mountains again with Jerry – both of us all 'grown up' by now, and we'd not shared a few days together like this for several years. The previous day we'd been fortunate that Paul's advice was sound as usual and we did the third ascent of *The Red Ring* and first of the year of *Nexus Direct* in the Pass.

Jez and I looked up at the Cromlech and laughed, recalling he'd been seriously cross when I'd fumbled his brand new Friend 2 whilst attempting *Right Wall* a few years earlier – it hit the slab beneath him but span off, his Christmas present lost on day one. That was when we were merely 'children' – throwing ourselves at life and nothing would get in our way. Ha! We climbed on double eleven-millimetre ropes then – for extra security. Jerry's was yellow, mine a mail order blue one from Alpine Sports in London. Andy B had taught me double rope technique on our usual nine-millimetres, but with two elevens – stupidly 'crossed' and causing a whole world of drag – I was approaching the 'furthest out from protection bit' of the entire route: I'm pumped stupid, but youthful and determined to reach the famous Girdle Ledge – so, telling Jerry to 'watch me!', strenuously drag through about six feet of slack and start slapping. But it's damp, slopey and far too hard and thus not to be, so I take the inevitable 'screamer' down the wall and come to a sudden whiplashing 'Agghhhh ... !' as the ropes pull around my (then) orange and white Whillans harness. What the heck? Jerry's **above** me! On the **starting** ledge and my feet are inches off the **ground**: 'Giz a foot Jez, please.' He wasn't happy and shouted at me about his Friend and how I'd now gone and used up one of the six falls his new rope was rated for ...

Anyway, dear Paul wasn't bothered with leading much – even though he could when he put his mind to it: think *The Weaver* at Tremadog, brilliant, and all Paul's own work – and much preferred being party to harder new routes (particularly if they were noteworthy), so he usually aligned himself as a seconder to the 'names'. Now that's not being disrespectful or disparaging to my old mate (God bless him), and to his credit it was his keen eye that spotted the majority of the 1980s' Welsh classics and shared them with the likes of Jim Moran, 'Big' Ron Fawcett, John Redhead and later little young me. I was indeed in privileged company.

I did though once psyche him up with a fresh, newly cleaned and bolted little 'toy' climb on Pen Trwyn's Hanging Rock: 'Ere ya go Dad, one for you, enjoy.'

It was the obvious central line and involved a strenuous 'pop' for a really decent hold from where you could easily clip the conveniently placed second bolt.

Roland Foster from New Zealand was with us and it was his turn to hold PW's rope. Roland and I had Paul primed and pumped-up on cafe coffee and 'sweet meats', but every time he got to the slap he went straight for the quickdraw and not for the hold.

'Paul!' (Cross now, so not 'Dad'.) 'For fuck's sake, you know the hold's a sinker, why do you keep grabbing the sling?' I admonished. 'This is too frustrating to watch.'

Again and again Paul got there, and again and again he'd throw two fingers into the 'biner, not four into the big incut. Another whimpering 'slack please' from Paul (as a car drives over my rope – 'be careful Roland, please') and finally a 'no' from 'Ro-ey' to PW.

'Fucking **slack** I said.'

'Nope.'

'I'll fckn kill you Foster, now last chance … '

'I told you, Paul: slack's for leading, not dogging!' … and I'm watching all this unfold, gently peeing myself. Now Paul was a big fellow and Roland a bit of a runt like me, so Paul lifted him clean off his feet with one huge bicep and clipped both the rope and the dangling Kiwi into the runner and promptly fell off … (I couldn't contain myself and just kept laughing and spluttering; that was *so much* harder than the move Paul was *meant* to be doing) … and when they shot past each other (Paul was by far the heavier of the pair) he threw an enormous clenched fist at Roland, and I completely lost the plot in hysterics.

It then got even more ridiculous as Ro-ey was now twenty feet up the crag, locked off on his belay device, and PW was on the ground with me. Roland was loathe to lower himself off and Paul couldn't untie with him hanging off the rope, so I stepped in and brokered a 'no bashing' deal before whisking Paul down to Parisella's whilst the Kiwi ran for his life.

After more cafe coffee and sugary treats we strolled back up the Marine Drive. I'd hold the rope this time and'd 'had words' with me Dad.

Minutes later … *De Torquemada* E4 6b … Led by Paul Williams, 24 July 1983, with a well-deserved 'Yes!' at the top.

'Let's go to the mountains next week, Son,' Paul suggested on the drive home. 'Get away from these crowds … '

FIRST IN, BEST DRESSED

Paul had only recently flogged me all the way up to this big, bold arête on Cloggy, the Black Cliff, because it was an unrepeated JR route, and the anticipated bold *bit* (read *lot*) was immensely enjoyable. 'I love this run-out shit, Dad,'

I shrieked down.

When I got home I asked my Mum, 'what's a flagellator?' And she said, 'that depends on the context dear … '

'Organ.'

Silence! … Then, 'oh, and how is Paul? Charming man, quite a dish too.'

'Muuuum … Euww.'

A Midsummer Night's Dream on Cloggy, third ascent, having followed JR on the second ascent the previous year; and *The Purr-Spire* as well with that terrific bloke Andy Grondowski, who'd joined us on some other routes and stepped in when Paul was away for a few days. Back in the Pass it was *Precious*, third ascent, led with muscle-bound Quentin Fisher from Sheffield; and *True Grip, JR, Hall of Warriors* (all under the tenth) 'cept *Lord of the Flies* where we got there late so had to make do with the twelfth ascent – sadly, well outside Paul's target – drat.

Now whilst the above and subsequent repeats were generally early ones anyway, it was Paul's intention, using his enthusiastic drive and determination, to achieve and maintain a degree of 'noteworthiness' in everything he pointed me at: 'Something for history lad, come back for pics for the sponsors.' I suppose he almost 'stage managed' me. To this end – in the mountains and on the sea cliffs – Paul was insistent that we 'tick' other people's routes, if not second then third. Pretty much 'shame on you' by the sixth and 'stop counting after ten, that's rubbish'. But, if not, our fall-back was that we **must** be the first **that year** to chalk up the holds, rather than follow the white dots of others. Throughout '83 and '84 we were the first on virtually everything PW chose – he'd always be on the lookout for 'first ticks' and had a phenomenal and current knowledge of who was doing (or intending to do) what. Oh! That reminds me – *The Cad* on North Stack Wall in 1982 when Paul was thirty-six and I'd just turned eighteen: 'Yer exactly half my age, lad,' he observed afterwards in his Minivan on the drive over to his new-found crag at Porth Dafarch.

'Yeah, but I'm catching up on you coz this time next year when you're thirty-seven and I'm nineteen I won't be half your age anymore coz two nineteens are thirty-eight Dad,' but he'd moved on to how well the Tories were polling at the moment, and we were pulling in to a new car park.

I remember *The Flakes of Wrath* and *The Smog Monster* well. Paul had done them with 'ropes and tackle' but said they'd be less strenuous to solo, being great big overhangs above a nasty drop into the sea. I soloed both in my pumps. Fantastic end to a great day and I hoped I'd lived up to Paul's expectations – **and** made amends for the 'Perrin episode' earlier on …

See, Jim had taken me bouldering a few times around Fachwen and on a little crag near his cottage around the corner from JR and Grettie's place, and I liked Jim. He told me he'd inspected a new route out in the Moelwyns, an area I'd not really visited, but reckoned it looked a bit stiff and run out. I recall hitching down from Ogwen on the day of our ascent. Entering Jim's humble abode I observed he had SMILE in great big letters painted on the column between his kitchen window sill and the front door jamb. It didn't register at first but there was a tiny little 'i' pencilled in between the tall neighbouring 'S' and 'M'.

Clever that Jim, what are *you* like?! I led him up it boldly and he followed without a struggle – Jim could climb very well when he put his mind to it.

Back at Pete's Eats the new route book was opened. I asked Jim what it was going to be called. Paul was stood next to me commenting, 'nice line that chaps, well done,' and Jim said, 'The Anvil' and sniggered. I could've died of embarrassment as he prodded me to write those two words. It was Jim's sly, 'diggy' nickname for PW and I felt somewhat set 'Up' and 'Up'-set. I apologised to Paul later but he had thick skin: 'I'm either "The Anvil" or "The Tick", Son,' he mused. 'Don't worry about 'em.'

But in '83 it was primarily Pen Trwyn most days. Obviously huge credit goes to Rowland Edwards for the vision to forge many of the early routes – albeit some with aid or a smattering of rest points, understandably though, as any cleaning was generally done on sight and ground up! It was ironically these aids that dragged our free-climbing generation to Pen Trwyn and the Ormes in the first place, so three cheers for Rowland!

We barely missed a day's climbing and if we did it was usually because we were cleaning and bolting up the next day's new routes, or guiding for Dryll Management Training, run by another of my old Prestatyn High School teachers, Chas Sewell. Dozens, if not hundreds, of new routes were done during that sunny, dry summer of 1983. Picture it if you can: back then there were barely twenty routes above the entire Marine Drive.

Of course, others came out to play too: Pete and Andy (the B's) were regulars; Billy 'The Bolt' Wayman and Fred Crook et al; the Lyon brothers – Chris and Dave, plus Dave Towse and his mates. Then there was 'Necky' Norman Clacher: 'Necky' because apparently he'd fallen off leading something so had gotten really cross, thrown off his harness, then soloed it! From across Stoke way came Gary and Hazel Gibson and their extended group of friends, and let's not forget the Sheffield Crew: Jerry, Martin 'Basher' Atkinson and Chris Gore; plus Chris 'Plantpot' Plant, Steve Lewis, 'Scotch' Ben Masterson, Mark 'Leachy' Leach and Mark 'Zippy' Pretty – the Sheffield scene was on annual leave at the beach ...

HITCHING HOME/O

Why me? Almost every bleedin' time I hitched anywhere I'd be propositioned by gay men. Never the gorgeous MILF with the short skirt in a Beamer with the sunroof down, or the nineteen-year-old 'hottie' returning from a yoga class: 'I've got a pair of Lycras that colour Andy, want to see *me* in them? We can go back to mine.' Nah! Never bloody happened did it. It was pesky travelling sales reps – virtually all of 'em. Must've been something about life on the road I guessed. It went on for years until I finally had my own van and could pick up hitch-hikers myself if they looked in trouble, or 'safe', or were Swedish girls, or had a rope around their sac.

There was an old Welshman who'd park at the junction just outside Llanberis and wait for hitchers – I happened upon him several times. Harmless old chap, not unpleasant; just wanted to chat for ten minutes about *your* sex life whilst he played his own game of pocket billiards, before running you into 'beris with the windscreen wipers on fast speed but the car in 'slow'. It was better than standing shivering in the pouring rain waiting for the next car to splash you, so I went along with his little games and (totally lying of course) told him about the latest secretary or nurse I'd slept with: 'Yes, of course they had suspenders on. Can we head off now please?' Honestly! He'd get me to Pete's Eats or the Padarn, however, and that was all that mattered.

Those reps though! I got offers of money, a brand new leather jacket, shoes, shirts, cologne, baby products (?!) and once as many teaspoons as I could carry, plus a couple of brand-new toasters (*useful* under Parisella's overhang!). **and a bible** too **ffs**. What's going on there? Over the years such propositions became par for the course, but it was always, 'Nopey, nopey, nopey … Sorry mate. Drop us here please … ' whilst hoping that my next ride might be from a pair of bi-sexual college students in short skirts who fancied 'a bit of rough'. It didn't bloody happen though did it? And anyway, in retrospect, I probably shouldn't've been hitching in pink tights.

HOW'D YA DO RON, RON, RON?

The 'big guy' was a regular at Pen Trwyn too, with then-wife Gill and puppy-dog Bill. They stayed over at Tal y Waenydd a fair bit – got the spare room and I got the couch – so we'd all pile over to the crag four or five times a week.

For the most part none of us were doing anything particularly 'cutting edge', but the routes were falling thick and fast. Some days we'd all team up and do half a dozen new or early repeat E3 to E5s together and just have loads of fun – with brews and ice creams from Parisella's between routes. Ron would've bolted that groove over there, say, whilst Billy Wayman floated up the arête to its right, and I got the overhang above it or whatever, and we'd simply just rattle 'em off one after the other; and Gary Gibson and Hazel would bolt or thread up every possible gap in between. That pair did get some flipping classics tho' and that reminds me – bolts weren't overly used as the crag lent itself nicely to offering up perfect thread or nut placements; but *in-situ* was the game if necessary and when the opportunity arose. Pen Trwyn was the testing ground for the 'new' ethic of bolt tolerance and 'French-style' was just around the corner.

Ron picked off loads of classics – I have to hand it to him – he certainly had an eye for a line, plus the talent to back it up.

He generally kept himself to himself and, bar the fun days out with Paul and me when we reeled off multiple routes, climbed solely off the radar with his missus. One particular rest day and at a bit of a loose end, Neil Foster and I heard Ron's car had been spotted parked up at the Rest and Be Thankful tea shop above the lighthouse, so we drove around there for a gander. Crawling to the top of Upper Pen Gogarth we had a clear view of Ron attempting to free-climb *Central Pillar* on Castell y Gwynt – this was a major line that I'd had in the back of my mind to check out. We watched for a good forty-five minutes as he repeatedly struggled with the first roof – his jumars on the abseil rope just out behind him. We wandered back up to the RandBT for teas and cakes with the cafe proprietors – I used to deliver their crisps with Jack.

As an aside … Jack's van had a Luton – the big, boxy section above the cabin – so on the weekly grind up the Marine Drive (underneath what I didn't have a clue back then was Craig Pen Trwyn) he'd speed up and lean the van over on the adverse camber of the bend beneath a big overhang at the headland. Now even though I was inside the van and only inches away from the rock face I still instinctively ducked as we rocked around without hitting it. Jack was an ex-ambulance driver and could drive anything! Well, it so turns out I cleaned that overhang many years later and climbed it with Dave Towse. I wanted to call it *Psycho* but Dave added 'phant' which sounded much better, even though I didn't know the meaning. 'Sycophant, a false friend,' Dave explained. 'Oh … OK … ' I replied, not knowing precisely which of us he was alluding to – we had an odd, rather strained friendship did Dave and I …

Anyway, Neil and I returned to see how Ron was going on *Central Pillar*. He was forty feet higher, alternately slumped on a bolt and straining to top-rope the individual moves up the pillar which petered out at a shield about the size of a large dinner platter. 'Must be desperate that, Neil, Ron's as fit as a butcher's dog at the moment.'

Ron and Gill rocked up after dark at the basement bar where we'd often hang out when The Cottage Loaf had shut for the night – I can't recall its name.

He said the route had gone down at 'hard' E6 6c, which confused me a bit as at that time perhaps only Jerry seemed capable of managing that standard in a day, and Ron had looked particularly troubled that afternoon!

'Bloody hell!' I thought, I really wanted that route – doing that free was one of the biggest plums on the coast. Five years later, in 1988 when I was on about my best-ever form, I ran into a highly respected old climbing chum down at Parisella's. It was Douggie Hall, perennial all-round 'good guy', brilliant climber, constantly 'up there with … ' no, bollox, *one of* 'the best' throughout the '80s and '90s; cool as a cucumber and obviously possessed of a healthy stock of bushels beneath which he hid his numerous lights.

Not keen on the limelight, 'our' Douggie (I actually feel qualified to refer to him as 'our' looking back from my there-at-the-time perspective) was happy to keep bang up to date with anything new and desperate by, well, just *climbing* it really … then wandering quietly off looking for the next one – as I stood wide-eyed, looked left, looked right, shook my head and asked myself, 'did that really just happen?' It was the same thing with Hamper.

Many of those eighties 'super route' Douggie repeats were very early on – and occurred in the same shadows Chris Hamper used to flit between – yet the limestone news in the magazines was always Jerry, Ron, Basher and sometimes myself or Leachy. The real 'rock stars' though were Messrs Hall and Hamper … as often as not anyway, and to be fair, up in Yorkshire John Dunne was really hitting his stride. The news wouldn't come out for at least six to eight weeks, even if it got past Jerry's latest 'super' – a *motorbike*! Or Dawes's latest Worcester to Padarn record. Not like now, live-streaming Adam Ondra doing a 10a plus (that's French not US), on your iPad in the bath.

Anyway, sorry, Parisella's in '88: 'Hey Andy, have you done *Central Pillar*?' Douggie inquired.

'No Doug, never got round to it, but I'm keen to do it. Looks brill dunnit?'

'It's a horror show Andy, bloody desperate, I didn't do it.'

'Bloody hell, if *you* didn't then it must be really hard Doug.' Obviously a totally free ascent of *Central Pillar* by Ron was, at that time back in 1983, an incredible leap in British standards. Of course, the actions and ethics of many back then were often slightly woolly, as Ben Moon recounts in a recent email exchange about our ascent of *The Bittersweet Connection*:

> **BM**: I recall you took several falls repeating the first pitch. If I remember rightly you also didn't lower all the way back down to the ground after your falls, but to some ledge or resting point – our ethics back then until we adopted the French style were always a little dubious …

AP: Fair point Ben … but this was hard and dirty E5 6b and the lower section was wet, slippery and mucky HVS to that ledge. I thought resting there was perfectly legit?

Whereas there were no such ledges on *Central Pillar* … it turned out that Ron's brilliant route was indeed an extremely tough proposition – it took me a full five days' work to reach the high point we'd seen him at – above the pillar and approaching what turned out to be a vicious and powerful crux, right when you're pumped-as. Reaching the in-cut edge on top of the shield it just simply fell away as if never really pulled on … I suppose five years' worth of birds weeing down the back of it hadn't done much to preserve its integrity! I hung there on my rope in frustration, shaking my head and cursing: 'Douggie's right, it's bloody desperate, and now I've gone and made it even harder.' A further three days of effort and I'd led it, with Zippy shouting encouragement all the way. I rather grudgingly claimed the **second** free ascent as without the top of the shield it was now rather harder, especially with the new redpoint ethics – bottom to top with no falls. It was solid E7 before I broke that hold and now was upper end. In comparison, it had taken me **two** days more than *Statement of Youth* (F8a), **four** more than *Masterclass* (F8a) and **six** more than *Oyster* (F8a)!

Douggie Hall, by email, May 2015:

> I remember doing *Central Pillar* on my next visit, still hard on the overhang, but made easier by chalk – most likely yours; got a feeling a hold came off and a slight variation was used from my first attempt.

Central Pillar is now introduced with these words in the 2014 Harrison/ Boorman *North Wales Limestone* guidebook:

> The big prize of the crag and little-known contender for the country's first 8a … the route has since shed 'crucial' holds, perhaps making it slightly harder than Big Ron's first ascent.

Fair enough. Ron got there first and that's all that counted back in the day!

Now, whilst **at that time** I doubted Ron had truly done *Central Pillar* cleanly, the initial 'How'd ya do Ron, Ron' had already occurred some while previously in the Verdon Gorge, south of France, and should have made me realise just how impressive a climber he was.

We'd done three long abseils in to the start of a super route called *Chrysalis* which had a particularly hard first pitch – Ron's pitch. He asked me for the quickdraws ...

'But you've got 'em, Ron ... '

'No I haven't, Andy!'

Then the most violent thunderstorm rolled in – we were 300 feet down, 800 feet up, and hanging off a shared belay. Rain? Never seen owt like it in my life ... thunder and lightning were blasting the opposite edge of the gorge and heading towards our side ... rapidly. It really was absolutely terrifying.

How **the fuck** (sorry, but never has the F word held so much gravitas for me) did Ron get us out of there? Fingering his way up a slick, featureless wall streaming with water; the violent storm shattering the tranquillity; just the 'biner off his chalk bag and the spare screwgate off my Sticht plate – I honestly still don't know to this day how he did it! How'd the F!!! Ron, Ron, Ron?

MINGLING WITH THE STARS

I'd started my love affair with France and the Verdon Gorge back in Easter '82, and my second visit, in spring 1983, provided perhaps my fondest memories and proudest moments ever as a rock climber – I'd been invited by the British Mountaineering Council to represent my country on my first international meet. So it was off to La Palud for my Verdon climbing epic with Ron and then a brilliant half day sat on my bony arse in the back corner seat of the private coach en route from La Palud to Burgundy's Rochers du Saussois, travelling through glorious French countryside, head-nodding and foot-tapping to The Stranglers' *Rattus Norvegicus*. To this day the base melody and keyboard of 'Sometimes' sends me straight back to France ... right there on that bus.

I was barely 20teen and respectfully took the corner seat so that *the* Ron Fawcett could stretch his long legs out into the aisle next to me. A few rows in front sat Louise Shepherd and Kim Carrigan – much respected climbers from Australia, then the talented American Scott Frye and France's Jacques 'Pschitt' Perrière and then, right up at the front, only the climbing world's very own supermodel – Catherine Destivelle! I wandered up and down the aisle, chatting to well-known climbers who I'd only ever seen before as pics in the mags. It was tough to communicate with the Soviet speed-climbers but, despite the Kremlin minders, we all agreed 'vodka in bar later, ya ... ' where I played a blinder with an empty Smirnoff bottle half-filled with water – dropped in a worm and sculled it in a oner, faking shudders before swallowing the poor creature whole!

Heck, I was the youngest by far and in exalted company indeed. Catherine had an empty seat next to her, up front by the driver, so I plonked myself down for a chinwag and ... oh, how I gushed! She giggled and snapped the denim of my stretch jeans a few times ... then went rub, rub, rub ... purring 'oooh Andeee, what thin legs you 'ave' in that oh-so-sensual French way. So, Ms Destivelle here, Louise in the middle, Big Ron up the back ... I didn't know who I wanted to sit next to most!

At slippery Saussois ... Ron and I alternately, almost-but-nowhere-near, 'doing' *Chimpanzodrome* (then one of France's hardest) in front of hundreds of onlookers. Merry-sur-Yonne – the nearby commune – had an annual 'Climbers Day' when no one went to work; rather they'd picnic beneath the crag along the banks of the Yonne and watch *les grimpeurs*.

That coach got switched out whilst we were all climbing and some of us never saw our stuff again! I'd lost Lizzie's Sony Walkman and all my tapes, others lost stuff too, but such things were relegated to mere annoyances by the friendly vibes, 'force of presence' and sheer aura of class emanating from my glittering companions. I was travelling on a bus sat next to *the* Ron Fawcett and that's all that mattered, particularly as we were also about to climb for the next two days with France's shining stars Patrick Edlinger and Laurent Jacob, then UK legend Steve Bancroft – who was Ron's mate already. Treasured memories indeed.

WE HAVE NEW MUSIC – AND NEW ROCK
Ian Dury and the Blockheads – Bobby Drury and the Slateheads.

Indeed there **was** new music; the New Romantics had arrived with their pretty made-up faces, Spandau Ballet and their lot, plus other genres more my kind, like The Cult and The Cure and Tim's favourite New Order. Funnily enough 'I wanna be straight' and 'Hit me with your rhythm stick' by Ian Dury still amused me when I threw the tape into my player. Even WHAM! And some of the gay 'boystown' stuff but not – no, never – Kylie and Jason's *Neighbours* songs. Give me John Cooper Clarke's 'Beasley Street' or 'Twat' or anything by Bob Dylan or some ska, and like most of 'our gen' I too got swept away by the Frankie goes to Hollywood phenomenon.

The band The Human League congregated in a massive house right opposite the hitching spot out to the Peak and you could hear them rehearsing loudly as I stood outside with my thumb out. They were on *Top of the Pops* the following week. We'd possibly even run into one or other of them at the pub down the road – as I had with the lead singer of ABC (actually they'd as likely run into you coz of their daft diagonal fringes that covered one eye).

Anyway, the quality and quantity of new routes us 'fortunates' were doing back on the Ormes was remarkable. There were classics just calling us on,

The Bearded Clam being a particular favourite with its pumpy start, fierce slap rightwards and 'out-there' headwall. All PW's concept and name of course, I just had to lead it as usual – that's all.

Geez, Paul was a hard taskmaster and didn't I just love it!

Then there was Norman Clacher and Keith Simpson's (remember, he of the *Great Wall* solo pics) *The Water Margin* – a 300-foot-long traverse along the high-water mark starting from the right-hand side of Lower Pen Trwyn. It's only HVS at best so, despite not being good in the water (I sink like a stone), I soloed it one hot day. You're mostly out of sight of LPT – my feet and legs kept getting soaked with the choppy tidal swell as it's rarely more than a few feet above the sea – so I was gripped yet excited at the same time, being all the way around the headland on my own. The traverse ended up at an easy gully approaching Pigeon's Cave and the water was calmer but deeper and the fun seemed to have come to an end all too soon. Continuing onwards was unclimbed but looked great – it was, and shortly thereafter I ran up and over the hillside, scrambled down the shaft with the rusty metal rungs inside and dropped into Pigeon's Cave for a great bouldering session. As the tide came in some of the others, including Jerry, were jumping sea-bound off its highest lip and Richie Brooks was there photographing anything that moved.

Pen Trwyn was brilliant of course, but was becoming a bit 'day in, day out' and not all our offerings were top-notch, despite many having 'interesting' names; for example, *A Touch Too Much* was based upon a strange incident in Bethesda (recorded in a striking John Redhead painting – see *colour plate 18*). You see JR had this gay old artist friend and the 'game' involved seeing who could hang from his kitchen rafter for the longest whilst he ran his hands further and further up the participants' legs – I let go first (hence the route name) and I'm not letting on whether it was Crooky or JR who won!

Back to the climbing …

The rest of North Wales offered so much more variety and adventure, so I often went for the solo hitch to Llanberis and either dossed at Paul's again, other friends' places, or over in the old quarry buildings beside Llyn Padarn. A few of us were slowly becoming intrigued with the new slate stuff that Redhead, PW, Bobby Drury and various other locals were raving about – even 'Gabbwt' – and he wasn't really a climber! Now good old 'Gab' was a local 'star' and was usually to be seen slipping and sliding all over the place in or around Pete's Eats or the Padarn – wearing tatty, worn-out climbing shoes: 'See these Andy? They're EBs, I got 'em off Leigh McGinley,' he proudly exclaimed one day, and I smiled (feeling sorry for his poor toes).

One day with Paul I'd gotten through this overlap at two-thirds height, having fingered my way up the most incredible slab – a feature **absolutely everyone** had seen from Pete's Eats, simply to dismiss as looking too blank; plus it was declared Out of Bounds by the electricity company who 'owned' it.

It was bold but safe enough and calf-achingly glassy. At the top I cried out loudly: 'Yes! that's the best route I've ever led!' only to be startled by cheers and applause from Steve Haston and Leigh McGinley, first ascentionists, who'd snuck up to the top of the adjacent wall to see how I'd go on Stevie's *pièce de résistance*.

'Well done Son, that's the fifth,' drifted up from Paul.

Comes The Dervish really **was** the defining moment in 'modern' slate's history and Steve Haston, now resident in Malta I believe, can be proud of that for life. I cannot imagine the number of ascents this easily approacha-ble super-classic has had since its first in August '82. Five thousand? Fifty thousand? I tell you what though, if we first ascentionists got royalties just like pop stars do, then Stevie would be living in a palace *à la Jagger en France* – off that route alone. I'd be falling out of coconut trees in Queensland clutching a vodka and orange and knocking myself out like Keef from the Stones did, but … who'll climb as Elton now he's had another tantrum and simply refuses to use his hands?[1]

I know! Sell tickets, I can visualise it now:

'A quid to lead *The Dervish* guv?' (Stevie on the turnstile.)

'Here's a tenner, keep the change Steve, we've waited years for this, hon-oured to meet you.'

Left Wall – smallest gold coin.

Cenotaph Corner – folding stuff and reservations only:

'September? That's two months away!'

'It's our most popular route mate … Can do you a special deal on Craig Doris though – some of t'holds 'ave gorn missing.'

Tim and I returned to Vivian Quarry and added a sister route rising in from the right to join and finish up Stevie's masterpiece. I was really pleased with that thin and run-out lead and, as my first big new route in that style, especially so. I knew right then I'd be looking for bigger and bolder things from that day on.

John Redhead and Dave Towse later added an independent finish, *Belldance*, and Dave, with Mel Roberts, crossed the slab to create the necky-to-follow *Swinging by the Bell*. On the repeat I was glad I led it! Abseiling down

---

1 *Editor's note*: Despite this being explained by AP, the editor still doesn't have much of a clue!

the left side of the slab I thought that the thin seam just right of *Reefer Madness* was possible, but no gear as such, so went for it anyway. Not too bad, bit snappy maybe?[2]

That summer standards continued to rise: back at Pen Trwyn E6 had not only arrived, it was almost passé. The Upper Tier was giving them up almost daily, and Lower Pen Trwyn (LPT) was getting lots of abseil inspections and some shiny new bolts.

But this idyllic summer couldn't last ... '83 would soon be shutting up shop, so I started psyching up for the big move over to Sheffield.

VIA LIVERPOOL!

It was precisely then that I received a phone call from my old Forwyn mate Mike Owen. By this time he and his wife Elaine had bought a house over in Widnes and Mike was the assistant manager at Blacks Camping and Leisure near the Neptune Theatre in the heart of Liverpool. Mike said there was a vacancy and did I want to help him set up a climbing department as they mostly sold clothing, camping gear and walking boots, and were the official Boy Scouts and Girl Guides outlet. I could take a room at theirs – it was five days a week in the shop, so I'd have my weekends, the money was way better than the delivery van and they lived really close to Pex Hill. Plus it was probably only for six months or so over winter.

So I deferred Sheffield, took the job, and moved into their spare room in Hough Green. We'd spend hours talking well into the wee small hours about the routes we fancied trying – Elaine too I should add – mainly over on Gogarth, as Mike particularly loved the place as well. North Stack Wall and especially John Redhead's routes were particularly inspiring, but I don't believe either of us were close enough at the time to have a serious attempt on them.

But, honestly, Pex Hill, what a place! I'd usually get in four or five sessions a week after work with Mike or on my day off. Everything was bloody desperate, I could barely get both feet off the ground. Mike could do them all and demonstrated problem after problem after problem. I was frustrated beyond belief coz I couldn't touch them. Admittedly I was wearing the first ever prototype grey Cragratz boots from Scarpa and they were way too stiff and the edging was all wrong, so I dutifully reported back to Berghaus – the distributors –

---

2 Vivian Quarry: Fifth ascent, *Comes the Dervish* E3 5c (at that time E5 6a). Paul said I **had** to do it below the sixth. 'Me Dad' was elated when I got to the top. I was just thankful the 'beris cafe lads hadn't bloody well egged me – I was a sitting duck and I knew 'Pengo' (Mr Haston) didn't particularly like me. First ascent, *Flashdance* E6 6a, 9 August 1983, with Tim Freeman. Third ascent, *Swinging by the Bell* E5 6a, with Dave Towse. First ascent, *For Whom the Bell Tolls* E5 6a, 29 April 1984, with Martin Crook and Julian Taylor.

and they had a different pair flown back to me from the factory in Italy (not exactly 'just like that' but soon after). 'This is more like it!' And all of a sudden I was running up the routes and chasing Mike in his Firés.

Joe and Gaz Healey's routes, John Hart's and many other locals' efforts were still desperate – but particularly Phil Davidson's. Heinous, tiny crimps and technical sequences on minute edges or smears for the feet. Generally not too high to really hurt yourself if you were being spotted – perhaps a sprained or busted ankle – but remember, there were no crash mats back then – bet it's paradise nowadays?

One of the brilliant perks offered by our switched-on store manager Mr Guy was for us all to advance our off-day by one every week. This meant each month we'd get the Friday off followed by the Monday after, so I could get back to North Wales on the train (or to the Peak if there was a lift going) on a Thursday evening and spend time on Gogarth or in the Pass with Andy and Pete or on the Ormes with Norm before train-ing it back to Widnes on the Monday night – usually still pumped. Brilliant! With Pex Hill every spare moment and a long weekend each month, my climbing didn't really suffer.

I resigned from the position after four months, but had learned much on those Pex routes and problems. That place was probably the singular best developmental aid to my climbing progress I'd discover – particularly for footwork – until wooden boards came along a couple of years later.

So it was, 'Thanks for the job Mr Guy ... and for everything, especially for putting me up you two ... call us if you're coming to the Peak, I'm getting a place – T'ra!' and caught the train back to Prestatyn. Mum picked me up from the very same platform where we'd met Dad after he'd fled those yetis when I was five.

With Basher below Malham Cove. **Photo:** Geoff Birtles.

8b.

SHEFFIELD: a NEW JOB ('what the..?'), ALFRED SMAKES, and that house!

I'd had a few trips over to Stoney to be with Jerry before moving to Sheffield and had done some of the best and hardest routes there like *Kellogg*, *Kink* and *Circe*, mostly in the presence of fantastic new acquaintances like all the local nicknamed climbers, Dirty Derek, Carny, Noddy, POD, Famous Chris, Chesters, Zippy, Plantpot, Big Smeg et al., plus the Kirk/Mitchell brothers John and Paul.

John Kirk recalls, May 2015:

Andy and Jerry arrived on the Stoney scene at the beginning of the eighties. Like many others they came out of nowhere. Andy was clearly driven, but not as cocky as Jerry. Quieter, more contemplative – he seemed a little more in awe of history and tradition. He'd shuffle up and down Windy Ledge working out what he could do to become part of that history. Each time I heard of Andy he had climbed something harder on limestone or in Wales. Splitting from Jerry he got involved in the Sheffield scene around the Porter Cottage pub and soon was living/surviving in the city. One of the first sponsored climbers, he was under pressure to deliver the goods in terms of new routes and repeats. He pushed himself to the limit on a regular basis, so much so that one of his shoulders wore out and needed repairing in his early 20s. This was something new in the sport. Training and crimping on tiny holds was taking its toll on the new generation. Andy got into drinking and women and the Sheffield scene began to get him down, but he was still climbing very hard routes, often with very little protection. I was a bit surprised when he switched to the gritstone to complete an epic first ascent on Curbar.

Paul Mitchell, May 2015:

> Yeah, I was one of the top lads along with Andy Barker until the Moffatt, Pollitt, and Moon generations turned up. I remember a young Jerry doing *Circe* with pre-placed gear, placed by other leaders. His technique was totally unrefined, but his massive determination was evident. The route had already been climbed no falls by Pete O'Donovan and John Kirk … I also remember you 'walking up' *Hot Rock* and thinking somebody had chipped jugs. They hadn't – you were talented and fit.

I caught up with Jerry when I finally made the move across to Sheffield. This was three days before my twenty-first birthday and Jack the Cake from back in Dyserth had let Justin and me use the little van to cart all my belongings over from home.

I'd barely been there two days – dossing at Neil Foster's place at no. 84 Hunter House Road, Hunters Bar – when Mr Guy from Liverpool tracked me down via my mum.

'Andy, you should call my fellow shop manager Martin Whitaker at the Sheffield branch, he's got a vacancy and is a climber himself – said he knew all about you.'

Well it *was* October, most of the limestone crags were drenched and I could still train down the gym or at home after work, knew Blacks' range – right down to the tents, woolly socks and dib, dib, dib badges – and so Mr Whitaker gave me a start on about my fifth day in Sheffield! Boss Martin's days off were always a blast and I'd play up to the max, trying to impress the gorgeous lass who worked in the shop opposite (was this a repeat of that earlier Forwyn infatuation with a T*** again?). Sometimes I'd don full mountaineering gear, stand dead still in the window holding an ice axe, and suddenly go 'Boo!' at people out front looking in; or dress up in full (way too small) Boy Scout regalia and have her in stitches over the road. Whenever I had the chance and her store was empty I'd ring the shop and we'd chat, laughing and gesturing to one another across narrow Earl Street as we spoke. We had clandestine meetings at lunchtime or after work in a cosy little bar around the corner, and one lunchtime caught the bus and went back to my place coz I knew the lads would all be out. What a kisser she was too! Talk about full-on passion – we were both 'hot to trot' and were all over each other 'cept I nibbled her neck a bit too enthusiastically and left the faintest of marks and she leapt up off the couch: 'My boyfriend's a bikie and punches anyone who even looks at me. He'll go ape if this shows up when I get home.' End of dalliance. Drat.

Anyway, I'd taken over Neil's loft room coz he'd moved out, but he'd kindly put in a good word to the landlord Alfie on my behalf. Now Mr Alfred Shakes apparently drove a bright pink E-Type Jag, was 'good with colours' and 'skipped puddles' (as they say) and 'You'll be in in a flash,' Neil reckoned, 'cept I'd be sharing with three others – all girls! Neil was good for his word – Alfie was most pleased when he turned up to meet me as I was wearing ballet tights and a small vest!

'I'll see these girls off,' I thought, just as soon as my signature had dried on the lease papers. 'This is gonna be a climbers' house' … and within weeks the girls started moving out, one after the other – I always left the toilet seat up which infuriated them, amongst numerous other deliberate annoyances like always having dossing climbers around and dropping the odd gut.

'Jez, there's a place going at my house, you'll have your own room and it's warm – you can't stay in that woodshed another winter,' I told him one bitter morning at Stoney cafe over a mug of tea and a brown bun as we hunted for isolated triangles on the Formica top of our table (a popular pastime back then as the squiggly pattern apparently had just one per table, all in different places), but he said he had a doss on Noddy's sofa now. A week later he came around with two packs and a carrier bag and the gender balance was equalised. The second girl 'gave up the ghost' and Chris Gore moved in. The last of the three girls fled – vowing never to speak to me again – so Martin 'Basher' Atkinson had a room too.

Chris Gore, March 2015:

Andy was very much responsible for putting together one of the great climbing households of the time, not that it was an intentional decision, more a gathering of friends. We all knew each other pretty well and even though there was a potential clash of egos we all got on exceptionally well.

Yey! Mission accomplished – and what a household it was! I'd just quit at Blacks (for the second time!) to train with my brand-new housemates for the new climbing season. But the training regime got somewhat sidetracked as I got into the clubbing scene: The Leadmill, The Limit or Barry Noble's Roxy discotheque. Picking up girls, and being picked up too. Loveless sex in strange beds, kitchens and alleyways. Animals rutting for pure pleasure whilst in alcohol or dope-induced states, often waking the next lunchtime to embarrassing: 'Oh God, I didn't did I?'s (The girls too on occasion no doubt.)

Mr Gore again:

Andy's nights out and consumption of ale and ciggies really didn't seem to affect his prodigious talent for climbing; strong fingers, precise footwork and fluid movement, added to a drive and determination coupled with a love for new routeing ... Andy's talent for climbing was phenomenal, but he also had another natural talent – women were just attracted to him, some sort of animal magnetism. As housemates we didn't understand what the attraction was, but it was most definitely there. When Andy wasn't in a relationship, he could go out assured that he would come back with someone if he so wished; now admittedly not all of them were beauties!

It'll not be news to you, dear reader/s, that the weather is often crap in the Peak, so throughout my years in Sheffield I'd often escape to the south of France. I much preferred Verdon to Buoux though and really wanted to try Jerry's route *Papi on Sight* but, for one reason or another, never got the chance. I'd sometimes spend a fair amount of time exploring Castellane, Moustiers and Avignon and checking out the bars and cafés and barely managing a 7-anything. I was at times simply burnt out and needed a good week or two off so I could go back home thoroughly refreshed – but shagged-out too. You see, I got to know (shall we say?) 'Brigitte' from the bakery in La Palud (rather well, ahem!) and loved her buns (groan).

Everyone made such a song and dance about the whole affair at the time and it's apparent that many still recall 'their versions' of all the sordid details. I kid you not though – hence all the fuss – 'Brigitte' was *my* 'younger Brigitte Bardot'. I often got amusingly referred to as 'Jagger-esque', so putting those two characters together you'd expect, well, something!

Back to Chris Gore:

There was one particular occasion that highlighted Andy's natural attraction for women. It was summer 1986. Climbing in the Verdon Gorge, France, was always a relaxing affair – the lake in the morning waiting for cooler temperatures, climb late afternoon and meet up at the bar in the evening. The drinks were served by the blonde, beautiful and buxom 'Brigitte' and there was an instant attraction. She would serve the drinks and then hang around Andy's table. He didn't speak much French nor she English but they communicated, albeit with a little help from John Kirk ...

John Kirk, via email, May 2015:

> We shared an amusing fortnight in the Verdon Gorge when I had more or less given up climbing. We were at the campsite with crazy Spaniards stealing our food. Andy found a local girl ... I will never forget him having to mop out the still slippery tent afterwards. On such details are legends built ...

A very young Steve McClure was camped there too, but I didn't know it at the time, in fact I'm not sure we ever met.

Steve McClure email, March 2015:

> At seventeen years old we arrived at the sun-bleached Verdon Gorge. Glancing around we soaked it up; Pollitt strumming his guitar from under a willow tree, Basher and Gore animating their projects and Moffatt's voice filling the campground. We had arrived right in the middle – guitars, lie-ins, Lycra, beer and dope painted the scene. The big boys were there, magazine heroes and front cover stars – far too big for us; we hung around like flies but something of them seemed to drift into us. We climbed harder, better, faster and for longer. As I'd come to learn much later, a rock star is usually just a normal person who happens to climb hard routes. But when hard routes are all you want to do these guys are elevated and beyond normal. Rock climbing is a simple sport, we climb for ourselves, but we draw inspiration from the characters who push the limits of our dreams ...

Anyway, back to the early days at no. 84 and I'd gotten home from some bedsit across town, and not surprisingly had picked up a dose of the crabs. Itchy little bastards they were too and I 'hosted' them for two days before (acting all casual even though I was desperate) asking Chris if there was a doctors' surgery nearby.

'Yeah, bottom of [whatever it was] road,' he replied. 'You alright, Andy?'

'Yeah, good as gold, ta.'

So I registered at the reception and in due course was called in. Doc snapped on the rubber gloves and I dropped my pants for an inspection. He said I was fine but my pubes had crabs so wrote me a prescription for crab cream. 'Thanks doctor, I've met a lovely lass and she's asked me out and I'm dead keen.'

'Well rub that in three times a day and they'll be gone in no time ... Good luck with the new girlfriend.'

'Thanks doc, bye.'

My first date with the future ex-girlfriend was ace and led to several more; then I was invited back to hers for supper and to meet the family. No probs, a pleasure I thought; she'd met my mum – who approved wholeheartedly – so it was now my turn to reciprocate. I was seated at the table with her, her sister and Mum when Dad walked in. Oh fuck me, it was my doctor! I wanted to crawl under the table and die but he was the model of professionalism and we enjoyed a delightful evening meal, even though I couldn't quite get it out of my head that he'd had his hands on my tackle a week before his daughter did! She and I were together for a year or so, but things eventually just fizzled out and we parted ways. She was a wonderful young lady …

It's funny really looking back at our time in that famous [infamous? *Ed.*] shared house – there was Chris, the eldest, followed by Basher, Jerry, and then me. Even though there were only a few years or even months between us all, there was a definite hierarchy or pecking order. If Chris fancied Chee Dale tomorrow, Chee Dale it probably was – even though only Basher had a car, a Citroën 2CV he'd named 'Uriah', coz it was a 'Heap' (a '70s' band you youngsters!). Chris wasn't bossy, I'm not suggesting that for a moment, but I for one looked up to him, and he called the shots on the majority of our 'family' affairs. He made sure the gas, 'leccy' and phone bills were all paid on time, reminded us of our rent and signing-on days and really was the glue that kept the household together. Displayed an often stoic yet somewhat magnetic personality I thought – from day one.

Chris Gore:

> It was the eighties, we were young. Political correctness had not been invented and we all lived in our own little bubble at Hunters Bar … no. 84 became our rite of passage, four young men exploring a new world that for us had no barriers. A constant fog of cigarette smoke, late nights, gatherings at the house, card games late into the night, sessions at the Porter Cottage and listening to Andy play Smalltown Boy on continuous replay, and of course the climbing. The household of no. 84 became responsible for some of the greatest routes of the '80s.

Chris occasionally made us all awesome meals as well, and one particularly 'high-spirited' lasagne night had us cracking up with tales of when he drove double-decker buses with Geraldine Taylor – top British female climber – as his conductor. 'Heel and toe, heel and toe!' he laughed – wiping béchamel sauce from his mouth – describing how *some* drivers would deliberately make the passengers stagger back and forth in the upstairs and downstairs aisles 'simultaneously' as they approached the next stop. I choked on my spliff and almost wet myself, and the soon-to-become 'JM Cool J' – 'gangsta' alter-ego of the best climber in the world – crawled behind the sofa and wouldn't come out. He'd turned into a mouse, so he advised, and was squeaking between fits of laughter as we'd just split open another six-pack and he really wasn't a drinker. Yorkshire's finest young star was there on that sofa too – grinning massively, having hit the wall and ground to a halt – focussing straight ahead and saying ... well, nothing really! Just grinning. He was, as we'd say at the time, 'way stead'. Eventually I wiped away my tears and begged Chris for another real-life *On the Buses* tale.

Now, I'll qualify (but can't really justify) the above by reminding you that this was the early eighties – a long time ago now and we were a group of young, fit, doley climbers and not, of course, the respectable, clean-living, upstanding pillars of society we each morphed into as maturity took its inevitable toll.

Ahem! But where were we? Yeah, bloody great climber too, Chris. Strong-as fingers and had terrific stamina. I seem to recall he'd smoked cigs when we'd first met a few years earlier, but had given up (wise decision – I haven't and still knock off forty-plus a day). I must admit though, we did rib Chris mercilessly over that famous quote from donkey's years earlier – the one that he would never live down. Chris had apparently screamed, 'It's only five ceeeeeeeeeeeee ... ' when, as a young up-and-comer himself, he took a monster fall on about the fourth ascent of Livesey's *Right Wall* on Dinas Cromlech.

For whatever divine reason, Basher and I just clicked. From day one. Humour played a great part and we'd take the piss with no quarter given, be it over his too-tight pants with proud package on display, or my scruffy hair or regular failures to 'trap off' with the hotter women. Whatever the excuse we were regularly in hysterics. We were both hungry-as for the rock and were trying to keep up with Jerry and Chris. In truth we weren't *that* far behind, but it felt like miles to us at the time. Certainly with the on-sight flashes, Jerry was leagues ahead – of *anyone*, anywhere on the planet. Jez, by his own admission, was not good with reading books, school work or the daily papers, but could read a climbing sequence in a nanosecond where, say, you or I would rock up, back down, feel around the other way and step down again wasting precious time and energy. Jerry would've sussed it, executed it and forgotten about it as he headed for the belay ledge. Yes! He was a phenomenal on-sighter.

One day Basher got home and was totally buzzing. He'd soloed *White Wand* on the grit and was bouncing around the lounge.

'Calm down, have a fag and tell us about it.' He did and it sounded terrifying.

I gather from the *Peak Rock* book launch video on *UKC* that it's a lasting memory for Martin and all these years later ranks amongst his best-ever days on rock, along with *Mecca – The Mid-Life Crisis* of course.

It was Basher who coined the title 'besties', and we were, there was no doubt about that. We went to Yorkshire together and I got to meet his family in Barnoldswick, lovely, and we did a couple of days guiding beginners up some scruffy crag for 'Hank the Wank', some old duffer who ran courses and liked his rock guides 'young and taut'. Terrible driver too – rarely went over 40 mph but his foot went up and down on the accelerator pedal constantly, so it was always a sick-making, rocking-back-and-forth journey. He paid cash though, so that was good. We also went to Malham ('Mayhem' as John 'Spider' McKenzie had cleverly renamed it) and ran into Geoff Birtles in the field below the cove. Geoff took a photo of us and a few days later handed me a print. I absolutely cherish that picture (the one I showed you a minute ago); it's one of my all-time faves. Oddly, the camera *does* lie sometimes and Basher looks emaciated and I'm **not** wearing a hair-covered Joe Brown helmet. Geez, we were young, fit and healthy then – ciggies aside (Basher's is behind him so you can't pick it out).

Eventually he moved out of no. 84 though, to live in sin with his girlfriend Fiona as their wedding was fast approaching. A day or so before the big event he was booked in to Plas y Brenin to give a slide show, so we drove over to Wales in Uriah and stayed at my mum's place in Dyserth (Mum adored Martin). Sitting next to the fireside at Walden Cottage after Mum had gone to bed I was particularly quiet, collecting my thoughts and on a bit of a knife edge: 'Biff, as your bestie, are you up for this, ya know, marriage and all?'

His reply couldn't have been more unequivocal: 'Yeah And, I can't wait … just what I've always wanted.' I was really pleased for Martin and 'Fiz' of course, but also somewhat glum – selfishly – coz I was losing my best friend.

So, Jerry was climbing harder than the rest of us but Chris was only perhaps a half grade (or put another way, a mere couple of days) behind him, certainly no more, it seemed to me. When Basher had first moved in to no. 84 he was only just leading the E5s and we all had a good few years' head start over him coz we'd led loads, plus a few E6s. Ha! Wouldn't that soon be reversed – in my case I mean, as my bestie's progression was remarkable! Our household tally of Es (points not pills, they weren't invented then), had we been counting, would've been staggering – especially during a period of frenetic activity by Ron and then after, when the four of us repeated his *The Vision*. Wolfgang Güllich was with us for that one, and I light-heartedly ribbed him regarding the German pronunciation of the letters 'V' and 'W' as he wanted to do '*The Wision*' in '*Vater*' cum Jolly.

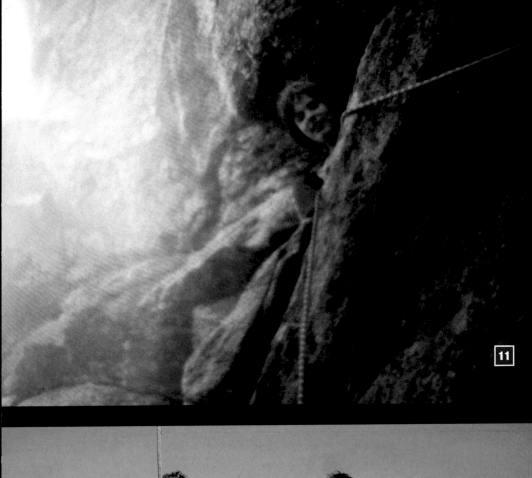

11

12

14

16

RED POINT, a range of packs which allow you to move quickly and easily on mountain, hill and rock.

Lightweight but durable, simple but efficient, RED POINT gives you the freedom to get closer to nature.

For full information on this exciting new rucsac concept and the complete range, write to the address below.

Photo: A. Rouse

Berghaus, 34 Dean Street, Newcastle upon Tyne NE1 1PG. Tel: (0632) 323561.

EXCLUSIVE RED POINT OFFER+FREE + RED POINT CHALK BAG WITH EVERY FLAME, EDGE OR WALL

'OK, I'll write it as I *hear* it Wolfie, you say it as I've *written* it, and we should be right.' He took it well and got the joke!

Then it was Dominic Lee's desperate (but cleverly named) *Obscene Gesture* where the crux involved sticking the middle finger up into a hole at eye level, followed by *Indecent Exposure*, *The Body Machine*, and *Prow* at Raven Tor – 'The Snore'. Then *Eye of The Tiger* and *Roadrunner* etc. Ron after Ron after Ron. Plus Basher and I regularly tipped in another thirty-odd points on returning from respective weekends away in Yorkshire and Wales, and Jerry was no slouch, having previously thrown in his own *Orange Sunshine* and *Rooster Booster* amongst others.

Chris wasn't a big new-router and preferred doing early repeats – but his anagrammatically correct *Ogre* in Chee Dale was indeed something of a beast. Chris continues...

> Andy had a fantastic capacity for new routes; for my part, I am always thankful to those unselfish climbers like him that put in all the hard work to do 1st ascents, so that I can go and repeat them. Andy's new routes ranged from the hardest trad to the hardest sport; his routes on North Stack and Raven Tor stand testament to his abilities. In the main we were good at climbing because we climbed a lot, like every day if we could; the routes were vertical to slightly overhanging, so you never powered out, you just ran out of steam. As routes became harder and more powerful they needed a more considered approach. This wasn't Andy's style, he was like 'Tigger' – bouncy, bouncy up he'd go, fall off, no sooner than he'd lowered down then he was off again, only to fall off again; but that was the way Andy did routes and success was never that far off. One of the most impressive aspects of Andy's climbing was his footwork, his feet moved very fast and with pinpoint accuracy, there was no scuffing them up the rock, trying to get some purchase; the foothold was seen, the foot placed on it first time then he'd move on up. It was always a pleasure to watch him climbing.

That first winter with Chris, Jerry and Basher was intense – for several bleak months it was pretty much a case of two or three days' training then a rest day before the cycle was repeated. Most of our training was at the Sheffield Polytechnic gym where we'd spend hours doing pull-ups and dead-hangs on timber edges screwed on to the horizontal bars, or wandering up the road to traverse on the small, sharp edges of Broomgrove Wall in the freezing cold. Jerry generally preferred bouldering at Tom's Roof or other areas in the Peak though – anywhere he could find a patch of dry, overhanging rock –

so would often hitch out there on his own or sometimes with Quentin Fisher or Tim.

It wasn't a bad start to winter really, weather-wise, so a bunch of us would head out regularly to Rubicon or High Tor, Stoney or Raven Tor. Rubicon was a lovely, sunny spot if the sky was clear, and had some pretty vicious little routes such as *Jaws, A Miller's Tale, Piranha* and *White Bait* plus the big, loose roof of *Rubicon* itself which (for some unfathomable reason) I soloed – chucking off half the loose holds along the way. What *was* I thinking?

Managing the first pitch of Jerry's *Little Plum* was definitely a watershed moment for me, as few could touch it (maybe just the Chris's – Gore and Hamper), but it took a further dozen or so visits – usually with the ridiculously talented but wastefully part-time climber Lawrence 'Loz' Francombe – until I'd worked out the top pitch and it had dried out enough for me and Gore to make the third and fourth ascents of 'both pitches in a day' following Hamper's repeat. I then reckoned I'd 'made it' in the Peak, coz all the other top climbers bar Jez, 'Christmas' Hamper, me and Gore had given up and wandered off dejected. *Hysterectomy*, next to the classic *Menopause* above Windy Ledge, with Loz, was the final route before the weather totally crapped out and the sleet began to fall.

Chris Hamper and I climbed a lot together at the time as the lads from no. 84 were back in Europe following the competition circuit.

Chris Hamper writes, May 2015:

One afternoon I managed to free *Menopause* at Stoney with Bill Turner [a fellow teacher at Chris's school]. I guess this was my finest five minutes. I'd repeated *Circe* the weekend before and Geoff Birtles happened to be there and took a photo. Somehow he got to hear that I'd done *Menopause* and rang me up at home to confirm. The result was a headline in *Crags* plus a little photo. Injury followed – it usually did – pull, pull harder, even harder, break! I still went to Stoney cafe at weekends of course, see what's going on, read the new routes book, mooch about the crag and find a party. We were athletes trying not to look like athletes. I would wear a pair of my dad's old trousers, a big woolly jumper and trench coat. No rucksack, just a plastic carrier bag. Turn up at the crag and no one wants to talk to you; all change when you solo the route they'd just failed on. I met Jerry who had just repeated *Menopause*, introduced myself and got the '**You** did that?' look.

At Matlock's High Tor, Phil Burke's *Tales of Yankee Power* and that other fine route *Bastille* became my all-time favourite climbs in the Peak and remained so for many years. We'd always laugh on the drive around to the cafe at the top, for each time we'd pass a little cul-de-sac called Pump Close. I supposed we'd been warned! *Tales…* wasn't desperate but required good footwork and was pretty run-out up to a little *in-situ* thread runner. Now that thread wasn't a tied loop of tape but a short sling poked into one pocket and pulled out through an adjacent one, so you had to hang there on a small finger pocket and at full stretch clip both open ends of it. I'll never forget John Codling, a big fellow, getting all the way up to the thread, 'Elvis leg' in overdrive, then making a grab for the tape … 'cept he only caught one side and of course it pulled through. He went *absolutely miles*! Oh how we laughed later on – with him, not at him of course.

One time Mark Leach and I went to High Tor with Bernard Newman to get pics on *Castellan* for his and Ken Wilson's upcoming *Extreme Rock* book. We both did the roof pitch but I was feeling sick as a dog and slumped on the belay wanting to throw up from the stance. Perhaps a big night before or the heat that day? I can't recall. It turned out to be another of my favourite photos, especially as you can't tell I was utterly wasted and had pulled my way to the top using every runner!

Extreme Pollitt: Bernard Newman, September 2015:

Andy and I worked together a lot on *Extreme Rock*. Which was just as well because I needed photos of some very hard climbs and climbers who could lead E5 at the drop of a hat, were keen to be involved for no material reward, and who looked brilliant on rock were few and far between in the mid-1980s. But Andy was more than just photo fodder, he was a mate and endowed with the boundless enthusiasm of youth. He was also one of the finest climbers of his generation – any generation.

Now my climbing photography shuns posed shots; I look for natural body shapes that are dictated by the route and the rock, not some artificial aesthetic, so I'd tell people just to climb and let me try to get the best body shape as it happened. Andy, however, needed no prompting – he moved beautifully and naturally – God's gift to climbing photographers.

So we had a few adventures and loads of fun shooting some superb climbs; chasing weather and light around the Peak and Wales – an often frustrating but ultimately rewarding pursuit.

Andy was a phenomenal rock athlete and could pull a big lead out of the bag in seemingly any conditions: like that crystal winter's day at Millstone when it was so cold I couldn't speak, let alone hold the camera steady, and Andy cruised *Great Arête* as Zippy and I became rapidly hypothermic; or a boiling afternoon on High Tor for *Castellan*, with the great Mark Leach.

Andy would just do it – take *London Wall* for instance. This is still a big tick for any high-end rock climber but not, seemingly, for the young pup. We'd waited for the crucial afternoon sun to glance across the face, pulling texture from the golden grit and making for great shadows. Andy led it effortlessly despite the buffeting breeze; I knew I'd nailed it but let slip that, although the black and whites would look fine (better, as it turned out), I wished I'd used colour. 'Well, let's do it again,' he grinned. I loaded the Kodachrome as Andy stripped the sparse runners and he cruised it – again. The whole session had perhaps taken half an hour.

But it's the fun I remember and the astonishment at how easy Andy made everything look. Oscar Wilde famously quipped that youth is wasted on the young, but not so for young Andy!

THE LAKES, SHRIVEL-DICK AND VAUDEVILLE

A few of us spent New Year 1983–84 in Ambleside in the Lake District – a beautiful place where Chris's girlfriend 'Roo' lived (Roo as in Rooley, not Kanga). Some friends of mine were staying in the town too, having just arrived from the Midlands, and this most certainly added to the 'Amble-iance' of the place, especially as they'd brought 'gear' with them. Loads of it, and 'Ha-Ha' us 'naughty' few laughed, demonically, as we took turns sniffing at the little packets.

Roo (*non-participator* in 'our' nonsense) had booked us in to Zeffirelli's – the more upmarket restaurant of the two in town that could be bothered opening – where we 'all congregated for supper and sang "Auld Lang Syne" gaily as the snowflakes fell outside the pretty, candlelit windows … '

Rubbish! It was degging it down and we were all rat-arsed, no one gave a toss about the snow and by my count at least three of us were off our heads … 'Upmarket my … ' – we were a flippin' disgrace!

Scotch Ben had spag bol or something tomato-ey all down his 'clean' shirt (clean meaning the lesser-worn one) and a friend of Judith's took this length of spaghetti in her mouth and … went 'Pwap, ahh' and licked her lips at the end winking at *me* … 'I'm in, defo,' I thought and went to boot my mate under the table but instead caught someone else square on the knee. 'Sorry lass!' Ben knew exactly what I meant and smirked quietly.

It was a welcome change from the Porter Cottage in Hunters Bar, as well as being my first-ever New Year away from my Welsh North Wales. 'The shoplift-ing's piss-easy,' I wrote on a postcard to my Mum. 'Surprisingly lax security for such a bustling town' – see if she ever read 'em, as Mum would've been more interested in the 'pretty photo' side depicting Loch Ness or whatever pond it was those Lakelanders were so proud of.

Just not the general store though: 'They're our friends, And.'

'OK, understood Jude.'

'…ith,' Chris chips in … 'It's … ith.' I thought he was lisping. 'Jude-ith, And.'

'Oh, sorry, can I have an "e" as in "And-*e*" then Chris*topher*?' And we're off … clutching sides in agony … dying flies, Stellas tumbling over.

I put on a particularly lovely hand-knitted woolly jumper – and walked straight out of the 'Particularly Lovely Hand-Knitted Woolly Jumper' shop wearing a 'touristy special' – a £99 price tag slapped over a 14-quid one hang-ing off the back and the hanger still inside the neck, a great big question mark sticking up. Hmm, naughty indeed.

I awoke that first Lakeland morning in the bed of Judith's randy friend – the spaghetti slurper from Zeffirelli's had struck – exactly as Chris and Basher had prewarned me she might!

First proper day there and Tim and I got to sample the thuggish delights of the Bowderstone after a lengthy 'hitch and hike' down (or is it up?) Borrowdale. This impressive boulder played host to Pete Kirton and Jerry's ultimate power problems. *Inaudible Vaudeville* was a classic and that afternoon is the first I can recall of feeling that initial vague, dull ache in my shoulders. Confession time: I'd snorted two thick lines of speed – my first ever, so threw and threw and threw myself at those severely overhanging problems, unable to sit still and rest between goes, garbling giggly gibberish at a million miles an hour with Tim, but loving every minute of life, totally 'whizzing'. Damn the cold. We ran down to the gate and back … garbling more about *The Bowderiser*.

More 'lines' that evening and round two in the fart sack with 'what's-her-face.' 'Does funny things to me that speed … ' I say, apologetically … previous night we'd 'banged like a shithouse door in a storm' … for ages … but now, 'down there', I looked like I'd just walked out of a freezing-cold lake. No penis. None. Not even a shrunken, tiddly thing – nothing! Gone inside. Not coming out to play … and I'm in a hot, nude chick's bed. 'Fuck!' Or not as the case may be.

'It's called shrivel-dick you useless prat … ' she mocked, not even feigning sympathy.

'How long does it last?' (Horrified.)

'A couple of days, see ya, I'm off out.'

'Aww, well fuck me!'

'I would if you were up to it ... ' and slammed the door.

Two more 'speedy' days and I hitched back to Hunters Bar, but spent a day and a half in bed on the come-down, curled up in the foetal position, sobbing, unable to get up and absolutely hating life, wishing I was dead. I swore I'd never touch that stuff again – and to this very day I haven't. Zippy, by then resident at no. 84, would pop up to check on me from time to time. I'll never forget that ... 'Top bloke', Zips, as we say in 'Upsidedownland'.

PUSHING BODY AND MIND

Ignoring the shoulder problem – thinking it was just a temporary soreness or something – I kept on training as hard as possible with the others back at the Poly gym, figuring the discomfort would subside in due course. It was a short winter and by late March conditions were improving by the day. Beautiful sunny days on grit, quite cold but clear. My diary entries record some of my best memories of early grit: leading *Pool Wall* at Lawrencefield then *Green Death* and *Great Arête* at Millstone, and soloing *Edge Lane* for the second time. The following week I flashed *White Wall* then led the fourth ascent of Ron's *Scritto's Republic* – in Chris's new Firé rock shoes.

Another brief trip up to Malham in Yorkshire with Basher was certainly well timed and I was fortunate enough to grab the second ascents of *Chasing the Dragon*, *El Coronel*, *Seventh Grade* and Ron's *Yosemite Wall* – back when it was hard and you had to carry gear (violins out please!). Ron recounts in his autobiography that he felt the route was diminished when it was retro-bolted for the sports nuts – I concurred 100 per cent with his sentiments when later repeating it on in-situ draws, all a few feet apart and right where you needed a runner.

I'd manage the first on-sight of *Cave Route Right-Hand* over at Gordale Scar a little later. Dead proud of that one I was coz all the previous ascents were done with yo-yos and the first on-sight was a major Yorkshire prize – I felt like a 'Peak Raider' , just like Big Ron a few years earlier when he'd come down to Wales and picked his *Strawberries*.

Despite all this eastern action North Wales was calling yet again and I now had wheels – a Ford Escort van with a mattress in the back. I'd wired my portable cassette player up to the battery so had music and, more importantly, freedom to travel where and when I fancied.

Now I'll apologise: I really didn't want this chapter to read like a bragging list of ' ... and I did this, then I did that, oh, and then I did that too ... ' – definitely not – but unlike Jerry, Ron and the two Johns (Redhead and Dawes), I never really managed anything particularly groundbreaking or ahead of its time, so it's difficult to devote twenty pages to one or two world-class climbs. In any case, these routes I'm referring to, although mostly upper-end-ish in their day, are undoubtedly well down the 'hard' list nowadays and the number of climbers operating around and well above those old grades is completely staggering! In truth though, I suppose most of the routes would even now fall into a 'respectable' bracket, so to this day, thirty years later, could almost be considered as 'rites of passage' – just like *Our Father, Menopause, Tequila, Indecent, Rooster Booster, Prow, Strawberries* and a million other true classic climbs were when I was working my way up through the grades.

My approach to becoming a better climber was to always attempt the on-sight flash, preferably placing all the gear on lead; but as styles evolved and redpointing came into vogue, it often never mattered if you were attempting a route on someone else's quickdraws – or they on yours. As long as it was always near or at my limit. Example: say you're regularly climbing F8b or above then *Chimes, Boot Boys, Arch Enemies, Thormen's Moth, Ruby Fruit Jungle* or *Over the Moon* aren't going to trouble you in the least are they? But aspire to them on your progression up through the grades and attempt them when they're a smidgeon above your best level, put in the necessary time, and you'll be rewarded tenfold for the effort and appreciate them for what they are – classics.

I guess I knew my place in the overall pecking order and though very prolific on the new route front for many years I just kept on plugging away, always a step or two behind the others in terms of difficulty. Arguably not for boldness though, but no one else cared for or 'got' that anyway really, except JR and JD and perhaps a small group of others like Paul Pritchard and Nick Dixon. The exception to that statement being, of course, Jerry's lead of *Master's Wall* on Cloggy! Now *Master's Wall* was the biggest prize in Wales, if not Britain, at the time – but I deliberately avoided taking a look. Firstly, it was JR's domain and I respectfully shied away – to tell the (pre-1984) truth, doubting my ability and certainly aware of Jerry's superior friction soles. However, I was coiled like a spring and eagerly awaiting the day when he'd pull it off so I could attempt the on-sight repeat – ASAP – whilst his chalk would still be there; but then the bolt was placed, and Jerry in his new Firés dispensed with both the bolt and the line, bagging the historic lead. I guess I lost interest ... but still wish I could have that route on my résumé ... regrettably I don't, and it never will be!

It was a similar thing with Johnny Dawes's *Indian Face* some years later. I had absolutely no interest in going anywhere near it. There's no doubt I believed I had the mental and physical capacity to attempt it, but I simply wasn't prepared for all the top-roping and pre-practice, not my style. JR's neither. Plus the walk-in: I never had the legs for it, did I? Obviously I was well impressed and respected Johnny for his super-bold lead, but was somewhat irked coz he'd only a couple of days prior seconded me on the first ascent of *The Hollow Man* on North Stack Wall – totally agreeing it was E8 and congratulating me on a fine lead. He graded *Indian Face* E9 – doubtless it is – and stole my thunder.

To be brutally honest, I should concede that my climbing 'reputation' or 'notoriety' (call it what you will) was probably as much a creation of the climbing media as any real talent. I was never camera-shy: always up for photo shoots for my sponsors and needed the most up-to-date pics for my annual slide show tours, and was, by all accounts, particularly photogenic. I guess I'd become everything John Redhead railed against: the well-paid 'loud-Lycra'd sell-out'. An 'attitude'. A new route – any new one (well not quite) if it got me back in the mags next month – being sufficient fodder for my insatiable hunger for more. More what though? Money? Publicity? Bragging rights? I'm not quite sure, but will happily concede I had an ego as big as the moon (I wasn't Robinson Crusoe there though was I?).

Having read JR's *…and one for the crow* (bloody awesome, my favourite book by a country mile) I now have a much better understanding of where he was coming from, but am confident in my qualification that those 1980s sponsorship quids permitted me untold freedom – bereft of obligation to my sponsors perhaps not, and I did retrace many of John's very own steps through similar mental turmoils. Generally always on sight and after the fact, 'trepidatious', *so* scared that you're not actually scared any more, more resigned to a horrible landing unless you can pull it off.

Do or die – literally.

Yes, one *must* be 'as one' with the rock as John put it; I'll agree 100 per cent with JR there, and I delighted in that adrenaline surge whilst preparing for the battle of a lifetime – *my* battle, no one else's.

Again.

Third time this month!

Don't push it Andy.

Why not?

Steve Lewis, me and Ben Moon in Parisella's Cave.

8b+

COMPETITIONS and FRENCH STYLE

Back on home turf at no. 84 things were changing. Jerry, Chris and Basher had all fully embraced the 'French style' – where they'd bolt-to-bolt, practise the moves, and pull their ropes down before 'redpointing' the climbs in one go, with all the quickdraws in place.

I wasn't pleased with the lads – made my feelings perfectly clear one evening when just the four of us were home, dosser-less for once. Said I thought it took the real challenge, adventure and sheer bravery out of climbing and dragged everything down to an inevitable, safe and positive conclusion – no matter how many days it took – no one counted anyway. I thought they were just chasing grades, and not even *British* ones any more – everything was 7-something not E-something anymore; felt they weren't considering the aesthetic line, exposure or finer elements of our sport – but they argued that by using these new techniques they could climb way harder stuff, in total safety, just like the Europeans, and that was all that mattered.

To be fair, they were mostly doing it on the Continent where it was de rigueur, but when they started going to competitions where stunning 100 per cent natural, sheer Alpine cliff faces were mercilessly chiselled to suit the required difficulty – and the boundaries of the 'routes' were clearly defined in bright red gloss paint slapped on six inches wide – they totally lost me. It was a most unpleasant realisation that times were changing. Pure, utter vandalism and the more the sponsors paid and the prize money increased, the more my housemates turned a collective blind eye to the desecration. Chris wrote an article about competitions for *Mountain* but I really don't think it swayed many people in the 1980s. Indoors? Maybe, but you can't do that to barren cliffs, so it was, 'Not for me thanks, things to do on North Stack Wall.' 'Anyone up for Gogarth?' Negative! 'Good luck at Arco next week then lads … ' Sigh. Left me in their wake they did – I simply couldn't keep up.

Mind you, during that undoubtedly exciting period for the lads, *they weren't* on another six magazine covers, two new posters, slapped across the walls at the Berghaus head office in six-foot-square wall hangings, featured in nine different print ads or giving sixty-odd well-paid public lectures, two radio interviews and doing a US cable TV programme. No, they were just getting better and better and winning money whilst their competition climbing on the chip-ups was being scorned by the vast majority. Absolutely lambasted they were when they tried to bring competitions to Malham – and rightfully so I thought, but, in their favour, they didn't go so far as supporting the chipping and the red line painting!

However, against my better judgement, I did attend one such outdoor event in Bardonecchia, Italy – mainly as we were to drive down there via Freyr in Belgium, nip through Luxembourg, stop at the Frankenjura in Germany, zoom over a Swiss Alpine pass, do the competition in Italy then head to Buoux for three weeks; but also partly out of curiosity and to appease my sponsor Berghaus, who'd sent me four hundred quid and encouraged me to 'go get 'em!' After several hours in the waiting area I was ushered out into the full sun in front of a massive crowd and introduced as 'Ondy Polite', whilst some 'Iti' tied me in. The first bolt was pre-clipped, so grasping the slimy, chipped starting holds I placed my left foot on the rock … stepped up with my right … left foot shot off … instant disqualification! Last place! Shameful, embarrassing – I skulked off with my head down. Gutted. 'No matter,' I thought … 'I'll just get back to looking for new routes on Gogarth when we get home from Buoux.'

Apart from genuinely loving that big Welsh sea cliff, I figured the lads would shit themselves if they were ever prodded with a big, pointy stick or held at gunpoint round that bulge, only to stare up and outwards at that protection-less layback up the twenty-five-foot flared flake on the second pitch of my E6 *Skinhead Moonstomp* – 200 feet above the sea – with a couple of shoddy runners way below and out of sight. Not that any of them would ever go there of course, I knew that. That was *proper* E6; so to each their own I suppose, and we agreed to disagree.

Amicably of course.

No. 84 Hunter House Road became the go-to place for itinerant climbers

– even on my very first night there I'd had three dossers on the lounge room floor and two crashing out in my own bedroom. The girls were well 'peeved' off! The overspill into mine were John 'Spider' McKenzie, one of Scotland's best climbers, and David B.A. Jones, the photographer, who was going to 'shoot' me for his book the next day on *Roadrunner* at High Tor. Unfortunately he snored really loudly all night; Spider kept kicking him and telling him to 'Shut the fuck up!' … wanting to throttle him. I wanted to throttle them both – had been looking forward to my new room for days!

Now Spider was an absolute hoot and had the sharpest, most laconic wit of anyone I knew – bar perhaps John Kirk – and we climbed together for a while … between fits of laughter. I really 'clicked' with the proud Scotsman (perhaps it was our Celtic heritage?) and shared plenty of memorable days on the crags. On one of his many visits down to the Peak, no. 84 was fully booked – there simply wasn't room for another three dossers – so his crew laid their sleeping bags on Karrimats out in a car park near Tideswell. In the middle of the night a gang of bikies, a dozen or so, pulled in all threatening-like and circled the lads, revving their Harleys and one – their leader – stuck the boot into the side of Spider's pride and joy – his blue Morris Marina. Now that was one *monumental* mistake!

'Fuck Spide, what did ya do?'

'Och, I got out of me pit, found me peg hammer and belted him so fuckin' hard in the chest the head flew off me 'ammer … they sped the fuck out of there … that's why we lobbed here at four this morning … case they came back.'

Spider was hard, but not stupid: 'Take out the hardest and meanest, Pollitt [Spider never called me Andy, ever], and yer right Jimmy.'

John was Glasgow – where they struck first and answered questions later.

Over the next few years it really was just a revolving door of the climbing elite. Pete Kirton – strongest boulderer ever – took Basher's room when he moved out to live with his girlfriend, Fiona; Nick Plishko, who was back at college, got Chris's spot when he married Judith. Zippy, who kept turning down the new hot-water system that Alfie had installed for us (but at the radiators, not the thermostat), sat shivering in a down jacket whilst all the boiling water was spewing into the back garden – not saving a thing, especially not the earth! He'd got Jerry's bedroom earlier when Jez went to Germany for his elbow operation. Finally, Spider took up official residence. Adrian 'Yorick' Hughes had to put up with the damp cellar. Didn't seem to faze him – he *was* 'allowed up' at mealtimes after all! For better or worse no. 84 became internationally renowned. Rather late one evening in '85, or maybe '86, when I was out of action with my shoulder problem and not long back from the pub, some total stranger – an American – turned up loudly announcing: 'I met the boys at Buoux, said I could crash here anytime … man!' He was Christian Griffith, apparently a US top 'gun' at the time – not that I was the least bit interested – and he just wouldn't shut up. I was 'ropable', sitting there fuming, wearing a bag of frozen peas on my shoulder whilst trying to watch something interesting on telly, and all I could hear was this loud Yank crapping on about 7b-plusses and 7-bloody-Cs. In *my* front room. Thanks lads.

Previously, Wolfgang Güllich – German climbing legend, all-round lovely man and a good friend of Jerry's – and his chums Kurt Albert and Norbert Batz had hung out with us too; but I think I upset Norbert when I said I was going down to the off-licence and did anyone else want some cans. Norbert said, 'I do Andy,' and I replied, 'bitter?' I realised later that Norbert felt embarrassed and apologetically said 'bitte' thinking I was pulling him up for not saying 'please'. I certainly wasn't … He didn't like the Tetley's I bought him – wanted Pilsner.

Then there was Antoine, one of the Le Menestrel brothers, and Jean-Baptiste Tribout and the American Alan Watts who was developing Smith Rocks. This was 1986 and Alan was – fair to say – taking European redpoint style to the States for the very first time.

They all stayed over, as did the Belgian Count – Arnould T'Kint (Basher's mate); and Randy Leavitt from the States dropped by once with Bernard Newman to pick me up so us 'Limeys' could show the American our pride and joy – Stoney Middleton. Randy was extremely polite – obviously knew how to exercise tact and diplomacy! It wasn't quite the Yosemite Valley but …

He asked whether people really 'lived' in that woodshed. 'You should see Derek's hedge, or The Land of the Midnight Sun,' I said – meaning the garage forecourt with the all-night security lamp.

They all came and went, but I was living alone injured for most of the year and disinterested, rotating my Birds Eye frozen veggies on the shoulder in twenty minutes on/twenty minutes off cycles, and chomping down ibuprofen tablets while Chris and Basher were tearing it up at Buoux. Hilariously, I only ever bought Birds Eye as they were the tastiest and most expensive brand – even though I never intended to actually *eat* them!

Luckily Tim lived a few doors up (albeit in a hovel) at no. 124, so I always had a mate around. One evening I took a six-pack up and, wading through broken glass, ciggie butts and other detritus – this was their lounge room, I wasn't taking a shortcut through the local tip – settled down on the sticky couch. But someone (there were a dozen or so 'co-habiting' there) suddenly shouted 'Singh' and everyone scarpered. They dove behind couches or ran upstairs.

One chap even stood bolt upright in the corner with a lampshade on his head whilst this frail little old brown face popped around the door and softly pleaded, 'Can I have the rent please?'

'Sorry, they're all out,' I lied, clothes glued to the sofa …

'So fuck off!' came from behind the telly.

1985 and a fair part of '86 was injury time for Jerry too. He had awful elbow problems, so was forced on to the subs bench alongside me. Had we just been over-training since our late teens and it had caught up with us, or were we simply doing the *wrong* training altogether? The 350 pull-ups a night I used to do – complete with diver's weight belt that I'd bought off Quentin Fisher – in 50 sets of 7 on the minute, on a quarter-inch edge nailed to the bedroom rafter: they can't have helped I'm sure? Our injuries appeared to be of the 'repetitive strain' genre; what had started as soreness had simply got worse by the day for the both of us. I can't speak for Jerry, but I don't recall either of us suddenly going, 'Ouch, what was that?' on any particular day, route or boulder problem.

Jez wasn't prepared to sit it out in Sheffield, so had packed up his stuff and left no. 84 to hang out back in Germany with his friends Wolfgang and Kurt. Mercifully we both found remarkable surgeons – Jerry near Munich, myself in Rotherham (via much helpful lobbying from Dennis Gray and the BMC I should add). After sixteen months or so we could both lace up our shoes again and get back out on the rocks. I honestly don't think the break did us all that much harm really – apart from the frustration of being cooped up when we were both hovering around our fittest, and waiting whilst a mishmash of potential cures were investigated: various and numerous anti-inflammatory pills, aspirated joints, physiotherapy sessions, frozen vegetables and Deep Heat were all trialled. We both most certainly came back as keen as ever and were fortunately – in a relatively short time – back where we'd been a year and a half earlier. Jez recounts his return to top form in *Revelations* and here's mine.

I was actually still fairly powerful but had soft skin, zero stamina and was most reluctant to pull too hard or try any right shoulder power moves. 'Gritstone, that's the answer!' I figured: get some mileage in and go soloing easy(ish) stuff – and lots of it. Second week back on the rock and I'd gone out to Froggatt with Basher on a hot, humid day. He was a few moves above me on *Artless*, a very thin and balancy steep slab, when he said: 'Andy, it's greasy-as … go back down … ' but I didn't listen. Slipping off the sloping rock-over I was lucky not to do more damage – my feet had landed either side of a pointy rock sticking out of the ground, but when my legs buckled on contact my coccyx took most of the impact and I rolled over in agony clutching my backside. I'd actually broken the top off that stone with my tail bone, damn it!

According to the X-rays at the Hallamshire Hospital my right heel had a nasty cracked bone and I ended up hobbling out of there an hour or so later with a really sore arse (six weeks sitting on a rubber ring), a plaster pot and flipping crutches to walk with. Bloody brilliant! This wasn't going to hold me back too much though: a week later I was out top-roping at Stoney with Tom Jones and Neil Foster, climbing with one boot and resting whenever my exposed toes hurt. Just no soloing on the grit for a while, or much else I supposed. I could still keep training with the nightly pull-ups though; cragging would have to wait several more frustrating weeks, that's all. When the cast was eventually removed and I'd handed back the sticks, I wasn't really much weaker than when I'd fallen: just uncoordinated and all over the place; but crucially the shoulder had handled a few thousand pull-ups really well and was feeling fine.

A DREADLOCK HOLIDAY

Looking back, a particular Llandudno highlight for me was making the third, and second free, ascent of *The Bittersweet Connection* on Castell y Gwynt. It was odd that Redhead had used a point of aid (eliminated by Fawcett on the second ascent). Maybe he was impatient or couldn't be arsed going back another day? I mean it was 'only' UK technical 6b. Probably just damp that day? I climbed it August '83 with a young dreadlocked kid from Kingston upon Thames who was barely seventeen.

In an email from February 2015, my second on that day recalls the trip with fondness. Ben Moon:

I was very young, very inexperienced but totally addicted to climbing – having just escaped from school and putting my years of education behind me, I started a new education. I was truly living the dream … and how lucky to be dropped off at Pen Trwyn that summer after hitching alone from Stoney? All my climbing heroes were there. All the people whose photos I'd pinned to my bedroom wall back in Kingston, including yourself. Here was the cream of British climbing all in one place. I had to pinch myself to realise that I really was walking up the Marine Drive with Andy Pollitt, top British climber and best friend to Jerry Moffatt! I know you only wanted a belay bunny for the day but I didn't care the slightest, although looking back I am surprised you took such an inexperienced climber on a hard two-pitch route. I remember being very reassured with your performance on the top, easier pitch which was in a very exposed situation – it didn't seem to faze you at all and we both topped out elated with our ascent. Happy days indeed Andy!

Llandudno 1984 was a continuation of '83 really and went along similar lines, though my visits there were becoming less and less frequent as I was directing most of my attention to the Peak and Gogarth.

We'd all doss in the dirt beneath Parisella's Overhang – as would the local wild goat 'Mean Mother' (now immortalised as a Steve Lewis Lower Pen Trwyn 7b!) and her two kids – or if it was chockers, under Pill Box Wall or in the nearby doorway to the old coastguard lookout. Hot baths were available if you had the 'front' to just casually wander into The Grand Hotel and find your way upstairs – it was, as Steve Lewis had confided in me, 'most worthwhile'. Unlimited hot water and as deep as you wanted. Of course, some thoughtless dirtbag went and ruined our scheme by leaving his filthy scum all around the bath, and wet towels on the splashed floor – the game was up! Fuck! What is it with some people, really?

Basher and I had a terrific few days on Castell y Gwynt and put up a clutch of pumpy and run-out new routes. However, far, far more importantly it was great spending time with Martin again, particularly away from the crowds – we 'picked up' exactly where we'd 'left off' when he'd moved out of no. 84 to get married. It's absolutely hilarious now to think that in *August 1984* Basher and I, in our early twenties, whilst resting beneath the crag between goes on our respective new lines, were chatting (well sort of grumbling a bit really) about our 'age' and about young Ben and how brilliant and hard his LPT *Statement of Youth* was: 'Amazing that for a kid, eh?' kind of stuff; and we figured Ben would inevitably be going on to greater things alongside us – 'us' meaning our no. 84 household with Jez and Chris, and the wider Sheffield scene. Yes indeed, 'our lot' could be in for a struggle if he does. And he did! Didn't he? And now he's at it again after thirty years!

'Come on then Andy lad, let's get these routes done and go back down to LPT this evening; though there's a new line there I want to do first.' We were each a day or two into working *Statement* ... [1]

---

[1] First ascents, 24–28 August 1984: Castell y Gwynt: *Blast Peru* E5 6b, Pollitt; *Sidekick* E6 6a, Atkinson; *Teenage Kicks* E6 6b, Pollitt; *Good Taste* E5 6b, Pollitt. Lower Pen Trwyn: *Under the Boardwalk* E4 6a, Atkinson.

Chimes of Freedom, Raven Tor. **Photo**: Richie Brooks.

9.

THE NEW PLACE

Our lease at Hunter House Road wasn't renewed (it was rumoured Alfie had some multiple-mortgage 'issues') so Nick, Yorick and I moved over to Sandford Grove Road in Nether Edge. An awesome place and I got to live in the attic again – accessed via a pull-down ladder from my 'office' and where I could only just stand upright beneath the ridgeline. Assisting females up there was always a pleasure ...

Our landlord, 'Genghis' (for obvious surname reasons), was a terrific fellow and made sure he popped over at least twice a week – ostensibly to ensure we were OK, but in reality to collect the mountain of government rent cheques (addressed to no end of 'family members', as he called them) that used to land on the doormat almost daily.

According to the postman there were sixteen people, all on welfare, residing there. We never met the other thirteen.

One evening Glenn Robbins, my Aussie mate and regular photographer, popped around to say his goodbyes as he'd be flying back to Melbourne in a few days' time. 'It's February Andy, you won't be climbing much here for a while so why not come down? I'll show you around Arapiles and the Grampians.' Nick had been to Australia and reckoned it was a top idea so I started making plans.

Now, Nick Plishko had come back to study in Sheffield, so had taken a room at no. 84 when it came up; he and I'd become absolute besties since Basher had moved on. Nick hadn't climbed for yonks – wasn't bothered, but still enjoyed the regular garage 'board' meetings and was obviously still immensely finger strong. He'd left a heck of a legacy though – albeit over in the backwaters of the Chew Valley where no one really visited from our side of the Pennines; though I did once drive to Wales via The Moors for a change, and it was really cold, really misty and uncomfortably eerie up there. 'There's still children's bodies buried up here!' I thought and shuddered – recalling the infamous Moors murders and double-checking all my van doors were locked, whilst resisting the urge to plough on through the mist at greater speed.

Nick's *pièces de résistance* were up at Wimberry – a stunning crag but too much of a walk-in for me. I'd read about *Neptune's Tool* and *Wristcutter's Lullaby* and was now sharing a house with the first ascentionist, who'd boldly led them ages ago in old-style EBs (and probably jeans or white baker's baggies too) but neither he nor the routes had gained the respect they genuinely deserved: here's to Nick *and* the routes!

My diary tells me I did *Neptune's* then jumped on *Wristcutter's*, which I didn't complete coz I simply couldn't find anything to pull on above the roof near the top, so traversed off left or something. First thing Nick did was to pull up my right sleeve and check out my wrist. It was trashed and heavily bandaged, with little red blood spots still seeping through coz – as Nick knew – the crux involved an enormous stretch out left and you had to drag your right palm across the rock to stay on but a tiny pin-head pebble at the end of the drag ripped you to bits. (Oh, and that's my equal favourite route name along with Basher's *Dream Topping* BTW.)

Nick was well out of the climbing scene by then and seriously not bothered, but he was right slap-bang there throughout my best ever years and probably put up with my crapping on more than anyone. Again, just like with Biff, something really clicked – our senses of humour, tastes in music, boxing, you name it; all these drew us closer together. I suppose these days you'd call it a 'Bromance'.

Nick didn't mind the odd pint either, so our friendship was really cemented over numerous beers and the drunken staggers home where we'd be in tears of laughter over some bollox we'd seen or heard down the pub. Long story short, I moved to Australia, Nick married Laura, we (Vertigo) sponsored them out here to set up the Sydney office, but it was simply too expensive so my bosses shut up shop and Nick and Lau got a transfer down to Melbourne. Great while it lasted and Lau accepted me 100 per cent unconditionally, purely based on what Nick had ever told her – as did I her.

Anyway, previously, I'd gotten my tourist visa from the Australian embassy on The Strand in London, delivered Mr Khan six pre-dated monthly rent cheques and lent our new housemate 'Tommo' the keys to my van.

'THAT'S OBSCENE!'

Well, my old mum Pam had visited me in Sheffield; she'd driven miles from Wales the poor dear, so what classier way to introduce her to the beauty of the glorious Peak District on such a balmy afternoon than by conn … err … asking her to run us out to a 'particularly delightful little valley … very picturesque, Mum'.

Meaning Raven Tor of course.

'Parched from the journey you say? There's a tea shack I'll take you to later, come on Mum, floor it will ya … '

'But I need a cuppa darling, please.'

'Later … alright?'

The Snore was chocker. Mum just complained it stank of poo and that there was far too much swearing going on for her liking. 'Why don't they build some toilets, this is disgusting,' she winced.

But Mum wanted her cuppa – badly now. Harped on about it she did.

Another 'fuuuuuck … !' followed by a 'bastard … !'

'That's obscene, Andrew,' tut-tutting.

'Not one of mine that, Mum,' as so-and-so drops his Lycras …

'And that's indecent … ' she goes, pointing.

'Nor that, Mum.'

Flipping clever how she got both route names right, eh?

'Does that charming George we met the other week climb here too?' she said as we left hurriedly (Mum covering her nose) for the Green Door Tea Shack cafe.

'Big George from the Ormes, Mum? No, don't think so.'

'Handsome specimen, ever so polite … I'm sure he would never swear like *that* boy … You don't swear do you Andrew?'

Of course, there's always more to mums than meets the eye: Pam was still occasionally acting on TV at the time, but under her maiden name of Rayner. She apparently auditioned for the part of Johnny Dawes's mum in *Stone Monkey*, but missed out as the agency advised they thought she appeared a tad too old. Mum never told me that for years … maybe, if any of us had known? … Alun Hughes and Johnny D would've smiled at the connection and been happy for her to do it: just think … both of us, in our own ways, acting out roles with JD!

'Right then!' I'd told myself in 1986, having finally received the all-clear from my surgeon.

I needed something to get fit on but wasn't prepared to embarrass myself flailing around on *Sardine* or *Indecent* for days on end, even if it was purely to regain my fitness, so abseiled down the Chris Craggs aid route *Free and Easy* – it was obviously 'on' for a free, but wouldn't be easy.

Chris was one of the older stalwarts of the Peak scene when I'd arrived and mostly hung about with Keith Sharples, Graham Hoey and their lot. Nice guy, sold me a super stereo system. He'd done a few artificial 'ascents' at the time but his effort down at Rubicon Wall was to become a faux pas of legend. He'd aided his way up through the severely bulging space left of the cliff's namesake climb, and then appeared to be waving a mocking and most deliberate red rag at us bulls when he named this line *Free that you Bastards!* Ben Moon obliged with *Zeke the Freak*. Rumours and uncertainty surround the exact chain of events, but there were accusations and denials regarding the chipping of holds by free climbers and the removal of such chiselled stains by the aid route's originator. Whatever really happened could be judged as inappropriate and is certainly not what climbing should be about. Unfortunately Big Chris was, at that time and in our circle, a bit of a fucking laughing stock.

I'd cleaned *Free and Easy* and placed a few bolts, but had decided to climb it ground up, pulling my ropes down whenever I fell (which I obviously would – and often) and try to do it in the purest style possible. No hang-dogging allowed. Virtually everyone else was climbing French-style and bolt-to-bolting – working the moves on their routes day in, day out, then redpointing within a couple of attempts once they had the moves totally wired. But I stuck to my guns and didn't waver for a second.

Mark Leach and I were climbing together most days – he had a short but extremely difficult project at Froggatt known as The Crack, so we'd pile out there several times a week. He'd give his new route a few goes, use up his power, then we'd head to Raven Tor via one of the cafes for a brew and sugar hit. Mark could've walked up my route with relative ease – as could Jez, Chris, Basher and Ron (I think he was away somewhere?) and Chris Hamper, Douggie, Scotch Ben and a few others; but they kindly left it for me to complete in my by-now old-fashioned style. Bloody good of them all, that!

So, thirteen days it took all up. Mark had already gotten over the initial roof by my third day of attempting it, yet it took me five to surmount. Then it was a relative cruise up the guts of the wall for a further fifty feet or so to reach the crux – a very fingery traverse left following the original aid route before a pumpy and technical few moves up rightwards to enter the final scoop, thence easing to a plod and the belay. I spent the next eight days getting through the roof, up the wall and to the end of that traverse, only to peel off backwards – staring at good holds!

Day thirteen and I'd bagged it. There was a stiff second pitch too but, as I discovered shortly afterwards, no one would really bother to do it. Dead chuffed I was and the route became immediately popular. The others jumped in straight away, having worked it during my attempts but never going for the redpoint, and a succession of very quick French-style repeats were made. Basher first from my recollection, and whilst the repeat ascentionists were most complimentary of my new route, Basher told me after his repeat he thought the desperate traverse left and the rightwards rock-over sequence into the scoop was contrived and unnecessarily hard, so he'd avoided it, staying where he was and making a fairly tricky move up rightwards then stepping easily left into the scoop. I'll admit that was the obvious scoop entry but I was freeing the original aid climb. 'But that's not the route!' I lamented to him and the others, but they weren't interested. Bloody hell, it's not like they couldn't have done it – course they could, but they all chose the easy alternative.

Some years later the big block under the starting roof fell off so the 'new' version was up for grabs – at last an excuse for Tim to rise from his slumbers: 'It looks even harder than your *Weedkiller*, Tim,' I told him; so enthusiastically he grabbed his pack, unused in months, and we headed out over the moors. After reminding Tim how to tie a figure of eight (OK, well not quite, but he was rusty) he bouldered out a complex horizontal sequence and swung out on the double crimp just over the lip. According to my diary I followed suit, so the whole route was a goer. Ben Moon made the first re-ascent and – nearly thirty years later, glued to my computer screen – I was delighted to watch Adam Ondra romp up it on sight. Top pitch too – strung together. Seems most people lower off just above the lip nowadays … [1]

SECONDS OUT, ROUND ONE – WITH NICK PLISHKO AS THE REF!

I always loved the boxing, and what a tremendous period in boxing history it was! Nigel Benn, Chris Eubank and Michael Watson were the top middleweights in Britain and we'd been through the Ali, Frazier and Foreman epics, Larry Holmes, Leon Spinks and Kenny Norton as kids, but it was the American middleweights we most followed: 'Sugar' Ray Leonard, Roberto 'Hands of Stone' Durán, Thomas 'The Hitman' Hearns, John 'The Beast' Mugabi and 'Marvelous' Marvin Hagler. Absolute legends the lot of them, and Sugar Ray was always our favourite. How come the top rock climbers didn't have stage names we wondered? Other than Martin 'Basher' Atkinson of course.

[1] First ascent, *Chimes of Freedom* E7 6c, 6a, 26 July 1986. Grade now hovering around F8a. Has anyone ever done it the original way … ?

Anyway, I went over to see the legendary Irish boxing trainer Brendan Ingle at his gym in Wincobank on the outskirts of town, and introduced myself as a pro rock climber. Showed him a few *High* magazine cover shots and said I was keen to improve my aerobic fitness and loved boxing.

'Can I join your gym please?'

'To be sure, to be sure – it's fifteen poond a year and a quid each visit,' he proclaimed Irish-ly.

'Thanks Brendan, see you tomorrow then.' Or something like that.

Three or four times a week I'd train there with the boxers, learning the footwork moves, criss-cross skipping and the seven basic ways of avoiding a punch on the chin; then work out on the speed ball, which I mastered quickly, and learned all the tricks like the double-up and elbow hit mid-session. Dead cool that one: you're going hell for leather one handed, double bouncing – and then introduce your opposite elbow without disturbing the rat-a-tat-tat rhythm. It took lots of practice and hand-eye coordination and I became better at it than many of the pros.

After the speedball sessions it would be a few hundred pull-ups on a quarter inch roof truss wearing my diver's weight belt – the boxing lads were totally perplexed. They had physiques to die for, ripped as ripped could be – six-packs, pecs and massive arms. Most of them had taut ebony skin glistening through oil and hard-earned sweat and I was envious-as. I explained to them when they'd collectively failed to do a pull-up on my little edge that we were at opposite ends of the physical spectrum. They needed weight and bulk and huge thighs and biceps for throwing punches and not falling over when some brute chinned them and made their heads spin. I required the complete opposite and needed no muscle mass – too heavy: it was all skinny legs and stamina training on small edges. Showed them a one-armer and front lever and they all failed again. They were a terrific group of very hard, fit young men – nicknamed me 'Jesus' coz of my long scraggly hair. They thought I was totally mad: 'Climbing dem rocks man!'

After a few weeks Brendan called over to my pull-up session and told me to glove up – he was one short for a professionals' ring session, so one of the older chaps taped up my hands and I took out my ear and nipple rings.

'Yey, boxing for real, but where's my gum shield and body protection?'

Stepping on the lower rope and urging me into the ring, Brendan massaged my shoulders and offered words of encouragement. I stood in the opposite corner to the British cruiserweight champion who was in training for his world title tilt – about six-foot-seven and truly menacing. Utterly terrifying, but Brendan explained I was to attack but that he was only allowed to block and defend, not hit back. Phew! 'That's how I do it here kid.'

We met in the centre of the ring and touched gloves, nodded and winked at each other and, as he was taking his first backward step before Brendan said we could start, I threw the heaviest punch I could muster and caught him square in the face. It was like hitting a lamp post or an oak tree – I actually felt my fingers crunch and thought I'd put my shoulder out. The monster of a chap was somewhat taken aback, but hadn't moved a millimetre. A broad grin came across his face and he cocked his arm but Brendan leapt in pleading, 'no man don't ... ' and probably saved my life! Brendan wasn't that cross with me actually, quite the opposite, and gave the pro an admonishing lecture on being complacent and dropping his guard – even though I was a mere pipsqueak and it was an illegal shot.

'Never underestimate your opponent, son.' Wise words – a bit like climbing sometimes?

My next round was with the Sheffield legend and British and European middleweight champ Herol 'Bomber' Graham. Again I could punch, but Herol could only bob and weave and dance and not throw any punches in my direction. Herol was the absolute master of avoidance and I threw all my best shots at him. Not a single one went anywhere close – even though he was standing only inches in front of me when I threw my best. Coiled like a spring he was and offering up his undefended chin, hands by his sides. I thought I'd out-fox him so dummied with my right and threw what to me was a thunderous left hook – hoping to collect him as he ducked around my left side. He'd obviously spotted my intentions a mile off and nipped behind me to my right and I was all disorientated having swiped thin air again. Herol tapped me on the shoulder from behind and called me 'sucker' – very Ali. I fronted him again but he sneakily stepped on my front foot and gently pushed me backwards on to the canvas.

Third round, and utterly buggered, I was to be on defence coz some young lad – an up and comer – was to have his go and this time it was me who wasn't allowed to hit back. Honestly, he was like a miniature Herol and danced around better than the cool dudes on the dance floor at the Roxy discotheque. I was about a foot and a half taller and roughly twice his size but he'd leap off his feet and pepper my face with jabs, hooks and crosses. I was swatting at him like a fly but the punches kept raining in. A left, two quick rights – coming in from all angles – then one right in the sternum that took the wind clean out of me: I got up at eight ... even though he'd smacked me at ten past four ...

But he wasn't just any *normal* young kid you see – his nickname within the boxing inner circle, even at that tender age, was 'Prince'. Yes, it was Naseem

Hamed … 'Naz' to his mates; a lad completely focussed on his life's ambition – just as Jerry and I had been back when we lived in the Tremadog barn. I admired and respected the spirit in that young fellow (even though I wanted to slap him). Prince grew up and went on to rule his division and pick up numerous world title belts. All flamboyant and explosive fights they were too. He had three 2-inch diameter ropes to protect himself and earned a hundred million quid or something off pay TV for giving the hardest men in his division a damn good slapping. I had a single ten-millimetre one and slapped my way up no end of the neckiest leads in Britain … and got two pounds five pence off Berghaus. Honestly! Where's the justice?

'Ow!' I said, rubbing my chin. 'Right you, you cheeky little sod, yer coming down Chee Dale with me tomorrow and you're leading!' So now it was *he* who went all wobbly-kneed – mentioned something about 'vertigo' and told me where to go – then chinned me once again.

I'd been clinically dismantled by a twelve-year-old boy! But who else here in the room can claim to have gone the full three minutes with Prince Naseem Hamed?

Nick Plishko, emailing in September 2015, still recalls my obsession with boxing. He and Yorick loved it too – we'd always ensure we were in when 'Feet Neet' (Yorkshire's version of 'Fight Night') was on ITV:

Watching re-runs of Sugar Ray, Marvellous Marvin, Hearns and Duran; rooting for Big Frank against Mike Tyson (get in there Frank), and Sheffield's Herol Graham (came close) – this was a regular Saturday night after the pub.

As was Andy's way, his fascination with the sport meant he had to have a go. Down to Wincobank he went, then after a few months: **'Herol Bomber Graham is amazing, so fast, so agile, he keeps his arms down and you still can't hit him'**. Then: **'come on Nick, try and hit me, come on, try!'** offering gloves and head guard. Eff off Andy, I've had a skinful and I'm trying to watch telly and anyway you're a rock climber, you shouldn't be able to get near him. Now **go away** or I'll give you a kicking!

All this at a time when Andy and Yorick had their first tiff. Hating each other and being the gentlemen that they were, what better way to resolve matters than 'Feet Neet'? It was on – Endcliffe Park on a Saturday morning three weeks hence. Yorick in the blue corner, Andy in the red and me as Ref.

Week 1
Andy – out for morning runs, drinking reduced to seven pints a night and high carb diet.

Yorick – 'I'm going to effing do him.'

Week 2
Andy – out for morning runs, drinking down to six pints a night and high carb diet. Sparring with the ref and sticking in the odd spiteful punch along the way.

Yorick – 'I'm going to effing do the bstd.'

Week 3
Andy – out for morning runs, drinking down to two pints a night (and three for the road), high carb diet, sparring with anyone who'd entertain him and relentlessly watching boxing vids for inspiration. Oh, and lone training in order to get angry.

Yorick – 'When is it again?'

Saturday Morning – Endcliffe Park
'Feet Neet' crew turn out to set up the ring, a slippy tarpaulin borrowed from our occasional employer. Regulation ring size but no rope – Ah well! Local folk wondering what the hell is going on. 'Feet Neet' we tell them!

Andy turned up with his corner man (can't remember who he was but I'm certain it wasn't Brendan Ingle), no big entrance but looking sharp. Warms up with his shadow-boxing moves and his Ali shuffle.

Yorick – Where is he? Ref goes to find him – asleep at ours down the hill, 'Wakey Wakey! It's Feet Neet!'

'Oh shit!'

'Why not stay in bed, call it a no show?' I offer.

'Can't do that,' he replied, 'and anyway, he's going down!'

Straight out of bed, up to the park, head guard and gumshield fitted along the way, and he's in the ring.

Round One
Pollitt straight in with a left jab followed by a right to the head. Yorick down on one knee for the count. Smelling blood, the crowd go berserk. Yorick makes it up on 9 to take a right to the face – legs buckle, snot everywhere and Yorick's on the tarp – counted out, the crowd still going berserk. Pollitt is the champ.

Yorick wants a 'me-ratch' or a re-match or something … and to go back to bed. Pollitt has his result and can go back to 10 pints a night. I gave the crowd a lift home then went back for Yorick. Bed to bed in 20 minutes.

It all made sense at the time!

THE TIGHTS, THE TIGHTS!

Well, if you've got it … as the saying goes.

Was I the height of 1980s climbing fashion or what? – popularising Lycra tights I mean – as Ed Douglas wryly observed some years later: 'Only Andy Pollitt could get away with it.'

I loved my Lycras, ace for ease of movement, but I also wanted to stand out. Berghaus and Scarpa had just taken me on as one of Britain's first sponsored climbers – as in *actual money* not just free boots or a gratis quickdraw – and I had photo shoots coming up with Al Rouse and Alan Hinkes for a new product launch.

So I bouldered, soloed, postured and posed whilst the two Als snapped away.

One of the full-page magazine ads featured Chris Gore and me. Chris sensibly attired, myself in lurid pink tights – with a **cigarette** dangling from my mouth!

Talk about a stir! Letters to the editors, complaints to Berghaus, the whole catastrophe!

The ad was pulled, but by then everyone was 'brand aware' and familiar with the Red Point range.

And thousands of climbers throughout the country started wearing Lycra. (Three actually took up smoking! Not a bad ratio when you come to think about it.)

Yes, this magazine exposure certainly did influence the next generation … and not all of it in a bad way.

Steve McClure, by email:

Like a well-trained dog I sat by the door waiting for today's post to drop on to the mat. Long anticipated, today was the day it was sure to arrive, as it did every month, the latest copy of *High* magazine. Packed with the latest news and articles and wrapped up in a glossy work of total inspiration, this was the highlight of my month, the front covers engrained in my mind deeper than any childhood memories or family photographs. I'd pore over the articles and absorb the pictures, even the adverts: Basher on *Choucas*, Nadin in the Verdon, Pollitt on *The Whore* and *Knockin'*, Dawes on *Indian* and Moffatt everywhere. Splashed with colour, the world of climbing was changing with increasing pace, dragged into a new era by what appeared a radically new breed of rock star. Tights, bolts, slate, big falls and massive grades flew like chalk dust in all directions. And the stars sat up high on the pedestals we placed them, up there with the gods blessed with skills and strengths we could only imagine. Just to see these guys would be a dream come true; maybe some of their powers would rub off?

Boot Boys, Raven Tor. **Photo**: Neil Foster.

10.
PAID TO CLIMB and A LADY OF ILL REPUTE

PAID TO CLIMB

Chris Gore:

> Andy was one of the first amongst us to become a sponsored climber, he had contracts with Allcord and Berghaus/Scarpa; it was through his influence that Basher and I went on to get sponsorship contracts of our own ... We also learnt a lot from Andy's work ethic with these companies – he was always very professional, always promoting himself with the sponsors through articles, slideshows and his guidebook writing. These contracts were initially gear contracts but they evolved into substantial financial contracts as time went on and we have Andy to thank for that ...

Back in the early '80s, Neil Kennedy, terrific fellow, was the advertising and marketing manager for Berghaus in Newcastle, who had the UK distribution licence for the Italian company Scarpa. He was given a brief, and a hefty budget, to promote Scarpa rock boots in Britain – and I was to become their first paid rock climber.

Six hundred pounds a year, no end of prototype and then production boots, travel and accommodation expenses reimbursed, and all the 35mm film our chosen photographers required. 'How good is this?' I thought, 'can do heaps with that'; but more importantly it gave me the chance to work closely with Scarpa to produce better footwear. Of course, I also got their latest rucksacks

– and Gore-Tex jackets too (which I wore **all the time** as Neil Foster noticed, then took the mickey with his new grit route *Andy Pollitt's Jacket*) plus they gave me a 'beaut' pair of the latest fabric hiking boots.

I suppose I was a good choice for Berghaus as I was 'at the cutting edge' (so they said), always in the mags and they'd get their advertising spend back by the sheer number of photos I appeared in – plus the spin-offs from other print ads, articles, books, slide shows, posters and the news columns. Any case, Ron had Hanwags (which looked great in colour but that was expensive to print, so images of these were rarely published – and I'd tried 'Handbags' for a while but they were like clumpy carpet slippers – Ron must have been good to climb in them!) and Pat Littlejohn (lovely man, wished I'd have run into him more often) was featured in Asolo Chouinard Canyons I think?

Anyway, the right-hand side of Raven Tor was well overgrown with bushes, brambles and nettles back then, and you only really ever tiptoed in there to go for a dump. Every stone had rotten bog roll underneath and some filthy buggers didn't even bother putting a rock on top of their excrement. It wasn't a pleasant place – believe me – and stank to high heaven. One afternoon I was rather taken aback to see an aid climber swinging around in étriers above the treeline, hammering and hooking his way up the crag, so I plucked up courage and thrashed my way through the little piles of poo to take a closer look. Amazing! There was a whole new little cliff in there and the line the aid climbers were taking looked brilliant. Returning the very next day I abbed down, checked it out and placed three bolt runners – I couldn't use pegs in the pockets – they were needed for fingers.

Ben Masterson worked out the first hard bit for me and I then pulled like I'd never pulled before, on one sharp mono or duo pocket after another, until out of the shade and into daylight – and breathable air! I won't attempt to describe the crux sequence other than to say it was most bizarre and involved a long reach out left for an under-cling, followed by tiptoeing the feet across, an underhand match before a powerful move and a slap for a little skyhook in-cut up right and then one final pull through to easy ground. Oh! I just described it didn't I? Well sort of.

I fell off at the slap for the finishing jug and was **not happy**.

Boot sales were booming, so Neil at Berghaus received a substantial increase in his advertising budget. I'd been summoned up to HQ in Newcastle for a meeting, so caught the train from Sheffield – at the expense of Berghaus of course – a luxury journey complete with British Rail breakfast, if such slop could be called that. Cutting to the chase, Neil said he had a whole pile of money to spend and if he didn't use it he might lose it from the next year's budget, so he was seeking my advice on other notable climbers who'd be interested.

'Well excuse me Neil, firstly how's about a pay rise for me? It's my third year and I'm only on twelve hundred quid! Jerry's wearing those new Firés and I bet I could also get a few bob out of Boreal; how much can you up the ante?'

Neil signed off on three thousand pounds, which I was more than happy with, plus it matched what I was getting from Allcord, CAMP and Cousin so I was 'rolling in it'. Add Mrs Thatcher's Enterprise Allowance Scheme payments and government rental assistance and I could climb, train or rest to my heart's content every day. So I did. For years!

Paul Pritchard – a mate of mine at that time – observed quite correctly in his brilliant book *Deep Play* that ironically it was the working classes (people who in general loathed and detested the Thatcher government and everything *she* stood for) who benefitted most from this scheme: if you were a 'doley' climber you could hitch around the country and climb rocks all day and every day without consequence. Her policies certainly suited my lifestyle so why vote Labour? They wanted to repeal the E.A.S. and make us **work** for the dole. **Yikes**! But suppose Mrs Thatcher had announced that she'd save one colliery between Manchester and Sheffield but it'd only take on unemployed climbers? There would've been a bloody revolt, make no mistake about it.

Sorry, no more politics. I was saying to Neil at Berghaus: 'Martin Atkinson and Chris Gore – they're our men, Jerry's with Wild Country and Boreal so we won't bring him across and Ron's changed to so-and-so at the moment so he's contractually obliged too. Be a great guy to bring across though. No idea about Dunne or Dawes.'

Neil sent free boots to 'me Dad' Paul Williams and Gary Gibson too – coz his name got mentioned about 345 times for every time mine did due to his maniacal new-routeing, and to Simon Nadin in Buxton as well coz we both agreed he 'looked promising' at the time. We can all laugh at the irony now can't we? Shortly afterwards, Simon was the first ever climbing competition 'Champion of the World' – and deservedly so. Not too shabby on the pointy end on real rock either was the delightful, quiet lad from Buxton.

Neil and I discussed a real 'kicker' too, and subject to the lads' agreement it would be implemented forthwith. Chris, Basher and I were to take on the entire sales-repping bit for Scarpa rock boots within the UK and we'd get commissions, per pair, based on our sales. Whatever the lads negotiated as retainers was their business, but we were all on several quid a pair.

However, things did get somewhat *light-heartedly* tense when our contracts came through and we needed to fill in our respective territories. We were slap bang in the middle of Sheffield remember – the climbing epicentre of

Britain – and Chris leapt in first and 'claimed' not only our city, but most other surrounding ones such as Manchester, Rotherham, Doncaster, Chesterfield, Derby, Nottingham and all points in between.

'Oh, and the whole of Greater London too coz I come from down there. Andy, you can have Wales and you Biff Yorkshire, and the two of you can argue over Scotland and the South-West, I'm not driving that far!'

Well something like that anyway. Brilliant, good of you that Chris, 'Mnoo, cheers' as we used to say, or think! Well, anyway, those were me and Biff's return facial expressions when our eyes met. Words sometimes don't matter – especially at an awkward time such as during that three-way 'business' negotiation – you don't need to speak if you're in the company of your best friend when a look or slight vocal alteration says it all.

'Don't dimp it, Andy,' Basher said solemnly as I was about to butt out my fag, and he proceeded to drag the last of that ciggie down in two heavy draws. I could read him like a book: just by his change in demeanour – and his smoking – I could tell Martin was stressed. He **was** trying to quit God bless him, so hadn't bought a packet in ages, but we obviously both thought Chris had over-stepped the mark somewhat. I sparked up another cig and, catching Basher's eye, our mirrored facial expressions clearly showed neither of us needed to utter a word. Chris was taking the piss surely?

So the three of us sat and discussed it like adults. We'd been housemates and trusted friends remember – each trying to support ourselves so we could *all* share the spoils and keep 'living the life'.

Chris ended up with Sheffield, the surrounding cities of Manchester, Rotherham, Doncaster, Chesterfield, Derby, Nottingham and all points in between; and the whole of Greater London – 'Coz you're from down there, right … '

Basher got Barnoldswick near Malham. 'The longest town name in Europe that doesn't repeat a letter,' he said with pride.

I got Llanfairpwllgwyngyllgogerychwyrndrobwllllantysiliogogogoch on Anglesey, which is – as I told them proudly, pronouncing it perfectly and probably spitting all over them with each of the double lls – 'The longest town name bleedin' anywhere on the planet,' and so 'top-trumped' the pair of 'em!

And we all happily shook hands and signed the papers. Well something along those lines anyway.

'We're in the money,' as the old song went.

Best thing though was that the name for my new, fierce little project in the shitty swamps of Miller's Dale came to me. Right there and then. The lads agreed it was a good name – for a great project. I gave it the British grade of E7 6c even though it was my very first-ever French-style new route. Douggie made the second ascent shortly after. Then Basher and Scotty. And Chris and, and …

'Oh give it a month for the mags at least lads, please!' They all said it was French 8a but the next person said: 'Nah, 7c+!'

'Well my British grade had a 7 and a c in it, didn't it?' I said. 'Isn't that how it works?'

Douggie Hall again:

> As for early repeats the only one I remember is *Boot Boys*, second ascent, after pulling my finger on the start move. On a personal note I never went back to Raven Tor after an altercation with a ghetto blaster! Why can't people leave them at home?

Great route all the same – up there with the best and hardest in its day – and I was dead happy with that one.[1]

Chris Gore:

> Andy's nights out and consumption of ale 'n' ciggies really didn't seem to affect his prodigious talent for climbing … strong fingers, precise footwork and fluid movement, added to a drive and determination, were coupled with a love for new routeing. Andy once gave up beer and ciggies for three weeks, which culminated in the first ascent of *Boot Boys*, probably one of the most fingery routes of its grade on the crag; however, he decided that his abstinence hadn't helped him and he went back to the beer 'n' ciggies … The household of no. 84 became responsible for some of the greatest routes of the '80s. All of us were dedicated to the common cause to climb hard and enjoy ourselves to the full … now this meant different things to each of us. Jerry would train hard and live off Eccles cakes and Fletcher's Golden Wheaten; Basher would train hard and live off cigarettes and coffee; I would train hard and live off flapjack from Hunters Bar bakery – but Andy really did live life to the full … he'd train sometimes, when inspired, but would live off beer and 'ciggies' and nights out, whilst we were all tucked up in our beds.

A LADY OF ILL REPUTE

In 1987 the 'lady' in question didn't really exist, she was a biblical metaphor, a 'Christian figure of evil'; a 'whore' created an awfully long time ago during the construction of the *Book of Revelation*:

[1] First ascent, *Boot Boys* E7 6c, F8a+, 10 April 1987.

'Babylon the Great, Mother of Prostitutes and Abominations of the Earth.'
My kind of girl.

I 'got to her' before anyone else and paid dearly for the experience – as one
tends to do in those circumstances. You see, the original *Prow* aid route
followed the first roofs and a polished little corner on to the main face before a
bolt ladder ran straight up just left of centre of the crag to the big break. Above
that it took overhanging flakes, then pegged its way over the capping overhang
at its widest point. When Ron freed *Prow* he avoided the start and traversed in
from the left (still a brilliant effort in its day, don't get me wrong) then followed
the original line in its entirety, which was stunning. Made for great TV too
and really reinforced Ron's claim as 'The Man'. Sometime later Jerry freed that
original start and christened what was then Britain's hardest route: *Revelations*.

A mere couple of paces to the right of *Revelations* existed a parallel line of
old bolts, 'golos' and threads that took an equally compelling and super-direct
line right up the longest and steepest part of the buttress – the old aid route
of *Brandenburg Gate*. I abbed it over a couple of days, brushed it and checked
out all the moves, but was stumped as to how to do the very start which was
a bit shaley and seemed almost devoid of any useable holds – well for me at
least. Thing is, the rest – a full rope-length – was all 'on' and a definite goer.
The moves were simply brilliant but it'd be long, hard and terribly sustained.
'Sustained' – I liked that and could do climbs of that nature rather well
I thought. Particularly for a heavy drinker and smoker.

So, pull on the first two bolts (despite what it says on the Rockfax data-
base!), link it free from the second right through to the tree at the top of the
crag, claim an aid reduction from gawd-knows-how-many to only two, then
get cracking and work on the desperate start. That was the plan anyway … and,
well, that's pretty much how the fifteen-day saga went. I spent days on end
working and working and working the moves, piecing together ever-longer
overlapping sequences on every part of the route, from the first move off
the second bolt all the way up to the big break on *Cream Team Special* where
I'd stashed sufficient quickdraws deep inside a vacant raven's nest to reach the
top – so another forty, pumpy feet to go … The eventual redpoint was the
absolute highlight of my career to that day – on limestone at least – and I truly
believed I'd produced something *very* special.

I gave it the highest grade on the crag – E8 6c. Bar *Revelations*, which was
short but ridiculously powerful, it was by far the biggest and most sustained
route on the cliff – and barely took a left or rightwards step. It was so much
harder than *Prow*, *Indecent Exposure* or *Rooster Booster* etc., and well deserved
of the grade – at that time and in comparison to its neighbours. Admittedly

it started fifteen feet off the deck, but many of the other routes were broken into two or three pitches where you could take an hour or so off – or even ab down and go for a brew up at the Green Door Tea Shack cafe at the start of the Chee Dale railway trail (having soloed Paul Mitchell's fingertip and footless *Urban Shark* across the little gritstone bridge above ten inches of babbling brook on the way – a Peak 'must-do').

Effing awesome was *The Whore of Babylon* (route name courtesy of Geoff Milburn whom I'd phoned for a suggestion – he was a Bible scholar, I was led to believe). It was by far my best effort to date but, problem was, nobody else thought so! No one except Geoff Birtles perhaps, so I made yet another *High* magazine cover. Maybe it was merely the best photo he had to hand at the time? Nah, he just wanted to use his latest witticism for the caption: *Notice how they don't carry gear any more … ?*

Didn't it make a Cousin Ropes ad too? I recall it may have.

My friends and peers basically scoffed and someone scribbled beneath my write-up in the Stoney new route book that I'd 'dragged Raven Tor kicking and screaming **back** into the sixties'.

Harsh that.

Over three originally wholly-aided pitches with probably a hundred-plus aid moves combined, I led it with just two at the bottom, in one single strength-sapping pitch that just went on and on – and I left an unaltered boulder problem start, open to anyone to completely free – yet I got utterly lambasted and felt quite sad. A bit cross and bewildered too I might add. My route, to the best of my knowledge, only ever saw one repeat ascent, by Mike Owen several years later; and since 1990 the start is free thanks to Ben Moon's *Hubble* – which lowers off at thirty feet – and the sixty foot mid-section of my old route forms the 'easy' romp to the belay of one or two modern-day F8-something-or-others.[2]

Ah well!

Raven Tor still holds a truly significant place in British climbing, a fact much appreciated by the very best on today's scene.

Steve McClure, by email, March 2015:

> Like a kid on a Christmas morning I awoke full of excitement. My present?
> A day's climbing at Raven Tor. Drawing back the curtains was like opening
> the wrapping paper; clear skies and a cold, crisp air would make for perfect

---

[2] First ascent, *The Whore of Babylon* E8 6c, 28 March 1987.

conditions. I'd be on *Evolution* today, Moffatt's masterpiece. I was close now, perhaps today would be the day …

Yes, this steep little crag has given us 'evolution' indeed! My first-ever visits to Raven Tor in the very early eighties had been to have goes on Tom Proctor's *A Little Extra* and Ron Fawcett's *Saline Drip* – two short, bouldery lines above the Council's winter grit pile. A couple of the toughest in Derbyshire many thought. Boy! I was ambitious. Did 'em both though.

Things have certainly moved on from those early days – however, the thoughts, ambitions and achievements of Proctor and Fawcett back then and Ste Mac above, attempting something hard *for its time*, would have numerous parallels.

Ron had certainly been king of this castle back then and … all of a sudden it was 'The Ron and Jerry Show' …

Poker faces. The atmosphere was tangible, the lines were falling: *Sardine* – almost 'old hat' but a true classic even before it progressed to solids.

Indecent Exposure – Bigger.

Prow – Better.

Jerry was in there like a flash. Repeat, repeat and … 'Here's one of my own – *Rooster Booster.*'

Imagine a television commentator taking up the tale … 'Fawcett stares him down and turns over *Body Machine* but Moffatt takes the upper hand with *Revelations* on the river and finally some *Verbal Abuse* gives Jerry the last laugh!'

Gore would generally be next, or Douggie, Basher or Hamper and Leachy and then myself. Raven Tor had provided a superb landscape upon which a brilliant chapter in the annals of UK climbing could be scribed.

Steve McClure sums it up:

Standing below that soaring wall history oozed, the zebra-striped vastness of stone towering above me, intimidating with its reputation but holding my hand and inviting me to join. The groove of *Mecca* stood proud, the scene of battles, and surrounding me, Fawcett's *Body Machine* and Pollitt's *Chimes*; their magazine images burned into memory stronger than any childhood picture. *Boot Boys* in the distance, and closer, but far out of reach, *Hubble*, another realm of climbing reserved only for the stars. The gallery of performance showed off its masterpieces.

A huge chunk of climbing history was written here; acted out to coincide exactly with my youthful keenness. It felt as though Raven Tor had always been right at the edge. Now I was on the stage with the masters, only a small part maybe, but just to be up there in the zone, following in the footsteps. How I'd dreamt of this before, and now I was here …

North Stack Wall, Gogarth. **Photo**: Bernard Newman.

11.

Go Garth !

(Who the heck is Garth?)

Ah yeah, of course ... I remember now!

Garth's not a person in the physical human sense, yet does exist and occupies valuable space in my addled brain's backyard (rather like the two still-taped-up tea chests in my garage from two house moves ago that I've never actually gotten around to opening. I figure if there was owt in 'em I needed in my life I'd have opened 'em up by now. They've sat there for nine years! Maybe I ought to take a peek inside?).

But wait ... pull the two words together and we have much more than their sum:

Gogarth. Anglesey. North Wales. Andy B took me there for the first time when I was leading HVS and seconding the odd E2. I was totally in awe of the place.

That day he led me up a few routes on the accessible Upper Tier, and whilst safe it felt way more adventurous than Forwyn or Pen Trwyn, but in reality it was still pretty tame ... He'd told me the rest was super-adventurous – meaning the Main Cliff and 'coloured' walls (Red and Yellow) and I wanted to be down *there* ...

We went a few times more – often four or more of us in two cars. After a number of visits I set off up my first Main Cliff E1 (advertised with some aid at the time) with Henry Clover holding the ropes, shivering. Yey! It was brilliant and turned out I'd actually on-sighted an unclimbed, particularly classy and *free*, 'direct' version of *Resolution* at E2 (!) and had now left my mark alongside Boysen and Ingle, Brown and Crew. I'd later go head to head with Moran, Fawcett and Redhead, but of course didn't know that at the time.

GEEZ! THAT WAS LOUD!

The foghorn I mean … nearly leapt out of my Lycras!

Gogarth was always one of my favourite venues – the variety of styles and the quality of the climbing being exceptional. Huge contrasts abound – from the severely overhanging dross on Yellow Wall (I don't believe I ever did a route on the Red Walls) to often balancy, off-vertical and green, furry boulder problems or run-outs on the Upper Tier – *Barbarossa* and *Blackleg* for example. *The Cruise* was a cracking pitch too – until the vile off-width rubbly chimney at the top.

Thuggery on the enormous Main Cliff – 'big' lines all of 'em, three, four or even five pitches arching outwards straight from the sea. *Positron*, *Alien*, *Dinosaur* and *Mammoth*, and with my direct start too. *Citadel* and Ron's *Wall of Fossils* and *The Big Sleep* and something **very special** of my own.

Easter Island Gully, the *Flytrap* bit, Wen Zawn where dozens of classics were to be found including a bunch of complete and utter 'headcase' lines from Johnny D, Pritch and 'Big' George Smith. These were eighties routes and typical of that era. They may well not be climbed much anymore coz they don't have a line of bolts and they also require total commitment. Mind and Brain and Body commitment I mean – this is not 'redpointing a clip-up with pre-practice and the draws in' territory. I'm honestly not sure, but would like to believe that the Gogarth trad scene is still happening. Somewhat like or maybe better than it was when I bode it goodbye a squillion years ago – secretly knowing it wasn't in particularly good health. The saying, 'what's old is new again' rings a bell and things often come full circle … perhaps they already have? Maybe in five, seven or ten-year cycles, but they do … apparently flourescent Lycras are next year's fashion 'must-have' and who'd've ever thunk that? But just a mo … allow me to remind you of Ed's words of wisdom: 'Only Andy Pollitt could get away with it!' So let's put a stop to that here and now lads, eh? Perhaps encourage the lasses though?

But it was North Stack Wall that really had me hooked, from the day PW pointed me up *The Cad* to early the following season where I on-sighted just the third ascent of Pete Whillance's harder and bolder *The Long Run*, with Derek Hersey watching my back. The cliff enjoyed full sunshine, was tidal so we had to check the tables in the newspaper, had huge old fog warning cannons rusting amongst the boulders beneath it, and at the top a pretty, white-washed stone wall surrounding the old fog warning station. A single telegraph pole – the last in a long line from Holyhead – carried the telephone cable and was the usual abseil point to get in. In to what though? A steady, well(ish) protected romp up *Blue Peter* or *South Sea Bubble* followed by a brew and cake in Bangor on the way home, or a delicate tiptoe a little way above bomber gear on *The Cad*? The third option down there was probable death. Severe hurt at least ...

We'll return to North Stack shortly – it deserves its own user manual, but one route stands out a country mile above everything else I ever achieved on the great crags of Anglesey. There's a lead-in which, when I think about it, was really all part of the build-up I suppose:

Tall, funny and affable Tom Jones had gotten through the aided section on a Yellow Wall route – a horrendous, ridiculously steep and sandy groove – but he didn't complete the pitch. It was *The Screw Machine* all over again – Tom freeing the move but not the pitch. It wasn't a pleasant experience, but I was chuffed to have made it through to the finish – only to belay on a threaded rabbit-hole in the dirt at the top with my heels dug in.[1]

A decade prior, Ron had reduced the aid on one of the imposing Main Cliff 'biggies' to two points, and later Redhead had bouldered out a free sequence but didn't quite get the totally free lead of the severely steep pitch, blowing his chance on the pumpy run-out to the belay when he ended up using one aid point. Nearly but not quite! Remember, almost everything was on-sight back then. If you fell, chances are you wouldn't go back. So, getting this one was a real highlight of my climbing career at the time. Steve Andrews takes up the tale:

> Sometimes you're in the right place at the right time and that was true for North Wales in 1984. Andy and I climbed a bit at Pen Trwyn and had free climbed a stunner called *Nemesis* over at Craig Arthur in the Clwyd limestone area. We met up again in Llanberis in May; Andy was going well and only had big targets on his list. I loved the Main Cliff on Gogarth, especially once I'd come to terms with its vast size, the often huge tides and soapy rock near the sea. The quartzite rock is hard and solid, nothing loose until near the top of the crag; the routes are steep but the holds are generally positive, best of all the protection is good.
>
> There's a discussion over our morning brew in Pete's Eats and the ever enthusiastic Mr Pollitt comes up with a plan: 'Let's go and free *Mammoth*.'

[1] First free ascent, *Ludwig* E6 6b, 10 May 1984, with Steve Andrews.

Gulp! It's only one of the biggest lines in British climbing that still has a pegged aided section after twenty years! But, as Craig Smith said later: 'The crux is leaving the cafe!' Andy's plan was to ab in first to check the state of the pegs, but it turned into a four-hour epic with two ropes tied together – I'm waiting patiently as time passes, more time passes, it's been a very long time, so I prussik down the taut rope to peer over the edge. Thirty feet below me is Andy, exhausted from jumaring back up – this was not part of the plan.

'What's happened?'

'The ropes were too short, I was left thirty foot above the sea – but the pegs are sorted.'

We make a long retreat back to our bags then scramble down to the foot of the route. It's a narrow, elegant groove that spreads out as it rises from the sea, hitting a roof after eighty feet or so, forcing a traverse left until the hard climbing starts. Andy climbs up and down clipping the pegs. After a long shake out he calls down: 'You are watching me … you are watching?' I assure him and he's very elegant and after twenty feet or so eases smoothly on to the belay. Mr P is very pleased!

I rattle up the groove and move left to the line of pegs. I warn him and start to climb, but where are the holds? There's twenty feet and only one obvious pocket and I struggle until calling for 'tight'. I hang there for five minutes then struggle up the next few feet, repeat the resting bit and eventually, exhausted, join Andy on the stance.

The next pitch is a lovely pillar of rock with nice holds in a fine position. Mr P looks very graceful as he launches up it and enjoys the climb. Conquering heroes, we return to Llanberis that evening for the usual debrief in the cafe and to fill in the new routes book. Three days later Andy's at me again: 'Let's go and climb the direct start, it's that huge chimney to the left!' I'm appalled – not only does he want me to flail up that crux I can't do again but I'm expected to crawl up some vast, dank chimney as well. I felt he was being particularly ambitious this time and ducked the opportunity, so 'Crooky' goes instead and I get to regret for the rest of my life that I didn't get my name in the book for *Mammoth Direct*.

Many years later my phone rings; it's Ken Wilson.

'Steve, you're a third-class climber.'

'What do you mean by that Ken?'

'Well you weren't one of the best climbers of your generation leading the new routes, and you weren't in the pack chasing them, but you were good enough to be seconding some of the best new routes of your era.'

Ken gets to his point:

'You were on the first free ascent of *Mammoth*.'

Ken's been reading up on the development of Gogarth and wants to know all about *Mammoth*. I point to the problems of the first ascent, the nice groove, but the very steep technical climbing on the crux that for their generation (the 1960s) was not quite feasible. We discuss the second pitch – originally given 6a, bold and up that lovely pillar in fine position – definitely the best climbing on the original route. *Mammoth* had proved to be a fine test, both for leading climbers of the '60s and now in the '80s.

So yes, I returned with my 'scally' mate and led the big chimney as a direct version leading into the bouldery crux sequence. It had an enormous natural thread runner at the top, off which one could winch an adrift oil rig shorewards. We were really stoked with that day![2]

Littlejohn's *Alien* – superb, third ascent with Steve A again. *Citadel* – not quite as classic as it's cracked up to be, *Dinosaur* similarly, but *The Big Sleep* by Ron was a standout! When I made the second ascent – again with Steve Andrews – I was on great form, in my element as usual, whilst my housemates back in Sheffield were bolt-to-bolting down Chee Dale and I was thinking how much they were missing out on, what with all that 'working', resting for ages and redpointing stuff. If only Chris or Basher would come with me one day – but they simply weren't interested and I couldn't convince them for love nor money.

---

2 First free ascent, *Mammoth* E5 6a/b, 23 May 1984, with Steve Andrews. First ascent, *Mammoth Direct* E5/6 6a/b, 26 May 1984, with Martin Crook.

Anyway, *The Big Sleep*. First pitch: direct up the *Dinosaur* left rib, a peg runner right where you feel like one, then yarding onwards to a questionable stance.

Pitch 2: Outer Space! A rising rightwards line aiming for the ledge on the arête about sixty feet away, winking at you from the right-hand side of the leaning *Positron* headwall, and where the hard climbing's all over.

Midway through that second pitch I bridged out on sloping footholds, shook out and was staring seaward and inwards straight down a blind and severely overhanging protection-less-looking, shallow and very round-edged flake that splits the lower half of this amazing wall; rising for about twenty-five feet to peter out at a flat-topped hold just beneath my widely stretched legs. It came from the lip of a bulge way below – with only crashing waves in the further distance, so I had no idea whether it was reachable from the sea-level traverse or not. It was love at first sight.

I lucked-in when I met Steve Andrews again in Pete's Eats – he was up for more adventure. He'd 'learnt his lesson' having knocked me back with *Mammoth Direct*, so we headed over the Menai Bridge on a direct course for the Main Cliff. A huge, open corner led to those bulges at the beginning of the flake I'd looked down on from *The Big Sleep*. I headed up it blindly, hoping to weave my way through. I was carrying tons of gear – including a ring of pegs and my trusty lump hammer – so every move felt pumpy, not to mention balancy, as the weight of all that equipment swaying left and right upset my equilibrium each time I leant one way or another. An obviously good hold out near the right arête beckoned – I pretty much jumped for it and swung around into *Positron* just before its first belay.

Next, all the real 'fun' begins: traverse out left, well below where *Positron* rounds the arête above, then bridge widely again and get a breather whilst fiddling in a couple of widely spaced protection pieces to the left and right beneath an alarming bulge. Ten feet above me, if I leant out far enough, I could see directly back *up* the blind flake that I'd last seen from above – it looked desperate to gain its flared, bottomless base – an experience that Joe Healey would soon discover, and then revisit over thirty years later in April 2015:

I was fortunate to witness the first ascent of *Skinhead Moonstomp* when Steve Roberts, Dave Jones and I were doing a photo shoot on *Citadel*. Whilst I was being photographed, I kept glancing over at Andy as he made his way up the flake of the second pitch. I probably had the very best view you could get of someone on the *Moonstomp* – it looked magnificent. The following day Dave and I checked Andy's route description in Pete's Eats and set off for Gogarth. The crux is establishing yourself on the flake.

It took me about an hour of up and down climbing before I committed myself to that rounded flake. Once on it I thought 'what have I done?' I don't
remember a positive hold for about thirty feet. It's extremely pumpy and
bold. I managed to get to where I thought was a good nut placement, but
my RP2 was too small, a no.3 too big. I pulled on the no.3 as hard as
I could and prayed it would stay in ... just as I climbed past it, it fell out.
Mike Owen, traversing the base of the cliff far down below, shouted up:
'Hey wad, if you fall from there you could eat a full English breakfast before
you land on the gear!' A few more trying moves and I got to the sling
around a poor knobble ...

Joe's spot on: that section is where one really just has to dig deep, commit 100
per cent and go hell for leather. I'd laybacked, laybacked and laybacked some
more to get there too – no gear, just clear air for 200 feet below – until a stretch
to gain the flat hold where the flake morphed back into face climbing. Drape
a miniscule sling over this lump, shake out, then it's straight into what I felt
should be the last difficult section of the route. One bouldery sequence and
I'd joined the intimidating-for-a-first-time *Positron* – that *mere* E5, but classic,
leftwards diagonal which crosses here: 'cept my fingers were clinging to its
worn-smooth-by-passage polished footholds, so another two hard pulls were
required. These moves landed me directly on to the crux finger holds of
Posi where it shot through out left, so I was now smearing on the polished
foot holds I'd just pulled on. It was, however, a most pleasant 'hang around
and ponder, admire the view' moment, compared to the battle down below.
What did Ben Moon call it? 'Where 6b is a rest,' or something? And remember,
he was talking – and I was climbing – in the 'old UK money' when he came
out with that classic.

As (I think) The Specials sang to Skinhead Moonstomp – the song of my
climb's name (could never learn songs properly ...):

*Put your faces together and your boots on feet, and give me some bold ...
moonstomping ...*

I hang there steeply on decent slopers and 'moonstomp' away to the ska
beat in my head – rocking left and right, lifting feet alternately off the right
then left footholds in that distinct off-beat rhythm whilst scanning my
surroundings for some 'good gear, man'. Ha-ha!

In my la-la land and, suddenly, what's this? A *Rat Race*-er crashes on to the
big spike on the arête over to my right with a jangling of gear and an 'ouch',
having been spat out of his horrid chimney around the corner.

We fix eyes momentarily, and I smile across.

He's awfully pale, sniffs the air then scurries away.

I overhear words of confliction emanating from his belay around the corner:

'Lunatic … only one runner in seventy feet; he's fuckin' dancin'. Singin' to himself.'

'Bollox, yer just scared.'

'No, seriously, I reckon that's that Andy Redhead guy, couldn't be sure through all the dark hair … '

Joe's feelings at this same point on this journey were similar to mine: 'What a relief and what a fantastic route!' All this fun, but we're only halfway up the main pitch, so shake out, shake out here all ye newbies … it ain't over yet … ask 'what's-his-name' … he fell off well above this point – the poor bastard!

Another short but OK section leads to the breather on *The Big Sleep* from where I'd first stared down this incredible flake. I'd now just climbed it, my ropes billowing way out from the rock beneath me. 'The Big Snooze' (ta PW) continued on its natural trajectory rightwards, but I was for going absolutely straight up. Good holds but pumpy … pumpy … ignored looking for runners, what I hope's a belay is only twenty feet above and ever-better holds led to a most remarkable little recess. Now if that belay wasn't the comfiest, airiest and most hard-won belay on Gogarth I didn't know what was! It was brilliant: imagine being fitted for a tailor-made rally-car seat. In-cut, back support, shoulder too on one side. Wriggle those butt cheeks in, snuggle back and there you are! Admittedly I was an arse size XXS and fitted perfectly. Ha!

Ahh … trad at its purest! It's a beautiful thing … and I tie off utilising a crafty jammed knot to bring Steve up. Letting my legs dangle over the edge of the 'seat' they just hung in thin air tickled by the breeze, so I had to bend my knees in for my heels to touch the rock. Sat facing outwards looking back down that long pitch and following the line of my ropes as they hung very 'out' but alternately 'pinched in' here and there before disappearing beneath the bulge, with only everyone's idea of a long-focus downwards view of waves pounding and 'sea-ey' crashing sounds and white foam 300 feet below – it was the best view of North Wales climbing I'd ever had, and ever would have. No doubt about it. Any readers sat there?

'The Bucket Seat' I'd name it. It genuinely merited a title in its own right.[3]

---

[3] First ascent, *Skinhead Moonstomp* E6 6a, 6b, 12 May 1984, with Steve Andrews. 'An outrageous adventure that is one of the best E6s in the country … It is not a soft touch and the penalty for those whose confidence falters or whose stamina fails, is long flight time!' *Gogarth North*, December 2008, Ground Up.

SNOOKERED
I ALWAYS PREFERRED GOLDEN WONDER TO SMITH'S
AND A FRIENDLY CHAT WITH A LONELY BOLT HANGER

I thoroughly enjoyed the game of snooker. Its angles, technicality and the need to always 'think three moves ahead' – so be mindful of 'position'. Always. And chalk your tips often too ...

We're being *very silly* young men on a quartzite rock face so are deserved of the wooden spoon across the back of the legs from our mums. Lord only help us when Dad gets home and finds out what we've been up to ... Quick, hide under the bed, I hear his clomping footsteps ascending the stairs.

We were on North Stack Wall that day you see.

Akin to a giant of a stowed-away billiard table – resting on its long side and leaning against the wall behind the comfy settee of the 'man-cave' that is Parliament House. Unused and unloved for quite some time. My fluffy old slippers and dressing gown set to one side. All my Rocks, tape slings and Friends scattered on top – thrown hurriedly so's not to miss the tide.

I took commitment and self-belief to extraordinary levels for an on-sight attempt to repeat *The Bells, The Bells!* It was six years since JR had metaphorically 'shook up the (climbing) world' – à la Cassius Clay back in the late sixties – but I believed (or had convinced myself anyway) that I could do it. I figured I'd have to get at least sixty feet up it without falling. To fall any lower would only result in permanent disability. Quadriplegia. Wheelchair and full-time carer for the rest of my life. Maybe one wink for 'yes', two for 'no' in ten years' time and all for a bloody rock climb. *That* was my greatest fear, not death; and I approached it, stewing all the same, in that headspace.

Mark Leach recently reminded me of a bizarre incident that happened shortly before I squeaked my boots and chalked up with butterflies and heavy breaths: after Bernard had dropped us at the South Stack car park Mark kept a safe distance behind me as we strolled across the heathery hilltop – I was not really talking. Quiet, deep – very deep – in thought, and psyching myself up for something momentous (Mark had an inkling and shuddered, thinking quite wisely that I was best left alone). But then I stopped dead in my tracks and bowed down, leaning over shouting something that Mark couldn't quite grasp over the wind. Quickening his pace he caught up – my face and hands were an absolute mess of bright red blood. I'd worked myself up that much I'd brought on a massive nosebleed and the claret was streaming out of both nostrils. All over the place it was, so we tilted my head back and I pinched the bridge of my beak, blood literally pumping out of both holes whilst I spat out great congealed blobs of the stuff that had run back into my throat.

He knew I 'got off' on North Stack Wall. He'd never been there before, so turning the next bluff and sighting that deserted and blank-looking face he knew I was having a case of 'the shivers'; he then shuddered once more.

We abseil in and pull down our ropes, committed.

So I set off up damp crunching barnacles till I'm above the highest water mark and can clean and resqueak my boots. Now, here's an opportunity to invite someone along – any takers?

'Come on, it's a Go-Pro view! OK, you'd rather not? I understand, I really do.'

Tell you what then: read this next chapter hanging off your door lintel. You can bridge against the sides but no Egyptian no-handers. And no under-clinging the far lintel, that's cheating!

'Tell us when you're pumped.' I was on the route for three hours ... just wishing there was a lintel-sized hold somewhere ... and a decent flipping runner!

'See ya at the top Mark,' I call over.

'OK. Good luck, I'm watching.'

So come with me now anyway; we climb 5b cracks up the start of *The Cad*, draping slings over spikes and weighing them down with the 'steelies', two apiece, clipping in only the left-hand pink rope until we gain an obvious line of flakes hovering above a faint rightward traverse covered in green fur. This sideways runner at the start's OK if I (we) were to fall *now*, as it also should go on pink – but will rotate and rip if I'm even five feet away and I'm going a good twenty by the looks of it.

'Anything else? There, here, fuck ... ' Keep traversing. Keep searching for protection. 'Still bloody nuthin.' It's OK climbing, 5c, 6a maybe, but there's no bloody gear and I'm weighed down with the stuff. There's a pleasant little platform waiting at the end of the traverse and we rock-over steadily until standing in balance, 'That wasn't so bad now was it?'

'Now, where are the runners for blue, see them?' I wiper-blade the rock and brush my hand over it to swipe off the fuzz, with eyes and mouth closed tight after a deep breath. Again and again I do this, covering myself in the arid shit until a tiny flake flashes a miniscule fissure. It accepts the smallest of nuts but that doesn't bite well. Hey, look, a little crack in the ledge we're stood on, so drop down and find 'get out of jail' cards!

Fiddling Rocks, fiddling RPs, sideways no. 3 or flatways no. 2? The 3 doesn't go all the way in but has further distance to rip. The 2 is all the way in but only just inside the flare. 'Which one do you reckon?' I go for the latter hoping not to fall, but am feeling much too heavy.

There are two more crafty placements for a keen eye – which should be useful to anyone ever here again. A pair of horizontal RPs in opposition – can you pick 'em out? This one is at least making an effort and trying, although that one's an underachiever, but by cleverly combining the two they may just take a short fall. We're thirty feet above the deck and this is all we have between us now. That 'pink' wire rotated and fell out ages ago and the spikes are too far beyond.

Let's step back up and take five. Get composed. I have a little eight-millimetre tape sling ready, it's clenched between my teeth and the peg's sticking out horribly fifteen feet up left ... 'Don't even consider clipping the eye. Choke it.' We rock upwards on reasonable half-finger-joint flakes and gain semi-balance. 'Any gear?' 'None that I can see.'

Wiper-blading away again with eyes and mouth shut – this is horrible. Everything's sharp – **poing** 'Whoa!' **startled**! 'Fuck that was close, see it snap? Almost off there.' (Meaning the boulders fifty feet below.)

Let's rock back down and regroup. All this bloody gear! This is pumpier than the ledge below and I'm not sure about reversing the rockover – so stay put. OK, am feeling it now, we're heading up leftwards but the best usable hold is that sidepull way up and right. I negotiate with it, exchanging a whispered 'I'll hold you against the wall, I promise' action in exchange for no less than a smooth layaway transition within an absorbing life or death sequence. 'What did *you* reckon? 6a into 6b and straight into 6a, without pausing and hanging off fingertips to shake out and chalk up?'

There's a decent-looking finger-edge up left and the peg's scratching at my waist. I don't *want* to stop but must crimp hard with my left whilst stood only on my right inner toe, left foot 'over there hovering in space' for balance, and fumble the tape over the peg and back through itself then pull up some blue and clip it. What a faff.

We've just clipped the peg but ' ... look at the mank ... fucking sad isn't it?' Another few moves up and we enter the 'death zone' so can relax a little – even though it feels somewhat chillier up here don't you think? I shut my eyes as I rest my forehead against this 'mountainside', just for a sec, breathing, breathing, then open them up and look all around me – blinking at the reflected light bouncing off the pale crystalline rock – up, right, left and down to take in, absorb and either embrace or rally against what I've just climbed myself into. And it's absolutely beautiful!

'Fucking hell! What a "space" to be in!' Very quiet, very calm. This is an altogether new place for me. I've never been this far out yet 'in' – as in 'involved' – before, you *know* that don't you? Oh, I didn't tell you. I asked God for a sign a while back, and a lone seagull drifted past above. I'm sure he noticed us.

We're balanced now precariously on tips of toes and locked on via steel fingers and forearms to two very small, creaky finger-flakes far, far above 'the red line', knowingly disobeying my old schoolmaster's rule that 'you could get hurt young Master Pollitt', and feeling laden down with useless gear.

Has the weight of the 'biner on that rusty old peg down there caused it to sag even further too? Oh, and my last remaining sideways RPs – those opposing ones – are still there but the others have fallen out from that cluster at around thirty feet … I'm now at eighty.

We're going for that thin horizontal seam running across above us, OK? Five thin-looking moves away. 'I've figured them out already, don't be worried.'

Crimp hard with the left, move left foot, pull hard as the right leg drifts away from the face as a counterbalance, and shoot and lock with right tips on that razor blade up there.

'Nice, well done!'

But, '**Agghhh**,' a sickening, tearing feeling, and '**fuck**!'

'**No**!'

There's blood!

It's pissing out of my right big fingertip and the next one's splitting too. Pump, pump, blood running down my hand. 'Quick Andy … ' Wipe shirt, wipe tights, right leg pops off suddenly, swing it in behind left and get balanced. **Quick man or you're on the deck.** Chalk more chalk wipe dab chalk chalk. '**Fuck**!' Reverse two moves quickly. Chalk dab wipe wipe inspect … ' … this ain't good … '

For the first time in my life I thought I was a goner and it was all happening in a weird 'sped up then slowed down again' timeframe. I was in a confused state where I knew but didn't know if this was all really happening. A fight for survival but strangely, oddly, really calm. I never panicked but remember distinctly emitting a sickly-sweet scent from my skin and I took its pungency to mean death. Attempting to reverse until standing on that peg then dropping on to it was my best option.

'Mark!' I shout down loudly. 'I've done a tip, going to try and reverse to the peg, watch us … '

A few moves down and my left big toe lands on that small matchbox-sized 'Thank God' hold I hadn't noticed on the hard bit passing the peg. Balance. Recompose. A lengthy pause then I make my decision: 'Am OK, going for it Mark … ' and we're moving …

We know the next fifteen feet and they pass precisely. Use the sharpie lower where it's blunter and stretch a bit further for the break. My fingers tickle left and right but it's too slopey. 'Shit, where's the good bit, there's got to be a good bit?'

Hold panic at bay, ignore all this weight pulling us downwards and hold tight. It's no good, my feet are too low. Reverse, shake out and flick fuzz off the newly intended footholds. 'No! Not in my eyes, wind! Owww … ' blink, blink, 'damn,' cling on and try and get it out with the other hand.

We're seriously way out on a limb here and I weigh a fucking ton and this is far too hard and thin for this shit to be happening. I'm seriously fearing for my life here you realise? My calves ache and I'm miles above shite gear with a longer move than I'd've liked. I shake the crap from my hair and face and spit out the bits then get the feet right up and stretch like mad. 'It's still no good … ' let's go the other way, over my head, **got it**! A decent hold and a runner too. Saved!

We're dragging ropes and are approaching the final groove, just another ten feet across and we'll be there. 5c, 6a maybe, like the start – then another platform arrives. The winter rainwater channel above teaches us how to swim and grovel desperately whilst remaining true to the traditions that The Leader Must Not Fall and should Maintain Three Points Of Contact.

What a hideous finish to such an amazing climb.

Earlier, gearing up beneath this route, going for the on-sight repeat with six years of sea-beard regrowth on it: a manky peg – more sticking out than was in, and by all accounts the odd shite runner in 120 feet of climbing. But what runners were they? I had no clue beyond *The Cad* spikes. My rack consisted of multiple sets of RPs, a dozen quickdraws, Rocks up to size 6, small and medium cams – Friends up to size 2, and slings with steel krabs on for the spikes before the real 'trip' began. Oh, and my tiny Leeper skyhook just in case.

So now I knew: apart from the slings low down with their weighty steel krabs, then the wire before the traverse, that cluster of three small nuts (two of which had fallen out), the one little sling and 'biner I'd tied off around the peg, and the single runner above the crux, I'd carried all the rest from bottom to top. Everything else – several kilos of it – was still hanging from my bandolier. I was utterly drained and lay there for a moment or two in reflection, gradually calming down before Bernard and Janine bounded down the bluff on their way to see us – moments too late for a historic snap, and then some other friends ran over and shook my hand and hugged me. Bernard Newman still recalls that top-out clearly:

> I remember that Jan got to you first and she describes your eyes – she'd never seen such a wild stare before – near death experience obviously – super adrenaline rush!

The Bells, The Bells! Finally repeated, and the utterly harrowing nature of the climb confirmed! That's roughly how one magazine reported it. 'Finally repeated.' Yeah, I liked that. It had been my goal and my dream for several years. Mike Owen and I had often fantasised over the prospect when I boarded at his and Elaine's.

All those months laid up twitching by the gas fire at no. 84 watching telly. The shorted-lived comeback thwarted by my downfall on *Artless* and the training and the laps on the fingerboards thereafter. Days on end working *Free and Easy* at Raven Tor – *clean* to get climbing-fit in a hurry, not to forget that prediction I'd made to myself below *Flashdance* that 'I'd go on to bigger and bolder things … ' Those tough days had paid off and the dream had just come true.

Funnily enough I was stuck for a doss that night and didn't fancy being outdoors, so Bob Drury invited me to crash in his caravan, which happened to be parked up in JR's back garden. I could see John inside the house, painting in his studio – the very house I'd stayed in so many times when dossing with Paul when he owned it – we're back at Tal y Waenydd, remember … from the Pen Trwyn days? John and Gretel live there now – they bought it when Paul moved down the hill to Bryn Crwn Cottage. I wondered whether John had heard of my ascent yet …[4]

☆ ☆ ☆

'Yey!' I exclaim to my 'taffy' mate as we park the van at the old quarry on the Holyhead side of the headland, 'bring it on … ' and I run this time, at a fair old clip – a heavy steel screwgate karabiner in each hand and clutching my trusty RP1, a tiny four-millimetre Perlon sling and one of those new-fangled Metolius TCU thingies a visiting American guest had gifted me as a thank you for a week's doss at no. 84. There were no other gear placements in any case, so why carry the rest?

---

4 Second ascent, *The Bells, The Bells!* 22 July 1986. On sight, and the only time in my entire climbing life I gave off that strange scent and honestly believed I was about to meet my maker.

Now, here's something I've discovered only recently – and shall now explain precisely how it came to pass: I, 'Andy P the climber', *did not* actually repeat the exact line of *The Bells, The Bells!* Simple as that. In his blog, Mike Owen states that he headed rightwards from clipping that peg – I rocked over leftwards and the peg scratched my tummy! Seems that – now I look closely at the photos of the wall – I actually totally on-sighted a new mid-section, which later became the best and hardest bit of my new line *The Hollow Man*. I then traversed desperately back rightwards along little white crystals to rejoin and finish up *The Bells!* So my error explains all those 'whoa, snapped' and 'green shit in eyes' moments on my 'ascent' of *The Bells!*: I was in unbrushed territory with much easier climbing over to my right – I'd death-defyingly misread the route! No wonder I bloody smelt 'funny' …

Maybe I should've gone for table-footy or a 501 best-of-three at 'arrows' instead of shaking scruffy hair out of my face on cold, damp holds … trying to find that bloody RP1 placement. I'd put it in around here somewhere before – prior to heading due left when first attempting to repeat *Flowers of Evil* with Mike 'Moose' Thomas, 'cept it took a real swipe at me it did, that route. I went at it having become 'Peak-District-fit' so it was only down to bottle really and I had a fair old reserve of that having just bolt-to-bolted for months. But it let a good, crucial foothold snap on me and I went thirty feet and took one of those over-in-seconds, staggered falls as the runners 'considered their verdicts' momentarily then barked snap, snap, then 'Agghhhh' – the lowest of the three holding, as my feet dunked down in a puddle on the rope-stretch and my boots got all wet.

'Oh! … Kin 'el! I'll have to dry 'em out now Bernard, and I've bust me favourite wire … Bstrds, bstrds … ' I grumbled as he dropped in having been taking distant shots from over on the lip of the cave (he was mumbling something or other to himself and looked extremely off-colour, most concerned).

'Hope you got that, B?'

'Pssst … ' I whisper to The Moose, ' … good catch,' then, nodding Newman's way ' … he just asked if I was going back up coz the light had improved … fuck me!'

'Ah flip, I've laddered me new tights too now fellas!'

I would return to complete that extremely severe climb with a most unexpected Peak mate and a sparkling new RP1 from the climbing shop, yet on that previous fall-equals-fail day, I was more concerned with dry boots for tomorrow's shoot and whether Bernard had captured that harrowing near-miss. That was a wake-up call for sure, and I questioned myself later why the heck I'd broken my own absolute, solid-gold rule and let a photographer anywhere near me on a scary on-sight? This would never happen again. Sure the foothold breaking caused a near catastrophe and I questioned whether I was getting cocky, but had reasoned I'd do it once only and not go back again for the cameras. Which was cocky personified I suppose?

Consider this: what percentage do we gain – or lose – if there's someone say, ten feet away on a rope with a long lanyard ready to pounce and clip you in if you lose it and 'Elvis' takes over?

I battle with myself in this dilemma; he's made all this effort to drive down from West Yorkshire, slogged in and brought different lenses. I can't let him down now; but I don't want to be here today, it doesn't 'feel right'. I want bolts. Bolts and ice-cream – not snapped RP1s and 'I-scream'.

I walk away from that fall, extremely shaken but physically unscathed, une-quivocally warned that North Stack's simply **not** the place to be gambling for photographs in such a manner. 'Don't take liberties sunshine, you ain't that good … ' I was dead lucky there – well one or the other, you can't be both!

I must say, however, that the above were *my* sentiments and mine alone. Mike Thomas was a most trustworthy and dependable climbing partner – particularly in such territory (not being afraid of the odd long run-out himself in the quarries), so hence 'innocent', and I was certainly under no pressure whatsoever from Bernard. Yes, I **did** want the pics for the article we were putting together, so had *I* – I wonder, reflecting from thirty years later – compromised *their* positions, even though Mike fancied seconding the route and BN needed the pics?

Whilst mooching around 'beris and using the Padarn payphone, I some-how managed to telephonically twist Ben Masterson's arm in *his* public booth, in what sounded like a riotous Llandudno bar. I coaxed him away from the tins of pop and 'sweetnesses' of Parisella's with promises of my, no, North Wales's very own Calanques just along the coastline: 'Pocket pulling at eighty-five degrees, Scotty,' I fibbed. 'Dolphins, whales, bikinis … and there's a bolt.'

'OK, OK, alright! We'll go to Gogarth then.' … Sucked in!

I'd repeated *Manic Strain* in the quarries that day and was feeling great. Redhead's again, and new hardest route over there. I'm not a stalker, honest … just gotta stay 'up there' – around the best. Snapping at heels, you know.

Then work even harder. See whom we can pass …

Ben followed me up *Flowers of Evil* and even suggested returning the next day as he wanted to lead something himself! We did, and he 'legged' it (where, as an eighteen-year-old I had desperately 'clung on' **all** the way up Ron's famous route), placing just a sling low down, a Friend 1 in the flake and a quickdraw on the bolt. I imagined Scotty up there chuckling to himself: 'Tee hee' or 'Nay bortherr' as he clipped the sad old hanger before sprinting to the top, probably unaware and unknowing of the historic steps he was retracing.

'Sad' bolt hanger you ask? More depressed really; the poor old sod was on tablets for his nerves! He was one of those first Troll caving ones with the really small hole. Aluminium – not good with salt spray. As I lost time wrest-ing Ben's 'biner out, 'our' conversation went:

'And that zinc bolt. He should've known us three wouldn't get along.'

Followed by:

'Well no-one liked the fact I was placed here Andy, especially me ... and I'm shivering me tits off all year round on me own, so do beg me pardon if I want people to stay awhile ... These tourists in summer love me. Ya should see some of the poor pricks' faces though, bloody hilarious! They should never have stuck us bolts on Gogarth. Or Cloggy. Call themselves the top climbers of the day – Redcett and Fawhead?

'We've all spoken and agreed; we've been around for years and we're simply not going to be any good any more. I used to have a brother nearby but he didn't last long; that Peter Whillans or someone – from up't Lakeland way I reckon – did for him, it was a quick demise so he's in a better place now. The ex-wife's Welsh nephew's son's girlfriend's best friend's neighbour's lad Dennis up on Midsummers is about to shit himself and my cousin Daffydd over on the crux of Manic Strain is 'worn-out' he said; asked why we couldn't get retired to a rest home where no one will bother us. A Gary Gibson route perhaps ... Well?'

And he was off ...

Oh sorry: 'Nice job Ben,' I call up.

I recall one of my boldest exploits ever was also on that blisteringly hot day (it was just after following Ben – seeing if I could speed-climb it quicker than he could take in. I could, couldn't, could, couldn't, let's call it a draw: 'Sorry Ben, got waylaid at the bolt.'). We'd scrambled down to the water's edge and dived in to check out two large seals who'd been watching us. Their big heads popped up right in front of our faces like overgrown black Labradors. Huge, inquisitive eyes with pretty lashes, shiny noses and long, impressive whiskers; 'Ugh', 'Phugh', they exchanged with one another – in their own language – seemingly unthreatening towards Scotty and me. 'Brrzqxionlweeeeeeeeei', 'Kgdemxzlhwooo', I probably sounded back in my language. 'Hello sealies,' was all I said. 'Sorry, no offence, don't go!'

Fishy breath? I honestly can't remember; they'd disappeared beneath the seaweed floating amongst the swell. It was eerie when we couldn't see them and I was protectively cupping, well, err *nothing* quite frankly, and flapping amateurishly with the other hand. 'They won't bi ... *splutter*, bite will they B ... B ... Ben?' whilst taking in a mouthful of Holyhead harbour's finest *Bin '87*. Even though I was bobbing up and down with the swell, every 'down' landed my feet on a submerged boulder, then as I rose I 'cupped and thrashed' for all I was worth – proper bold or what?

A memorable couple of days for sure![5]

Back again for more on yet another occasion, but I was now heading off up rightwards on the first ascent of my 'direct'.

That putrid stench and the big, bright red nose and colourful baggy pants and braces were only ever discernible on the blankest of faces between those 'safe cracks' where you were essentially facing a hundred feet of Smith's crisps splattered randomly up the face – like a piece of Pro Hart artwork.[6]

Some were held on as if by Blu Tack, and fell off when merely tapped with fingertips. Others were part of Mother Earth, but who was to know? Not me. 'On sight' more often than not, and in what precise sequence did I have to ballet dance, improvise, then tippy-toe my way up? Some would snap off if pulled on to the left, others to the right. Dr Dolittle's 'Push-Me-Pull-You' came to mind.

With Yorick watching attentively as ever, the crux involved repeated rock-ups to feel around, then scuttles back down again to its one, solitary, decent hold before committing; I 'read' the rock as best I could and knew I had something of a juggling act to perform. I was particularly concerned about the best of the fingerholds – I needed them for my feet a move above, and didn't want to snap them off. Be pretty stuffed then, believe me, so pulled extra hard with three tips and an opposing 'thumb-sprag' – on a *cheese and onion* of a crisp until widely bridged on the *smoky bacons*. Creak, Creak. I was entering *salt 'n' shake* territory now – the packets with the little blue bag inside, but I wasn't shakin', just yet …

Golden Wonder always made more flavoursome crisps in my view …[7]

☆ ☆ ☆

You'll recall that I'd developed a familiarity with such thrilling experiences back in 1982 when Paul suggested I was about good enough to lead *The Cad*.

'*About*, Dad? *The Cad*, Dad?' Was this his test – see if I was all I was cracked up to be? Does he want to invest further time in climbing with me? We'll see …

---

5 Second ascent, *Flowers of Evil* E7 6b (now given E6 6b). Attempted on a cold 3 February 1987 with Mike Thomas, then completed on a scorching-hot 9 August 1987 with Ben Masterson.

6 Kevin Charles 'Pro' Hart, MBE, born in Broken Hill, New South Wales, was considered the father of the Australian Outback painting movement and his works are widely admired for capturing the true spirit of the outback. Hart revolutionised the Australian art industry and the world with his unique painting techniques and extraordinary pieces.

7 First ascent, *A Wreath of Deadly Nightshade* E7 6b, 20 May 1988, with Adrian 'Yorick' Hughes.

On another occasion JR and I had abb'd down a blank wall apiece – he got traumatised on his lead and then, straight after, I mimicked his actions like a star-struck hanger-on.[8]

Reclining at about eighty-five degrees so as not to topple forward, its baize a poor-quality 'spray-on tan' of arid pale-green sea-beard. Nasty stuff it is too, burns my eyes, then again Gogarth *herself* could turn nasty on the merest of whims.

Just don't 'go in off the black,' that's all – or the game is lost!

As I've said before, consider 'position' at **all** times and where you'll end up when you commit to your sequence, coz there's no going back nor 'replacing the black' once you've touched it – the ref doesn't allow that. Neither do Father Time nor gravity, so this is your *one*, your *only* chance of escape and you'll rue poor route-finding decisions – if you live that long, coz yeah, muck up and you're gone!

Those 'safe-crackers' climbing the protection-guzzling and very 'safe cracks' on a sunny day when the wall was basking and being submissive were always pleasant to witness, but that zawn would start to shiver and awake from its relaxing afternoon nap as the shadow line crept silently, almost unnoticed, across its flank. Often as not it would wake in a foul mood and become 'cranky', and if you were still down there at teatime you'd better watch out – count your fortunes, then get the heck out of there. Hurry up. Run.

Sh, sh, shiv … err. I'm 'channelling' Redhead, but there's none of his usual love or warmth. No, he's hisssing in my ear: 'Petrushka's around Andy, take care youth.' I fear that one of his blessed clowns will appear, then my thought-bubble bursts and I snap back to reality – only to find myself way too far beyond *The Cad* flake for my Friends (two in the flake and Steve Andrews down below) to be of any real use. 'Redhead' had, moments earlier, warned me so pointedly that this was the spot *he'd* most likely come swooping in, so I had nobody but myself to blame for my predicament – stuck, confused, horribly overcommitted by misreading the sequence that landed me where I stood – wrong-footed and cross-handed with a trembling bottom lip. I have an idiot (?) on my left, a comedian (?) on my right on the *safe cracks* and I'm 'Stuck in the middle with you', you evil bastard, sod off you clown … (thx to Stealers Wheel there …)

---

8 First ascents, *Birth Trauma* E6 6a, *Art Groupie* E6 6a, 27 May 1984. A lead and a second apiece, with John Redhead.

Not that I actually ever 'saw' a clown, I make no such claim – other than my own reflection in the mind's eye for buggering up the sequence so badly, but JR and Dave Towse swore blind the clowns were real and had both seen 'em with their own eyes. So John, Dave? I inquire: what's that unpleasant, acrid scent that wafts across the wall just as the fog horn goes off when the mist rolls in off the Irish Sea, and your tea went cold hours ago?

Reheated, soggy fish fingers and chips to look forward to, if only I can extricate myself from this by my own hand. Well, the belayer, Steve, may just as well unclip me and go home – he's of no assistance this far out and there's no one to call for a rescue line anyway. Even if I could untie one rope and let Steve jug out with it and lower it back in, I was way out of time. That'd take forty minutes at best. I doubted whether I had forty *seconds* so it was fruitless. Even if there was sufficient time I realised we'd not left an abseil rope, rather pulled ours down, so were in a potential predicament from the get-go. 'I must leave a rope and bring my partner jumars next time,' I promise myself.

So I'm all at sea, high up on the frictionless tilt-slab of a billiard table that is yet another Redhead horror show, itchy green shit in my eyes and pumping out … tick, tock, tick, tock … thirty-two seconds and counting …

But wait! What's that? I spy the minutest of cracks just above me. Can I reach it before I run out of juice and peel off backwards only to land on the 'down' escalator to oblivion a hundred feet below? 'Ref,' I plead under my breath, 'I need a rest … '

Making some godawful contortions I stretch above clutching my 'biner of smallest RPs and manage to wriggle in a zero. But my fingers are uncurling so I make an all-out grab for the bunch, pull up one rope and, clipping in immediately, slump off. How it holds I can't fathom, but Steve lowers me down ever so gently whilst taking in on the rope running through *The Cad* runners till I'm equally suspended, then lowers me more safely to the boulders below the cliff. Next try – tick – Paul *will* be proud. Why on earth did I go up there again and why am I so 'into' all this terrifying shit?[9]

Anyway, that unpleasant olfactory assault I assumed to be the revolting body odour of a *demon* – with a German accent. I read some years ago that my own surname is part-Germanic in origin, perhaps that's why I was left unpestered to complete a seriously long and thin run-out *without* my scant protection being interfered with by an invisible hand once above and 'going for it'.

---

9 Second ascent, *The Clown* E7 6b, on a chilly 8 January 1987, with Steve Andrews.

Redhead hadn't been so lucky when the silly bolt he'd placed unfathomably unclipped itself as he approached the excruciatingly technical and bouldery crux about seventy feet up only to – at the worst possible moment – realise he was simply trailing a useless and weighty pair of ropes.[10]

I suppose I was just about the only other climber back in the second half of the eighties to venture out 'between the cracks', uninspected and unrehearsed, but I believed I could understand and speak the 'language' of North Stack Wall. Funnily enough my old mate Mike Owen, who was also my manager at work and *my* landlord at home, was the only other person who ever really showed any genuine interest in the place around that time … Then again, I'm sure I probably badgered him constantly about it, I mean, it was bound to happen – cragging, working and living together seven days a week! Poor Mike and Elaine probably just snapped one night and agreed to ab in … if for no other reason than to shut me up and have a quiet evening meal for once.

Sometimes my descriptions of climbing on North Stack would be verbal, at others in written form in magazine articles, so now I may as well regurgitate a hackneyed old musical analogy too, so here goes: whilst I could play 'Fmaj7' both left and right-handed it was the 'sympathetic', 'diminished' and 'minor' shapes that I struggled with the most. North Stack is littered with the darn things.

John and Dave were obviously cursed to some extent, because their next big route, a rising traverse, was interrupted during the change in leads – on doubtless a questionable-at-best belay – by a *fiend*. Did the little RP they shared for a hanging stance slip, all by itself, down the crack – only to half-bite an inch or so lower whilst the two brave men stared at each other's shocked, white faces whilst both wailing 'Agghhhh!'?

The faint, eerie tolling of distant bells shortly before dusk as I 'hold it together' high on the face a million miles out from non-protection – having brushed a thirty-foot thin streak above where I previously almost died.

Images of Clowns, Demons, Evil Flowers and graveside Wreaths.

'One last time,' I vow to myself. 'Just the once!' Then … 'No more Andy, get up to Cloggy … they say it's dry and *Master's* awaits.'

I shake my mane furiously to clear my head, dark scraggly hair all over the place. It's windy today so I'll 'throw it my caution' and toss away my fears. Put the blinkers on like a thoroughbred – pointless even *thinking* of all those bomber nuts twenty feet either side, they're unreachable.

Yeah, be focussed and 'Hollow,' man, this shouldn't take long …[11]

---

10 Second ascent, *The Demons of Bosch* E7 6b (sans bolt), 12 August 1988, with Paul Williams.

11 First ascent, *The Hollow Man* E8 6b, 2 October 1986, with Johnny Dawes.

Arch Enemies, Dovedale. First ascent. **Photo:** Richie Brooks.

12.

MY WEB OF ADDICTIONS

Much as I liked the far end of Chee Dale, it was a terror for access and egress – that path was far too steep for my skinny legs, so every time I made the slog back out I'd need to stop halfway up for a breather … Looking back down into the dale, the commanding prow of Plum Buttress hung well out above the surrounding greenery, offering a particularly dominant profile. 'Wow!' I thought. 'Now there's a line … and a photo op!'

After seeing this prow for the umpteenth time I decided to drive out there one day and throw a rope down it. The top was pretty loose and I had to be particularly careful when chucking off wobbly flakes and blocks in case people were walking up to the crag from below. There was a fair amount of old, *in-situ* aid gear – pegs and a bolt or two I think, and they seemed half decent. On reaching the main roof I was heartened to discover some very good and very solid holds about six inches above the lip, but feeling around underneath and flipping upside down for a look I couldn't see much to undercut off. I never owned a cordless hammer drill – though had borrowed them on occasion – so usually had only my little Petzl hand kit and a small lump hammer … it took ages placing an upside-down bolt to aid in on for a look. Hanging off that I placed another bolt (or a peg, I can't remember) in the break at the back of the roof and clipped in with a short sling. This allowed me to pull the slack through my 'Stop' as it was dragging me outwards with the stretch; I could then play around and check out the moves across the roof. 'Yep, that works, but feet need to be there … ' and 'Yey, that's a long reach, that'll get 'em … ' and other such mutterings to myself; but I figured out a sequence and semi did it. I say 'semi' because the sling I was attached to wasn't long enough for me to do the thing in one and had to be unclipped from the peg at the back then transferred to the upside-down bolt part way across, so I actually did it in two halves. At least I knew it was a goer and thought that on lead it wouldn't be *that* hard. For someone with my wingspan anyway.

This latest new line that I'd cleaned, prepared and got all ready to go was the old aid route *The Spider*, and I'd need to be having a really good day – problem was I was drinking even harder than usual around that time; my relationship with my girlfriend was not in a good place either, which made matters worse. Often I'd scold myself on getting home from a day at the crag with my mates, because I knew the booze was starting to slow me down and my great friends (and personally, my very own limestone 'barometers') Scotch Ben and Chris Hamper were burning me off on a daily basis. If they took two falls, I'd take six; two days, five days etc. … I could do better than that. They knew that and I knew it too, except whilst they went home and had proper, healthy meals and early nights, I went to the pub and got smashed.

Forty smokes a day and a lousy diet didn't help – I was writing myself off seven nights a week, getting to the point where I'd often need to throw up in pub toilets or in people's gardens on the way back home before crashing out. Not good, Andy. Not good.

However, I did do the route but was having 'another of those days' and was really pretty half-arsed with my attempt. The climbing was steady to that crux section I'd done in halves on abseil across the roof, then eased off towards to the top. No big deal. We'd often all do two or three of these grades a day. Leaning out from the break, placing my feet where I remembered I needed them, I launched out and stretched for all I was worth, 'cept my power was way down and I was sagging and simply didn't have enough in the tank to get up close enough to the horizontal roof so my positive ape index[1] would land my fingers on those good holds just over the lip. Damn! Second go and I struggled 'from go to woe', used the bolt under the roof for a handhold, and claimed the route with one aid point. I could've/should've gone back any number of times but never bothered.

I should give credit (and award kudos) to my climbing partner on that occasion – Rory Gregory. We'd not climbed together before, never did again I don't think, and Rory was a mate of a mate and had the biggest biceps known to man. I certainly admired his physique but didn't have a skerrick of envy coz

1 *Editor's note*: long arms – more later.

A DIFFERENT KIND OF POKKETZ PRODUCTION © Alan James 1991

he'd be heavy carrying all that – I was a stick insect by comparison. Calling down to Rory on the ground to begin following, I started taking the rope in – foot by foot, 'cept it felt like I was sinking in little, jerky increments every time I took in. Long story short, Rory was that strong that he just stood there, pulled and pulled on all the holds and the cliff gently sunk into the ground until eventually we were at eye level, me tied back to a tree, and all I had to do was unclip and step off the top of the buttress right back on to the ground where I'd started. Put it this way, the man was strong. Very strong. As if by magic the cliff was sticking right back up out of the hillside again the next time when I went to get my pics for the mags and slide shows etc.

I happened upon the title idea for this chapter 'My Web of Addictions' quite by chance in 2013. I'd decided on 'Arachnid' as my working title even earlier, but then I was net surfing – delving into the psychological and physiological effects of addiction vs dependency vs holding down a decent, responsible career whilst basically just loving a bit of booze – it was genuinely enlightening. My Web … seemed perfectly appropriate. Some of the case studies were enough to make the heaviest of drinkers quit on the spot (as I discussed later with my mates up the pub as we got rat-arsed one Saturday evening … 'Sad cases them lot,' one goes, 'Yeah,' says another, 'we're nowhere near that bad!').

UNDERNEATH THE ARCHES

Being upside down is great – I can vouch for that living here in Australia. The gravity pushes me ground-wards along with everyone else, so we don't really notice it that much to be honest – and nothing suddenly flies off into space.

Flicking through old mags and guidebooks one day at Sandford Grove Road, my eye was drawn to Reynard's Cave in Dovedale – just along the path from Ilam Rock where Ron had done his classic *Eye of the Tiger* – and there it was: *The Flying Circus*, an old aid line which looked simply stunning. Up, under and out through a natural rock arch near the top of a steepish gully.

Abseil down, give it a brush and chuck in a few bolts, simple. Not quite, and it turned out a tad harder than I expected, so I had to go back a few times to do it in a 'oner'. Called it *Arch Enemies*, what a bloody ripper of a route: Zippy and the rest of my close friends reckoned so too, all having repeated it within days – again – wish they'd stop doing that![2]

However fine that route was, it paled into insignificance when compared to my next project.

---

2 First free ascent of *The Flying Circus*, to give *Arch Enemies* E6 6b, F7c+, 9 December 1987.

Thor's Cave had been pegged and bolted by the aid climbers going back decades, so Yorick and I took a day trip and went for a gander. We aided *Thor* although it was seeping like heck and, surprisingly, it looked like the holds were all there for a free effort – yes, there and generally huge. A straight line of water solution pockets in the ceiling ran for twenty-five-odd feet, totally upside down and horizontal, so whilst I was hanging in slings I fished out old spiderwebs and general grot then replaced most of the perished tat with brand-new threads. To this day my left hand carries a small scar where molten Perlon dripped on to me as I was blowtorching off the old slings. We redid the start and gave it a good cleaning and placed a few new bolts. The route was ready – if only it would dry out. Returning a few days later with Tim (yet again out of 'retirement' – but only coz it was a roof) we both bolt-to-'threaded' it – the sequence across the cave roof was utterly stupendous. Problem was it was still weeping and needed rags stuffing in the pockets after every move.

I returned again with Yorick, having once more borrowed Jerry's blowtorch, and soon had the route dry enough for an attempt. The start and little traverse left were a bit scrappy, but then the entertainment began: a bomber two-finger pocket, toe hook in a big hole, reach through in an almost-upside-down crucifix and grab the biggest jug in the Peak District. Swing off that to a similar pocket, then throw both feet into another hole and hang bat-like for a breather. Best no-hands rest in the Peak that, bar none. I never had the core strength to do sit-ups, so had to hand over hand up my own leg until I could get my mitts back into the roof (that doesn't constitute aid does it?) whence followed a further fifteen feet of upside-down craziness and a 'king swing' out to an absolute bucket around the lip. The belay ledge was another fifteen feet above – I was pumped out of my brains – on reaching it I slumped down, gasping for breath.

The best way off is to just … jump … the enormous thread at the lip could anchor the *Queen Mary*, so off into space I stepped. You go about thirty feet or so but at least it's a nice warm-up for doing the Monsal Dale viaduct rope swing, and the route has as many stars as you can give it.

A few years ago, twenty-plus after the fact, I used the *UKC* search engine and punched in *Thormen's Moth* (taken from a Catherine Cookson novel that was lying faded on the rear windscreen shelf of Wild Country's Roger Withers' car when he and his missus had kindly given me a lift home from Provence a few weeks earlier). I delighted in the comments on the thread:

XXX: Best 8a in the Peak.

YYY: My favourite British sport route by a considerable margin.

And then the tale of ZZZ who was so pumped on lowering off that he had to lie down for twenty minutes to get his breathing and blood pressure back to normal, dry-retching from the effort. Couldn't even untie his own rope or remove his harness – his mates had to do it for him as they sat there next to him hoping he was OK.[3]

'WIMMIN'

I was in a rather stagnant union with a young lady, predominantly due to my own personal 'issues' – we were pretty much in limbo and, to be honest, both struggling. Her new university friends that she'd hang out with 'wore denim dungarees', shall I say, and didn't appear to shave their armpits or legs, and it felt as though they disliked me simply because I was male; so it wasn't a particularly pleasant environment when I went around to visit, even though I never had an issue with their sexual orientation and certainly didn't fancy them (one of their girlfriends, yes!) – but why be so horrid to me? I honestly was the perfect gentleman at all times.

I'd always assumed my GF was 100 per cent hetero, and I'm not saying she wasn't, but was stumped as to why she wanted to live in 'Dykesville, Arizona' (OK, it was Sharrow) and take up reading hard-core feminist writings? The bookcases, the coffee table in the lounge room, and the shelf next to the toilet all played host to such publications as *Why All Men Are Bastards – No Exceptions*, and *You Know You're Gay, Come on Out: Join The Sisterhood*, and *Ditch him and Cum With Us*, and an instruction manual which was predominantly about the pleasures of girl–girl oral sex.

So what's this got to do with climbing?

Long Tor Quarry, down across the river near High Tor, was a hidden and rarely visited place (a bit like the GF's 'intimates' at the time) but it had a stunning, gently overhanging wall of excellent limestone with a terrific-looking line of widely spaced edges. I gave it a brush and placed a few bolts and it was as crimpy to climb as it looked – I rather surprised myself by getting it in pretty good time. It turned out to be a little gem and I named it *Ruby Fruit Jungle* after the 'coming-of-age' lesbian novel next to the bog back at that shared 'wimmin's' house in Sheffield.

E-something 6-something in the old money. Reckon that'd be an F7- or F8-something these days wouldn't it?[4]

---

3 First free ascent of *Thor*, to give *Thormen's Moth* E7 6b/c, F8a, 14 June 1988.
4 First ascent, *Ruby Fruit Jungle* E7 6c, F8a, 19 May 1988.

THE FREE CAFE

Mrs Parisella owned and ran the cafe at the Happy Valley (just at the start of the Marine Drive around Llandudno's Great Orme) with her gorgeous identical twin daughters – her son had an equally beautiful girlfriend, who was utterly delightful also; amazingly we're still in touch to this day! I guess Mrs P had only really been used to serving, and the girls wiping up after, old-age pensioners – by the busload! The old-fogey men wore cream summer blazers and dribbled on the napkins, so when the first ripples of what was soon to become a tidal wave of rock climbers arrived she went out of her way.

End of the first afternoon there in '83 with Paul, Ron and Gill, Mrs P began taking in the tables and chairs and we all automatically leapt up going: 'No Mrs P, we'll do that for you, please let us help'. Taking in the outdoor furniture became a nightly ritual and it circulated around the Pen Trwyn scene that whoever was there at closing time was expected to follow suit – assist the ladies and 'No Questions Asked'.

Totally unwarranted or desired, Mrs P simply wouldn't accept us four's money from that day on, and our two or three tea breaks a day became gratis: 'Grab some pastries and cakes lads, fancy a 99, Gill?'

'No thanks, all good, see you in The Cottage Loaf later or in the morning? Thanks for everything.'

Of course, human nature being what it is, some idiot had to go and spoil things, didn't they? I was in the queue ahead of Paul, Ron and Gill, with some scumbag freeloader idiot ahead of us – Mrs P was on the till. The oaf had piled his plastic tray with pastries and a 'large' cup of coffee. 'That'll be two pounds twenty-five please,' or whatever it was.

'Yer what? I heard climbers ate for free here.'

'Some do, not you sonny boy, That'll Be Two Pounds Twenty-Five Please!'

'Yer fckn kiddin'!' he argued, so Paul reached past me and silently squeezed him around the scruff of his neck and effortlessly lifted the little bugger clean off the floor. Bringing him right up to his face squirming, Paul quietly suggested he pay up or he'd smash him to smithereens, then gently set him back down.

The cheeky lout coughed up the requisite funds and Ron asked, 'What happened there then, a bit of bother?'

'Nowt Ron, all sorted,' Paul replied.

'No pie or sandwich today, Andy?'

'No ta, just desserts thanks.'

A few years later on I had a clutch of super new routes lined up on Lower Pen Trwyn (LPT) so started bolting and climbing them. *Libertango, La Boheme, Night Glue* etc., and later still *Over the Moon* (E8 6c, F8a) on 30 June 1986 –

my hardest first ascent to date. This was all very well but when preparing the next one, and with apologies to all, I went overboard with the hammer – my sole indiscretion.

There was a small finger-pocket with a funny, crumbly fossil-thing in it and I overzealously dug it out in my haste to produce another decent route. I stupidly thought at the time that it seemed a shame to have a stopper move on an otherwise delightful, flowing and mid-grade climb that heaps of people could enjoy for years to come, but I was simply short-sighted and greedy and my mates were justifiably disappointed in my actions and I realised the error of my ways soon after. There's a sure-fire way to tell if a hold is improved or chipped at Pen Trwyn, because once the weathered surface is penetrated the rock 'sweats'. I attempted to anti-perspirate the little hole by painting it, but the supposed grey Humbrol dried bright silver and 'winked' at everyone when the sun shone.

I desperately regretted that stupid misdemeanour and it could well have cast doubt on my overall ethics and personal integrity – two things I'd always held dear, but had idiotically compromised. Thankfully there was no great fuss (at least of which I was aware) and we all moved on. Apparently the chains were lowered in the early '90s due to chipped holds at the top. They aren't mine – just that single, slight enhancement lower down – but yeah, 'just desserts' indeed![5]

'CIGARETTES'
'SUNGLASSES'
AND 'BOLLOCK-CHOPS' THE SAVIOUR

The first two items are what I screamed for the umpteenth time. Usually followed by: 'You deaf bastards!'

This wind, really!

I'd just led the first vertical frozen waterfall pitch with ease (I never mentioned finesse). This 'proper mountaineering' malarkey's piss I thought – being halfway up what was supposedly North Wales's harshest winter route; though my poor shoulders were telling me all was definitely not good.

'Belay's crap though, I'll give it that. Now which way does this thing screw in again?'

---

5 First ascent, *Café Libre* (The Free Café) E7 6c, 2 July 1988.

Editor's note: The lower-off was resited near its original position at the top of the route by Pete Harrison in 2009 after he had excavated resin filler from a chipped hold near the top. The 2014 guidebook grades the route F7c+ and comments: 'The challenge has been tainted by a chipped hold high in the scoop, but it's just where you need it – impossible without?' Fortunately for AP a typo in that guidebook means the route has been credited to Paul Freeman on 10 July 1991 … Oops! Definitely, as the 1992 guidebook says, a route with history …

I lower the barely-scratched axes ninety feet back down to Biff coz he'd come 'Malham prepared' with what was tantamount to 'me granddad's old Alpenstock and these spikes I found in 'is shed up t' allotment' and his trusty little geologist's hammer from when he studied chemistry or whatever at uni …

Oh, here he comes now, look …

'Honestly Biff! If that guy seconding the pitch ahead of us sends down one more big chunk I'm gonna deck 'im,' I yell through my itchy balaclava as Martin scrabbles with his knees/feet/ten-pointers to get on to our belay going, 'Yer what, lad?'

Whoooooshh … another one! 'That shit! It's coming from those careless fuckwits above … '

'Giz a tab, lad, forgot mine,' says I and laugh once more at his bendy-soled hiking boots and old-fashioned tie-on walking crampons with no real front-pointy-bits!

We shared Martin's last two fags but they got all wet like everything else and fell to pieces as we huddled a hundred feet up a particularly runny-nosed Craig y Rhaeadr, high above the Llanberis Pass. I yodelled down to the 'mountain climbers' on the scree below, trying to catch their attention, then threw out our ropes, yelling and pointing towards our sacs. You see, some garishly-attired 'mountaineers' at the foot of the buttress had scoffed when we'd arrived shortly after first light: 'What d'ya think you two are doing up here … ? Chalk's not gonna be much use is it lads, or sticky rubber? Ha, ha!' Smarmy sods.

Another pair were tickled by the banter – I could tell by their expressions, so shot them a wry smile back as they huddled over their stove. Rock stars! Busted, this'll be fun … Ha! But hey! I have an ace up my sleeve you pedants over there – check these babies out, ta-da!

I'd advised Berghaus and CAMP we were going snow climbing, ' … you know, "punter" stuff Neil,' so Kennedy – my man at HQ – sent down a pair of snazzy white Scarpa plastic double boots from the warehouse in my size. And a Berghaus windproof. 'Colour coordination Andy man,' Geordie-ley. 'Maximize the product mix, and logos are on both sides this time.'

'Will Bernard be photographing or Glenn?'

'I can get a-hold of Brian Hall or Al Hinkes … man.'

As CAMP too had 'come to the party,' I was able to pull two devilishly violent-looking ice tools from my sac, ripping off the Italian factory wrappers admiringly – right there under that enormous frozen mountain. Splitting open the next box, out fell a pair of sabre-toothed, rigid, snap-on Foot Fangs.

Brilliantly shiny and red. 'I really don't want to scratch these,' I thought to myself.

That shut the smarmy ones up – for a second, till they started guffawing again as, feigning the bleedin' obvious, we 'pretended' to figure out which way on the Fangs went. 'Any heel hooks in the description, Biff?'

Anyway, we're on the stance and my ropes have just landed a good thirty feet away from where I'd hoped, but somebody'd thankfully managed to retrieve them. I scream and point some more, but it's useless giving the V sign with 'Dachshund' mitts on and I'd heard you could lose an exposed fingertip in no time on Mount Snowdon, or catch that 'Cerebral Oedipus Disease' most of 'em got at *this* altitude. Mitt off, mimic smoking, mitt back on, thumbs up and a bloke clips on my little waterproof fag-bag. 'Sunglasses too please ... in the carrier bag ... with the bickies ... ta.'

Up until then they'd thought us dropping the ropes meant we'd had enough and were bailing out. Ha! As if!

Basher was going to lead on through and his pitch was supposedly the crux so, being traditionalists, we paid respect to our predecessors – and had a Woodbine at twenty-six thousand feet, err, inches – a bit like Joe Brown and our mutual friend Martin Boysen in virtually *every* expedition picture we'd ever seen of them. And we scoffed too – our few chocolate Hobnobs, whilst dodging the debris hurtling past from Bollock-Chops above.

'Did your mum buy you tartan shirts every birthday and Christmas and red woolly socks when you first started?' 'Yeah, mine too.' 'Reckon they thought we were walking up "round the back?"' 'Mine *still* turns my pictures sideways and goes "my goodness, well look at that"'... 'Yeah, why do they always do that, infuriating isn't it?'

Martin now has the ice picks and a very pink nose. I pass him our three screwy-pegs and just before he sets off I amuse myself again comparing the two axes. One has an adze, the other a hammer. What if yer left-handed? You'd be whacking yer knuckles with the hammer with yer less functioning hand, surely?

'OK off ya go, the light's fading.'

I heard chopping. Chopping and 'scraping-away' sounds from around the corner and giggled at the thought of Basher cutting away perfectly decent ice to reach a good crimp or expose a finger-jam – ice tools dangling from his wrists; but I was paying out rope so he was at least making steady progress. He was terribly slowed down by the team ahead and I eventually followed just as God flicked the switch for the night. We'd been all bleedin' day!

Thankfully Bollock-Chops stayed back with Biff rather than scarpering off like his mate had, and guided us both down to safety with his head torch.

Top chap. Never got his name.

'That's alpineering ticked then hey Biff? Wait till I tell Jim Curran and Rab down the pub tomoz!'[6]

---

6 *Cascade*, a tricky ice climb back in the day, millionth ascent but not really our cup of tea. No photographers showed up. I later worked out (by dividing my combined salaries by 365 days) that Berghaus and CAMP had wasted two pounds and 5 pence apiece, as well as a fair bit of never-to-be-used-again kit!

Nati Dread, Arapiles. **Photo:** Simon Carter.

13.
NEW YEAR'S, DEAD OR ALIVE

'You Spin Me Round (Like a Record)' was a big hit at the time ... and is possibly an odd introduction to a chapter but it should make sense by the end.

He was something of a brat when he first arrived on the Sheffield scene around 1984. Young, boisterous, loud and often annoying, yet had oodles of self-belief and I couldn't help but admire him for that, and I warmed to him even though many took the opposing view. He took a lot of working out though – a bit like *The Guardian* cryptic crosswords that Tim and I used to compete over at weekends.

Let's imagine ... we're in particularly 'high spirits' and Christmas has just come and gone and New Year's Eve is in two days. A new century, Y2K and the whole world's collective hopes that our computers wouldn't all crash at midnight – and we all 'magically' assume Sheffield in 1984 is Melbourne in 1999:

I'm heading into the big city to see *DJ Shaw on NYE* (as the posters promote). *He owns Y and J* – Young and Jackson's, Melbourne's most notable old pub/hotel – the one with the neon billboards on top, opposite Flinders St. railway station and St Paul's Anglican Cathedral that I sometimes pop into in times of reflection and solace (I *do* mean the Cathedral not the boozer); the hotel houses the world-famous portrait *Chloe*, and Shaw always puts on a great trance night at New Year's.

The 'he' I refer to was cryptic indeed. A bit of a conundrum, an anagram – hence the otherwise nonsensical wordplay above – so I'll simply refer to him as 'DJ'.

DJ was like one of those little rubber power balls we played with as kids. Tons of energy compressed into a tiny little package, but by heck he had the talent to back up his braggadocio. Incredible on grit and pretty much untouchable for quite some years. It would be unfair to pigeonhole the brash young lad – then man – as just a gritstone master though, for he transported his supreme skills down to North Wales and stuck his neck out, often further than most.

I remember chatting with him on one of numerous occasions in Pete's Eats – at the time I *think* he was trialling some new Calma rock boots but wasn't too happy with them so reverted to Boreals. He'd just put up an alternative 'escape off to the side' finish to the desperate upper pitch of an existing route but – pen in hand, new routes book open on the greasy table we were sharing – was scratching his head for a name. 'How's about *The Fire Escape?*' I said, 'pronounced *Fee-ray* after yer boots.' He loved it and that's where the name comes from. (Course if it were mine I'd have called it *Scarpa Off Left* or something after *my* sponsors.)

We went up to the Cromlech one day coz we both fancied doing Ron's traverse across the *Right* and *Left Walls*, but you could only really do it if there was no one else climbing upwards through you, or your trailing ropes would be under someone's, over the next person's, back under again – and no end of bickering about sharing runners. If anyone slipped it would've been one off, all off. Luckily the Pass was pretty much deserted. Great fun to climb with he was, and I led the *Right Wall* traverse and he led the *Left*.

Our second trad route together was something truly momentous I had lined up on Gogarth – North Stack Wall. He'd probably done *The Cad* and a few others but had stayed well away from the Redhead 'scarys' for some reason or other. I didn't really like the fact he'd checked out *The Bells!* on abseil with Nick Dixon and Pritch, but they'd all said, 'No fckn way!' Told me so in the Padarn one evening just before I did it, and they were my ultimate motivation coz I always felt the second ascent of *The Bells!* – and the first on sight – was for me, and this was six years after the first ascent. As they'd all inspected it I sensed top-rope practice then a lead attempt was in their heads, but I couldn't countenance that.

Yes, the old top-rope practice thing – a real bugbear of mine it was!

Anyway, back to DJ and North Stack Wall.

Having done an established major route – albeit the second ascent, I abbed down the unclimbed 'direct' version and it was obviously a goer. Very thin and bold but had a bomber nut placement at around ninety-five feet – just before you top out. Bugger all below but something to aim for at least, so over we went for an attempt.

Harrowing as it was, I was comfy and 'in my element' on North Stack Wall and floated up it in no time at all. Pretty easily from memory. A steep, familiar start then thin, crimpy and balancy climbing on sharp edges – all the way to ninety-five feet facing a deck-out fall.

Looking back down the wall between my dangling legs I watched him second my first ascent – I was most impressed, even though he faltered and wobbled a couple of times as he struggled with a few of the longer reaches. Plus the odd flake suddenly creaked.

'I'm going E8 this time,' I said as we were packing up our gear. 'Damn right Andy, bloody well led mate.' It was the boldest route I'd ever done at the time and to have DJ's endorsement was most satisfying.

I must admit though, I was willing him to fall off seconding me, all the way up, but of course he didn't.

Question: Had I just inched my way up Britain's first legitimate 'big cliff' proper E8 or not? I felt I had. There was the first claimed one done on gritstone, and desperate no doubt, but 'comparatively' only thirty feet high and only two moves long, so I settled for a UK second, and possibly the world's.

'Ooh, make the mags big time this one definitely,' I thought, but was dreading the prospect of having to ring Bernard again and return for the photographs.

Then he went and outclassed me and Britain's second E8 was overshadowed by the first E9.

He was obviously a 'survivor' though, and no matter how many times he put his neck on the line he managed to pull it off. I suppose JR and I did too, but so many others were not so fortunate.

Oh, silly me, I meant JD not DJ; so to end my barking-mad nonsense, for anyone who didn't figure out the anagrams before, your prize is to '*Wash JD on NYE*'. So run the bath on December 31st. and prepare the loofa, I'm sure he won't mind!

☆ ☆ ☆

Hmm, baths, that reminds me of Derek Hersey.

'Dirty Derek' was amongst the first of the 'dosser' or 'dirtbag' climbers, led the way for a lot of us, and what a great bloke and good mate he was. He'd get ribbed coz the back of his Helly Hansen jacket was almost waterproof from all the grease that came out of his long, scraggly hair, and he never gave a toss about anything but climbing and having fun – then a chip butty and a few pints if he had any money. Coincidently we share/d a birthday, Derek the elder by seven years, so were both Scorpios.

I'll choose my words carefully – having seen that charming little interview with his mum and dad shortly after he'd fallen hundreds of feet to his death soloing in America, and the obituary videos too – but suffice it to say he was a genuine ragamuffin and was/is sorely missed by many of us who knew him … I recently read (with several tears yet a smile on my face) a piece in *Rock and Ice* regarding his passing. It was about a gift from the afterlife … I shan't spoil the story; you can google it.

'Salt of the Earth', working class from Manchester, 'cept he never actually 'worked'. Ever. As far as I can recall.

We'd agreed to hitch to the Cheddar Gorge near Bristol to get photos on *Crow* for Bernard's *Extreme Rock* book and would break the journey with a day at Craig y Forwyn and a good feed at my mum's back in Dyserth.

'You can have a hot bath, Derek.'

'Woooo, nooo,' shaking his head, ' … don't want one fanks yoof … '

Unfortunately Mum wasn't impressed one bit as Derek's table manners were absolutely atrocious – he talked with his mouth full and reached right across Mum's plate to grab more bread and butter with his filthy hands, then wiped his mouth on his smelly sleeve and belched.

Mum 'had words' with me in the morning and requested I didn't bring Derek home again. (My father's name was Derek as well, so that was two of 'em not welcome back!)

Mum much preferred ' … that lovely Bernard, your photographer friend,' and then asked, 'how is young Jeremy from Leicester?'

'You *do* mix in funny circles don't you, And?'

'Yeah Mum, but we all have houses and Derek lives in a hedge at Stoney Middleton – all year round.'

I (we) have lost many good, close friends through climbing and though I hadn't seen Derek for a few years since he'd moved to the States, word of his death was particularly crushing – but not totally unexpected, as he was really pushing the boat out. I figured he'd have been falling for ages from that height so would've had time to think about his impending doom, and I wondered what goes through someone's head in that situation. Fear? Or simply resignation? (I seem to recall an interview on YouTube with a guy who jumped off the Golden Gate Bridge but survived. I think they may've asked him that question.)

Huwie Watkins I mentioned earlier, albeit suicide, though Brian Jones intimated that there were questions asked, because around that time Huw had gotten himself into some awful tangles with ropes whilst not concentrating. A sad loss whatever happened.

Neil 'Noddy' Molnar fell from around sixty feet so it would've been over before he knew it – he was soloing around his highest leading level and had rejected our offers of a trip to Tremadog or Gogarth that day; the Pass was damp, but he hitched off to go soloing anyway. Paul Williams positively identified Neil's body for the coroner, and Chris Gore took it upon himself to relay the sad news back to Stoney where Jerry was his best friend. Chris used the payphone at the Padarn where we were all mooching around sad and grieving. 'Croaked' was the actual word Chris told me he used. I'd never heard the term before! How did the message get through? Not sure as Jerry was bouldering as usual at Stoney and we didn't have mobile phones back then. Probably via someone at The Moon or the cafe in the village.

My first experience of loss to a cruel, early demise was that of a photographer chum from down south. Andy Brazier was a terrific fellow, an accomplished lensman, and fit as a butcher's dog. Sadly though he carried a defective heart condition – one day, having just returned home from his evening run, his ticker simply gave in and he collapsed. Aged about thirty-two I think. Awful, just awful.

Then another: Phil 'Jimmy' Jewell. Jim slipped off from well up a simple Severe on a filthy, wet day at Tremadog – nobody could survive a ground fall from that height. Jim was soloing E4s and 5s, which, like Noddy, was pretty much his leading limit, and many of us sensed it was 'on the cards' yet again. Just not off a beginners' route though. It was shades of Derek – an easy romp they'd done a million times before ...

Wolfgang Güllich. Simply the nicest man on the planet – lost his life in a car crash in Germany. I felt particularly upset for Jerry as they, along with Kurt Albert, were particularly close friends. Kurt died a few years ago too – yet another climbing accident.

Alex Lowe, American all-rounder, gone! We tandem on-sight-soloed *Edge Lane* at Millstone together, me going 'hurry up you're smearing on my handholds'.

Ed Wood from Sheffield. Used to train and climb with Mark Stokes and they both looked like bodybuilders. Sadly Ed's professional and personal lives took a wrong turn and he ended up in lots of fights – often with the police, so was regularly banged up in the local cells. All too frequently when he was released we'd see him wandering around Hunters Bar covered in bruises and with a black eye or cut lip – twice even, desperately, wearing a long flowing yellow floral dress ... bulging biceps stretching the sleeves, a few days' stubble and a couple of fresh scars! He'd go from pub to pub 'mine-sweeping' – brazenly picking up other people's drinks and sculling them. Nick and I often bought Ed a pint, and though wild-eyed he was always calm and pleasant around us two. Very few people wanted any trouble, so merely went and replaced their drinks and moved across the room. Those who took offence usually got knocked out and the cops would be called yet again. Ed was discovered on a park bench one frosty morning. Stone dead. What a dreadful demise – Ed's passing upset me rather more than that of many other friends. I mean, here was a terrific guy in need of a hand with life! Maybe everyone did what they could but … ?

Giles Barker was a really keen climbing historian and was collating a book he intended to call *Peak Performance*. Giles made several taped interviews with a variety of local activists, myself included, but tragically lost his life in a caving accident. Thankfully Phil Kelly and Graham Hoey took up the challenge and, based on Giles' early efforts, produced *Peak Rock* – an absolute belter of a book, which I'm confident Giles would have been truly delighted with.

Dennis Kemp was a war veteran. He lived near Mold in North Wales when I was just starting out, and we'd see him all over the local crags. A charming, delightful and really interesting man. We reconnected at Mount Arapiles in 1990 when he'd become something of a regular down here for several seasons; he was hugely popular. Whilst chatting in my caravan one evening, Dennis told me that his injuries meant he'd lost the ability to reproduce so he'd thrown himself into climbing. He was sixty-seven when he led his first-ever grade 23 (around UK E3), but the huge belay flake that everyone used – even someone moments before his ascent – suddenly went 'crack', peeled off and took him down with it. We all held a tearful wake along with some old friends of his who'd come out from Britain for his burial at Natimuk Cemetery. I recall there were some heated discussions between his funeral director and the graveyard guardians – apparently Dennis could only be laid to rest with his feet pointing in a certain direction. I never discovered what that was all about.

Paul Nunn. I was glued to his Peak guide from the first time I bought it as a kid in North Wales. By the time I got there in the eighties he was one of the elder statesmen at my locals in Sheffield – The Byron, Porter Cottage and The Union. Ridiculously intelligent and a total hoot as well was Paul – a highly regarded lecturer at Sheffield Poly, something to do with economics I think, and sharp as a tack. He was a regular on the Sheffield pub scene, along with Geoff Birtles, Rab and Sue Carrington, Jim Curran, adorable Pat Lewis (oh how I gushed) who owned and ran *Mountain* magazine, Steve 'Banks' Bancroft (oh how I positively didn't gush), and limping John Gerrard who'd done some of the first aid routes on Raven Tor before getting smashed up in a motorcycle accident. Paul lost his life due to a desperately unlucky bit of timing, when a monumental ice fall swept him away on a long traverse moments between the party ahead and the party following.

Alan Rouse. We all bode Al farewell and 'safe trip' the night before he headed off for K2. Never to return.

One day at my desk at work I took a phone call from Chris Baxter, the editor of *Rock* magazine here in Melbourne. 'Sorry to advise Andy, but Paul Williams died yesterday.'

'Ohh, no, not Paul, please. He was "me Dad"!'

But it was true and yet again desperately unlucky. Paul was out soloing on the grit and something went dreadfully wrong. He didn't fall too far but landed badly and bled internally. I wept that night. Still do every time I think back.

Another call to my office much later: 'Chris Baxter passed away yesterday.' The Big C this time.

Cec Delaney from The Willows, the milk bar in Natimuk. 'The D's' were many a climber's friend, psychologist, bank manager, cook, cleaner and bottle-washer and perfect hosts for dinners and board game nights, so a 'life-support crew' shall I say? One hundred per cent mine for sure, and I'd have done anything in return. Anything.

Marion rang me in Melbourne and very matter-of-factly suggested I come up the next day. This was years after my climbing days, and I could tell by the brevity in her message and the tone of her voice that it was almost Cec's time – he'd been in and out of chemo but was desperately weak – so at dawn I headed straight off up there on the four-hour drive. From within about a week of our first meeting when Glenn introduced us, Marion and Cec had become pretty much my surrogate 'Mum and Dad' as well as the dearest possible friends, so it was just awful to see him in such final, dreadful health. Marion wheeled Cec out into the back garden and we sat for twenty-odd minutes and chatted. Sort of reminisced I suppose. He softly uttered he hoped his precious Carlton team would get a Premiership soon and we chuckled, but that set his coughing off and Marion came outside to check on him and bring a glass of water – which I took and gratefully skulled (no I didn't ...).

Cec's hushed penultimate words to me were, 'If I were a dog they'd've put me down ages ago Andy. I just want to go now mate.' Determined not to burst into tears, ever-so-gently I hugged Cec but he sighed 'Ow' and I apologised. He took my hand though and held it tight with all his failing might. I'll not repeat our final words because they're with Cec, me and God.

I hugged Marion, very quickly, and fled – unable to speak, and she fully understood. Rang me later that evening:

'How far did you get?'

'The *100* sign and had to pull over.'

'I thought as much.'

(That's about fifty metres.)

Cec passed away two days later.

Le Blond, Patrick Edlinger. My French mate who I'd first met in the early '8os and then on numerous further trips to France where he'd shown me his 7b party piece *Septième Sot* – in bare feet – up, down and back up. I couldn't do it in rock boots. Merde! And whose film crew I'd guided around Arapiles and the Grampians a decade later. Dead. Suffered terribly with depression and alcohol abuse post climbing career – accident at home I believe ...

And more recently my old mate Peggy – the King of Rifle. Dave Pegg took his own life ... he was only forty-seven ...

There are others, but please forgive me if this is getting depressing and sad. Recalling them all is *celebratory* surely? Sad, Damn Shame. Tragic, Untimely. Call it what you will, but I still value the memories – as I'd like to think most of us do.

On the 'cheating death' side, my dear friend Pete Bailey from Dyserth was bloody lucky to survive when a falling block the size of a TV set near wiped him out on a hanging belay part way up some multi-pitch route in the mountains of Spain. Leiva was the crag, near Murcia. Massively broken up Pete was, with a cracked vertebra, dreadful crushing injuries to his ribs and a collapsed lung; but thankfully a difficult helicopter rescue high on the face saw him reach safety fairly rapidly. Four days in intensive care and a fortnight in a Spanish hospital. Pete's made an unbelievable recovery and no doubt counts his blessings (as also after the 'Huwie incident' at Forwyn way back when) on a daily basis.

Doubtless too does Joe Simpson, who uncharacteristically thrashed me at pool in The Broadfield a day or so before flying out with Si Yates. Surely *everybody's* read *Touching the Void* by now? If not, how come?

Neil Foster was about to have his foot amputated after a horrible landing on grit but *one* of the three surgeons reckoned he was worth a try at least. Success!

Gary Gibson and Norman Clacher – they had dreadful accidents but lived to tell the tale and are still out and about new routeing.

There's Paul Pritchard obviously – another old mate going back years. Pritch's determination to get himself physically fit again whilst carrying some appalling disabilities is testament to his strong character, and he's to be lauded for his truly remarkable progress. Great writer too.

Finally, *Alas Poor Yorick*. Adrian 'Yorick' Hughes was Nick Plishko's and my great chum and housemate at Sandford Grove Road. Yoz and I climbed heaps together and he was always great fun. Once he'd gotten out of bed that was! He was an odd-bod of a kid though. Several years younger than Nick and me and recently 'departed' from college. He'd head off to sign on when Nick or I reminded him, but no dole cheques ever arrived so Nick and I had a 'slate' that grew and grew. Yoz and I were great mates and shared everything: My house, My food and My climbing gear (thanks to Bernard Newman for the loan of that one) but when the slate hit a thousand pounds we hauled him in for a chat. Turned out he'd not been signing on at all and for fourteen weeks had lived totally off Nick and me.

'Why Yoz?'

'Couldn't be arsed lads.'

'Well you're fckn going tomorrow coz we're taking you!'

He had an **extraordinary** hidden talent though, and made us totally authentic Indian curries – took two days to marinade the chicken and spices. He also produced simply amazing pizzas with superb toppings and dough he prepared himself.

He still owed me a whole bunch of money though so we (sorry, I) arranged that I'd pay for him to come to Buoux with me and Scotch Ben for a fortnight and I'd do an insurance job on our gear when we got home. Sadly for all concerned, that trip went rather pear-shaped – and before we'd even reached the motorway! Now Ben and I were in the front of my Escort van and the feet of our travelling companion in the back absolutely stank to high heaven. Ben was driving the first leg and I was in the passenger seat arranging the cassette tapes.

'I'm not going thirteen hours with this stench coming from the back, Andy. Sort him out please.'

'Yoz, I told you to have a bath and get to the launderette.'

'Slept in, yoof.'

'Sorry Ben, I did tell him yesterday.'

I don't think Ben spoke to me until we got to the ferry terminal in Dover, other than when we wanted to switch drivers or take a pee. The windows had been open all the way since leaving Sheffield in an effort to filter out the filthy green haze – but Yorick promised he'd have a shower when we got to France!

One day during the first week Yoz and I were ticking off the routes on the delightful Styx Wall and he was to lead the last route over on the right-hand side – which he did, and very smoothly (although he rarely, if ever, led a route).

Lowering Yorick back down I started congratulating him as he got within earshot 'Brilliant lead Yoz, you looked great, wanna go back and lead that one you liked earlier?' ... just as the end of the rope shot through my figure of eight and he landed at my feet with an awful cracking sound and literally bounced past me into the scrub, screaming in agony. Poor Yorick was busted up all over. Leg, ankle, arm, foot and very grazed and shell-shocked – scratched, bleeding and screaming even more so when attempting to move.

This accident was undeniably my error – no, *fault* – as belayer, and was inexcusable. Thank God others leapt in to offer immediate, split-second assistance; quite frankly I was somewhat befuddled for a few seconds and just stood there like a stunned mullet, shocked out of my wits. We somehow managed to carry him down to the van, probably against all first aid best practice, then I gassed it down the winding mountain road to the hospital, with him bouncing around in the back begging me to, 'Slow agghhhh down!' (I couldn't win.) At *L'Hôpital d'Apt* he was rushed straight in for emergency surgery ... and ten days' recovery as it thankfully turned out.

During Adrian's first few days on the ward – all wired up to *the machine that goes 'Bing'*, (ta Monty Python), on a drip and covered in bandages with various limbs braced – I was wandering somewhat aimlessly between the town's bars and cafes under what I felt was a *visible-to-climbers*, great big down-pointing, accusatory finger, and feeling a whole world of embarrassment and shameful guilt. Hell, did I berate myself!

But, I was also furious – no apoplectic – with the bloody French: that route was five metres longer to the fixed lower-off than all the others in a long procession from left to right so you'd need at least a sixty-metre rope, yet there were absolutely no warning signs at the start (or, I assumed, the finish) so how were we to know a fifty-metre rope – the world standard at the time – wouldn't do it? It had for all the other routes. Yes, I learnt the hard way to *always* leave a knot at the end. It was such a basic, silly error on my behalf and I cursed – and have done since too on occasion – dropping my climbing partner and housemate like that.

The surgeons did a tremendous job in saving Yorick's foot in particular, and Ben and I duly picked him up on his release day for the long drive back to Hunters Bar. The irony of homeward-bound was that Yoz had been thoroughly scrubbed up and shaven, had neat, shampooed hair, and his clothes washed and pressed. He smelt all sanitised, soapy and 'hospitally'. Scotch Ben and I probably reeked compared to Yorick – what with the sweaty armpits and bad feet!

A month later the *Hôpital's* bill arrived. Then it was Reminders and then Final Demands. Thousands and thousands of pounds – but the insurers refused to pay out as 'adventure sports', including rock climbing, were expressly excluded from his policy.

Yorick started atoning for his sins when his giros eventually began to arrive, but I'd still send him into the city through driving sleet to pick up my 'choof' and our dinner from the baked-potato man on the way home. He never once complained and often as not went out in a vest and no coat. In all weather!

Yoz commenced paying down the slate at twenty quid a week but soon reverted to sponging again, so I covered his bills and bought his food, smokes and beers out of guilt as he was still in plaster. Hundreds of pounds more – my sponsorship money for trips away – but it was becoming ridiculous and we were falling out big time. One evening I just 'cracked it' and told Yorick he was to be out the next day.

'Find a doss or I'm taking you to the hitching spot and you can bugger off back to yer nan's!'

Now considering Nick was absent, I was, technically, out of order and Mr N. Plishko, being the joint lessee (though owed hundreds himself and fed up) would've been far more accommodating I know.

But that's what happened. I left the poor lad at the start of the Snake Pass on crutches and in two casts, in the drizzle with a couple of carrier bags and a sign for 'Stalybridge Please' and never heard from him, or of him, again.

Sorry Adrian, Yozza, if you ever get to read this. Poor form on my behalf that!

Photo: Neil Foster.

14.

DISS SIR CHRIS, A FRENETIC FEW YEARS, OH! AND A GOODBYE WAVE AS WELL

The Cornice, Water-cum-Jolly, is like an overhanging, frozen South Atlantic wave, and about as wet too for eight months of the year damn it. A bit like something the surfers perform on in the briny or like all those snowy ridges in Sir Chris Bonington's books, except this one was rock solid ... and at ground level. Much more my style. A few of us were standing around beneath it and I was wearing my brand-new yellow Berghaus Red Point vest with the red writing running down the side (just to be creative) and a small, tight pair of denim cut-down shorts. Plus I had Vuarnet very dark sunglasses, big hair and lip gloss (and shoulder pads too!) ahh, the eighties! No need for all those thermals, layers of down or oxygen masks down 'ere Sir Chris.

OK, I fibbed about the shoulder pads. Those enormous, powerful, bulging shoulders were all natural (giggle). I never wore lip gloss either for that matter. Eyeliner occasionally maybe, and the big hair was all mine. And still is!

I almost had the pleasure of talking to Chris once, at a function somewhere or other; I don't think he was Sir Chris in those days, so I'm not being disrespectful. He was, after all, a world-renowned and most highly respected mountaineer, and the top consultant for Berghaus – along with Al Rouse (sad loss, terrific man, and author of *Positron* too!) and the other Alan – Mr Hinkes. And then there was me; their new 'star recruit' on the crags, who'd read all Bonington's books as a kid – thought *Everest the Hard Way* a real classic. Oddly enough our paths had never crossed, so I'd never got to shake his hand or get a book signed.

So, there we were, ending up about two feet apart at a function one evening, around about the mid-eighties. 'Good evening,' I croaked, offering out my hand courteously – not quite bowing and scraping but just being genuine and somewhat in awe – but his reaction was nowt but a cursory glance down his nose as he turned his back on me to wave at someone across the room: it was Birtles! 'And after all I've done for you Geoff!' I thought.

His Highness Chris wouldn't recall unless he were a diary keeper too. Who knows? He may've written: 'I heard that young Pollitt lad was here this evening so went to find him and introduce myself, but this scruffy pedant interrupted me so I fled ... Oh no, not that bloody Birtles again! After all I've done for you Geoff ... '

The place filled up and got noisier and noisier, so I slid quietly out of the door and wandered off back to the bar feeling somewhat put out. I never got to talk with my boyhood hero and when I rang Mum later and said: 'Guess who I met today?' she hardly believed me and was really impressed. 'It was brilliant Mum.'

Sadly that couldn't be further from the truth. Doubtless our National Treasure wouldn't deliberately have been so rude, so I shrugged it off, disappointed, and he was immediately forgiven. Never forgotten though, hmm ...

Unfortunately, I never had the chance again. First impressions. Sometimes they go wrong. Never mind, I wanted to meet Evel Knievel or Muhammad Ali more anyway, and as a kiddie had even written off to *Jim'll Fix It*. I think my little sister Elizabeth may have too. Something about Duran, Duran or Adam Ant I think. Knowing what we do now I'm so relieved we never heard back, as little sis was about twelve or something, so was spared from the clutches of 'Sir' Jimmy So-Vile.

But WCJ ...

It was Tim Freeman's excellent free route *Brachiation Dance* which first breached the rearing wave of The Cornice – really showed the way things were going and alluded to what could maybe come next. I started abbing down the old aid routes to the right and checking out which, if any, would go free. One very steep line of old bolts and pegs down the far end of the crag was certainly a possibility and it scrubbed up well – was soon clean, dry and I'd replaced the rotten *in-situ* gear with three or four new bolts. In truth though there was a year and a half's gap between cleaning it and climbing it – it just sat there with no one else bothering to try while I sat watching *Oprah* and *Days of our Lives* with a chip on my shoulder. A bagful actually – frozen ones.

In between this line and Tim's classic about thirty metres to the left, the crag was at its steepest and the capping roof at its widest point. So abseil over (I recall the belay tree was bloody miles away – Staffordshire possibly), reverse-aid on the manky old pegs, and give all the holds a feel and a cursory wire brushing. This one'll be really hard, I knew it – too hard for me – but if it's still unclimbed next summer I'll come back for a reappraisal.

Not long back from my sixteen-month lay-off and shoulder surgery I was raring to go. I really got a grip of my climbing and did many repeats and new routes in the mid to late eighties. The following record is included here for two reasons. Two.

1. To attempt to convey how lucky I was to be around at such a time in British climbing's evolution – yes – I know all 'old farts' reckon their era was the best, so perhaps I'm simply following tradition?

No, bollox, ours *was* the best!

2. The other reason is to say: 'Hang in there and be patient,' to anyone who's injured and forced to watch telly all day with the frozen veggies on. You'll be getting better by the day, frustrating as it is – believe me – and there's every chance you'll come back fitter and stronger than ever.

Oh, and you do realise I was kidding about Geoff Birtles don't you?

☆ ☆ ☆

We'll leave The Cornice for a while … coz … well … this bit's the part where for publication I had to defer to the advice of not only Mr Boorman, my editor, but the publishers at Vertebrate too. See, my original draft contained a bit of a 'list' – rather lengthy it was – of new routes. But, the way I see it, their collective advice was, basically, 'shut the fuck up and stop bragging, they're all easy nowadays, you're embarrassing yourself'.[1]

So I have shut up – but not quite, coz you see 'Andy P the climber' had cleaned, bolted and done a whole bunch of new routes which were alright for the time but are probably overlooked these days – so fair enough. Perhaps I should change tack and tell you about the woman who wore a wig, the one I almost trapped off with in the Porter Cottage? Basher was on hand as technical advisor that night and when the lady joined me for a glass of … whatever … she whipped out the photos of her brain operation and flashed her enormous ear to ear scar … I think I caught sight of Biff as he legged it around the corner. My excuses for leaving were slightly more protracted – I caught up with him about ten minutes later, breathless!

---

1 Not *exactly* what we said Andy! *Ed.*

Basher never let me down, but neither did the Peak District, where we'd regularly wander down the dales passing literally dozens of blank walls and old aided climbs – some of which looked brilliant.

It was only ever really Ron who had 'the vision' to give 'em a go back then, and what a record *he* has of First Free Ascents!

Perhaps book sales will reach double figures if I mention Yorkshire I thought? So here goes:

Cave Route Left Hand at Gordale Scar: I'd made the first ever on-sight of the *Right Hand* but this was at least a grade harder. Another on-sight flash? Well I flashed the easy start! But then fell off the first bulge, twice. Next morning twice more but, after a brew and homemade teacakes at Pete Livesey's Malham cafe (rather humorous seeing this one-time legend, my old hero, serving behind the counter in a shocking pink pinny!), bulge number one finally succumbed! I then on-sighted right up to the easy groove where the two routes converge, but it was running with water and the wet streak ran right over the finishing holds. Pulling into the groove my fingers slipped off and Dominic Staniforth held the 'whipper' beautifully. Having dried it a bit with my T-shirt, I got it next shot – so sacrificed a runner and lowered off. 'Good enough for me that,' and ticked it off in my 'RK MESTO' guidebook, the one with Basher on the front cover doing his brilliant *Pierrepoint* but half the book's title is lost in the shadows of the overhang (due credit to Neil Foster for that 'RK' observation!).

The upper headwall of the two-pitch aid route *Masochism Tango* to the left looked amazing from below ... so I cleaned it and replaced some old gear. Unfortunately the approach pitch (which followed a series of depressions – five if you count quick ins and outs) was scrappy and loose and everything wobbled ... pretty much as I did at the bulge near the end – so grabbed my quickdraw before the hold (pitch even) fell off. So, of course, I copped a demerit point – my first for using a point of aid on a new route!

As for the top pitch? Pretty bloody 'out there' is all I remember. Perfect grey-white rock, right up the top of the gorge and lovely, exposed climbing.

Know what? I got laughed out of Yorkshire! I was fully aware of the 'rivalry' with the Peak, so put it down to that. That climb had a fantastic all-free top pitch, but both the route and myself got judged on the mound of rubble piled up beneath the start. I believe the top's now enjoyed often, and I was proud of all of that brilliant pitch – my first and only new route in Yorkshire – harrumph![2]

---

2 First ascent, *Emission Control* E5 6b, 6b 1pt. 27 July 1984. AKA *Masochism Tango* with aid reduced to 1pt on first pitch. As all the best guidebooks say, 'the second did not follow' – although in this case it wasn't that he couldn't, but that he wouldn't, as he was hiding below the overhang for fear of getting nailed by falling rubble!

Oh, and we'll visit another, altogether different, 'series of depressions' later on – where it seemed *everything* was falling to pieces around me … Scarier than Gordale for sure!

Before the editors notice, I'll attempt to mention a ten-minute, second-go solo up *Perfidious Primate* at Raven Tor (The Snore) without using the bush. The French lads who tried it straight afterwards, from what I observed, seemed to reckon it was French 'Merde, Putan!' (whatever grade *that* was) as they collectively kept dropping the first undercut pull up.[3]

I guess I was about my fittest and keenest ever between '87 and '89 – an enforced break does that to you, ask Jerry and look at what he accomplished following his return to fitness.

Back to North Wales and Ben Moon's *Statement* was erased from my to-do list – the fourth ascent too. Redhead's brilliant *Wrinkled Retainer* in Ogwen, third after Fawcett. Then another Jez route – *Masterclass* back on the coast, fifth ascent for that one and given F8a now! Well happy with that day!

I always mixed in the first ascents with early repeats – the earlier the better – and it's important to point out that being a somewhat prolific new-router I always strove to keep up with current events and the stupendous efforts of my mates and contemporaries. That was really the only proper way to gauge one's progress, and to be taken seriously one had to do each other's routes for comparison – not to mention the fact that they were mostly brilliant rock climbs.

Glad to be back from injury? You betcha!

Allow me to re-emphasise – this is not me saying 'Look how good I was' … far from it. The point I'm trying to get across is how unbelievably fortunate I was to even be around (a climber and not too bad at it in my day) during that period, when many of the best new routes *hadn't even been abseiled down* by other, better climbers.

On a personal note though – and I find this difficult to say for 'you big-headed wanker' reasons – I *did* leave you some bloody classics to look after … didn't I?

The Bearded Clam and *Night Glue* at Pen Trwyn, *Flashdance* on slate, *Resolution Direct*, *Skinhead Moonstomp* and *The Hollow Man* on Gogarth, *Carousel Waltz* in the Crafnant Valley, *Knockin'* on the grit and then the upside-down hilarity of *Thormen's Moth*.

Sure! That life was just too good. And I was getting *paid* to live it: I'm with the best bunch of mates ever, flitting between North Wales, the Peak, Yorkshire and the south of France in my van with the cassette player wired to the battery;

3 First free ascent, *Out of my Tree* – had to be really didn't it? F8a, 20 June 1987.

and I get big cheques every three months from Berghaus, Scarpa, Allcord, CAMP and Cousin; and do thirty-plus public lectures every winter and loads of people come and hand over their fivers to watch and listen – then afterwards, when the applause has died down, I get another quid for each poster on the way out. I do recall my lectures were well received and I did put a lot of effort into making them as professional as possible.

Yes, how lucky was I to be around back in those days with all those ripe plums just waiting to be picked? I suppose they're 'rites of passage' now as the young 'uns get better and better on their way to doing Basher's *Mecca* and the other Raven Tor desperates?

Pen Trwyn had less than twenty routes, mostly scrappy – some aided – when I first went there around 1980. The Derbyshire Dales were riddled with aid routes just going begging from '83 to '90, and in Australia even the great Taipan Wall was host to a mere eight climbs on my first, memorable visit.

Fortunate indeed.

Over the Moon I was, back down on LPT, having redpointed the first ascent. I gave it E8 6c. (And despite what some wag suggested on *UKC* – no – my fingers were definitely **not** resting on a nut at the base of the top crack. Cheeky blighter.)

Four days off from Pen Trwyn on a top-secret mission, but I could still just about make out the climbers above the Marine Drive – specks in the distance from where I was hanging. On my own and shivering while they were in full sun. Two single fifty-metre ropes joined together should do it. **Wrong**. Jug back up, hike back over the hill to my van then trudge back carrying a third. Exhausting.

The Diamond Buttress on the Little Orme is a seriously big cliff and I came *that* close to abandoning my objective. Not so much for the effort involved, more coz the last abandoned and starving fledglings high up on the wall freaked out as I abbed past them and about six of the eight leapt for their lives, only to plummet to their deaths in the cold Irish Sea 400 feet below. That really saddened me, and I still feel the guilt. These days there's an agreement between the BMC, local and visiting climbers, and the various conservation bodies that climbing should not take place here from March 1st to August 15th each year (or until the birds have 'flown' their nests).

But my new route? 'Yey! It's on for sure ... Yey!'

I avoided the sopping-wet start and came in to the line from the right, about twenty feet up. Jugs, jugs and more jugs. Perfect overhanging rock, rough and great friction. Odd that, around here – and it was now going free, and brilliant climbing too. The first-ever free route on the Diamond. I looked at the other unclimbed possibilities – particularly over on the left-hand vertical side –

but thought no one else would ever come here, so returned to the more popular Great Orme. How mistaken I was![4]

A further first repeat (on sight again) of yet another North Stack Redhead horror: 'Want a complimentary bolt with that?' 'No thanks, I'll do without.' (A bolt had been placed by the first ascentionist.)

Thinking back to another of John's, but this time on the Gwynt: *The Bittersweet Connection*, third ascent, second free, and John was right when he said the top pitch was 'Cosmic'. Oddly appropriate given my belayer's name was Moon.

Was I shadowing JR or what? Over the next few weeks it was his *Ryley Bosvil* in the Pass – a brilliant little gem – but then 'apple carts' got upset: one late August day in '87 I eventually eliminated his deviation off-route for a breather, stringing together *Menopausal Discharge* (his sister creation to *Manic Strain* over in Vivian Quarry) in a ten-day-to-oner. I renamed it *Kleinian Envy* and upped the grade a notch to E8 7a.

I was chuffed to get that one – as much for the effort and constant flappers I kept getting as for 'the grade' and the one-upmanship towards my old hero and sometime mentor. I can honestly say that John and I never, ever, had a falling-out; I suppose it's just that after those few early years we'd drifted into different circles and things, well, became a little 'prickly' on the odd occasion we'd meet.

Now whilst our respective circles often overlapped, the competition was definitely 'on' – I was being 'sponsored-climber-guy' and usually plastered in advertising and using sparkly new free gear with a photographer off to one side. I knew this commercialism irked John – to his back teeth – as *he* was undoubtedly the 'name' the companies would've wanted more than anyone's, but I can only suppose he never asked (one had to back then), let alone begged. At that time I wondered whether JR was being slightly hypocritical in that he wasn't exactly one to hide his light under a bushel and always participated vividly in any ethical debate (magazine letters etc.) and made for great print media; but then my own 'lightbulb moment' – you only get *self-publicity* for that, you don't get *paid* – and I remembered Berghaus were paying for my next two weeks in Buoux. John could easily have come along, fully laden with new shoes and ropes and jackets and a bunch of 'free money' – but this was anathema to the free-spirited, self-proclaimed 'image-maker who climbs'. So he stayed in 'beris as the rain pelted the windows of Pete's, probably smiling sympathetically as Gab slipped about in his old EBs!

---

4 First free ascent (pitches 1 and 2), *Wall of the Evening Light* E6 6a, 6b, F7b+, 7 July 1988, with Mark Pretty. On a superb August weekend in 2015 over forty climbers visited the Diamond and three new routes were completed. There are now well over thirty high-quality sport routes on the crag ranging from F7a to F8c+.

Oh, and by the way, in the time it took you to read the above Ben Moon promptly on-sighted *Kleinian* – that's no falls – and took it down about three notches, and the route name reverted to John's original (even though PW changed it to *Misogynists'* in his guidebook). Why did Ben do that to me? I thought we were mates, and then he'd gone and made me look like a right old pillock. I could understand the whole *Hubble/Whore* thing, there was a logic to that, but surely this was 'putting the boot in' – maybe it just didn't occur to him that I could be so sensitive? But anyway, bollocks to it, Glenn and I split the 300 quid we got for the pics – I just took the money and ignored the chuckling in the corner of the Padarn …

'He took how long?'

'And Moony flashed it?'

'Ha, Ha, Ha.'

'Yeah, yeah lads, settle down please.'

I wasn't up for reacting, just wanted my bed – Dover to Calais ferry to catch tomorrow courtesy of my chief sponsor, and neither I nor my van could out-pace Dawes, whom I'd arranged to meet at the caravans we'd booked in Apt.

'Kleinian Envy', by the way – and I'm sure at least one of you two readers will already know – refers to a particular type of mindset. For example, 'If I can't have it (him/her, whatever) then I'll destroy it so no one else can have it either'. The concept was constructed in Germany years ago by a clever chap called, you got it, Professor Klein. I came close to patching that route back up and chucking the bolt hangers into the freezing, blue lake below – I was that frustrated. Got it eventually though.

On course for Buoux again, but Scotch Ben led me to a gobsmacking but rarely-frequented place called Fontjuval or something and sent me off up a 7-something – it may've had a + on the end but I can't remember. Similar thin face climbing and angle to North Stack Wall but with bolts, so we got on famously 'cept all the hangers had been removed from the second twenty metres of the route – but we didn't know that, did we? Bloody miles out from the last bolt I hit an impasse and was facing a seriously long fall. Pulling a rabbit out of a hat I somehow bouldered my way through that sequence and landed in easy territory. Ben fell off that crux seconding. Twice. Both times where I faced that whipper. Now Ben was way better than me on the French stuff and I think he was genuinely rather taken aback at my run-out lead. I know I was. I think he may've mumbled 'Good effort Andy'

or something, but that might've been wishful thinking on my part coz he was angry. With himself.

'Au revoir France – eh up t'dales.'

Raven Tor with Yorick again and another first free ascent. This time it was one of the lower, thinner left-to-right traverses. It was crimpy, hard, crossed unclimbed territory, and was sustained – all my favourite things – but I doubted anyone would ever bother doing it again. Pity, it's great climbing. I dread to think how the heck anyone could do it nowadays with all those 'up' routes between *Indecent* where it starts and past *Rooster Booster's* second pitch where it finishes?[5]

☆ ☆ ☆

Let's return to The Cornice in Water-cum-Jolly: try another new route – or rather try it again – that big one right through its guts. I down-aided it on abseil from that tree I mentioned earlier – the one bloody miles away near Simon Nadin's house in Buxton. Cleaned, equipped and I was on my seventh day, but we were all going back to France for a fortnight coz the Peak was *still* bloody wet and we'd need to be back in twelve days for that pesky signing-on thing the government made us do just for giving us a paltry forty pounds a week and paying our rent. So I left the route incomplete – I'd gotten right through to the final leap for the finishing jug but was knackered and couldn't latch it, so yet again flew off out into the treetops.

Ace France trip this time but got seriously burnt … off by the lads as usual and skin-wise by the sun. 'Check out me tan.' Daft. Skin cancer from UV is a serious killer down here in Australia; I can't believe people are still basting themselves up with coconut oil and falling asleep in the direct sun just to get brown. Tanning salons and home machines were banned recently, since a young lass in her early twenties developed melanomas and died. Absolutely tragic.

On returning from France I headed straight back down to The Cornice but it was still dripping wet. Bugger! And I was fit-as. My good friends Chris and Hilary Hamper and Rab and Sue Carrington were heading to Cornwall with Martin and Maggie Boysen, so Glenn Robbins and I tagged along. Chris was something of an 'unsung hero' in many respects, but to those in the know, boy – could he climb! We climbed together most of that season and

---

5 First ascent, *Terence Trout D'Arby* E6 6b, 6c, 6b, 29 October 1988, with Adrian Hughes.

I think I only ever beat him to the ascent of a route one time, twice tops. Maybe Chris *was* indeed merely mortal and actually had off-days too? Who knows?

I got in touch again in May 2015 and Chris wrote back:

> When reading famous climbers' autobiographies I am always amazed by two things: first, how did they manage to remember all that stuff [they're called diaries Chris] and second, how come they never remembered me? [I've never forgotten you] … Still at school, sitting at the top of *Vector*, an older lad soloes up behind me; it was Ron Fawcett. Did this really happen, I've heard several other climbers telling the same story, did he do this a lot?

We enjoyed our South-West trip but the fare down there had far too many 'chips' for our collective diets so we bailed back north.

☆ ☆ ☆

Chris Hamper was there right up until the end of my UK climbing career and he sums the Sheffield period up pretty well:

> There were many climbers' houses, two of them were on Hunter House Road – 124 and 84. My first experience of staying at one of these houses was at 124. There was a party and I slept there … I'm not totally sure who lived in 124 at the time but there was a motorbike in the hall and food rotting on a plate in the sitting room. Everyone had nicknames. Compared to sleeping on Windy Ledge [Stoney Middleton] staying at 124 was, well … worse, but 84 was much better so that became my doss of choice. When I first started to stay there Chris Gore, Andy, Basher and Jerry lived there. All with real names except for Basher.

> I broke my pelvis climbing in Poland, actually I broke it falling not climbing. Often when you read about a climber who died climbing it will say, 'Well at least they died doing what they love.' If I die climbing I don't want anyone to say that; if I die it will be because I fell off and hit the ground and that is what I have been trying to avoid doing all my life.

> I climbed mainly with Andy. Maybe it was because our girlfriends lived in the same house? [Prior to the wimmin's house.]

Andy had two climbing lives at the time: the death-wish life and the happy-go-lucky fun life. I remember reading an article he wrote about his death exploits, *Knockin'* and *Hollow Man* I think – not the Andy I knew. Different partners for different routes.

Andy put up quite a few routes in the Peak – *Easy Skanking* was an early entry next to *Little Plum*, *Boot Boys* a later addition at 'the snore'. *Easy Skanking* was named after a Bob Marley film but *Boot Boys* was named after him and his mates working for Scarpa. I wish I had worked for Scarpa as I might have been climbing in better boots. Andy's other contributions to Raven Tor were *Chimes of Freedom* and *The Whore*. I repeated *Chimes* before the block fell off but *The Whore* at the time had two points of aid so I never bothered.

When looking through first ascent lists the memory becomes clearer and Andy's contribution begins to stand out again – *Empire Burlesque* and that route next to *The Vision*, etc. etc.

When a new route went up there was always a lot of interest. I mean limestone sport routes of course – when Johnny put up a new gritstone masterpiece there was immediate disinterest which lasted some years. Simon Nadin was promoted from gritstone oddity to top dog after his [world climbing competition] win in Lyon. He soloed *Menopause*, yikes! *The Inch Test* was one of his sport routes which Andy and I went to repeat … took us longer to find it than climb it. I say we climbed it, I think Andy did it but I fell off the top when a hold came off. [So did AP but through a broken spirit!].

We spent many days down 'Smee Dale' (might've just made up that name) and I added to all those fishy routes with *Name that Tuna* … 'Gritstone 6b according to Chris Hamper' … what do I know about gritstone 6b? One might suppose that the move was some sort of full-body, torquey, opposition compression sequence on slopers and friction. It's a jump. Gritstone, limestone – all the same to me, crank or jump. *Unleashing the Wild Physique*, another upgraded route, my tick list looks better by the minute – as long as they weren't footholds that broke I can't see it making much difference. *Powerplant* was another route Andy did that I couldn't. Chris Plant had been pretty quiet up to then … *Powerplant* indeed … it turned out he was!

Andy was so pleased with *Thormen's Moth* (great name) that he dragged me down there for an early repeat (I think it was Andy). The guidebook says it's always wet but Andy climbed it to place rags in all the pockets then climbed ahead of me taking them out. I have no idea how he did this but that's what happened.

Another upgraded route, I wonder which pocket fell off?

☆ ☆ ☆

After the trip to Cornwall with Chris I finished climbing in Britain within days – back down on The Cornice in WCJ. This would be the last new route I'd do before my emigration to Australia, so it really was a 'wave' goodbye; and the lads reckoned it was worth an 8 again, so I was leaving Britain on a high. I'm kind of lucky because Jean-Baptiste Tribout had worked it when I was away in Cornwall, but deliberately took a rest coz it was my project.

'Merci beaucoup! J'apprécie enormement Jibé,' as a French chum of mine up my local boozer showed me – a much better place to learn French than Prestatyn High School![6]

☆ ☆ ☆

Well that's about it really as we're off to Australia in a page or three … just a few final thoughts …

THE WARM-UP MAN
In all live TV comedy, sketch, interview or game shows – anything where honest, spontaneous laughter is required in preference to the overlaid canned stuff – the live audience need to be nicely warmed up prior to the cameras rolling: cue the 'warm-up' man or woman. This is the time to make a mark and progress their comedic careers (a bit like mine at times) before unsuspecting audiences, producers, talent scouts and their peers (and hopefully their girl-friends' cute friends).

Two ex-warm-up guys come to mind. There was Peter Kay, warm-up for Sir Michael Parkinson's shows – he's hilarious, gone on to show genuine comedic genius. Then there was Alexei Sayle – well, not actually him but one

6 First ascent, *The Rumble in the Jungle* E7+ 6c F8a+, 11 August 1989.

of his alter egos, Bobby Chariot, 'World's Top Warm-Up Man', who was 'on pills for me nerves and livin' in me Jag' (same pills the *Cad* bolt was on?). I'm showing my age now so 'apols' to the young 'uns.

I was browsing *UKC* after work one evening and the opening banner video was of a lad who'd just redpointed *Mecca – The Mid Life Crisis* at Raven Tor, and in a ridiculously fast time. It's 8b+ and he was fifteen years old! I was due to email my old bestie Martin – the first ascentionist – anyway, with well-wishes for his retirement from heading Wild Country, and I thought once more about our ages – just as we had beneath the Gwynt in '84, and I pondered again over how come the kids got *so* good *so* quickly these days, and why were we only seconding VS's at that age? Humans haven't evolved *that* much, so there must be myriad reasons – and coming together within twenty years is perhaps staggering when compared with any other sporting interest or discipline? Of course, climbers achieving such feats have started out at a much younger age; the gear, training methods and facilities have all improved dramatically – and we're talking bolted climbing not trad – yes, a world of difference!

My own retirement strategy (as I choked back tears of envy to answer Martin's question) was 'Another twenty-five years at this rate Biff' (sob), and I went on to congratulate him on his legacy to Peak – no, to world – climbing.

Mecca is undoubtedly a benchmark, quality classic these days and, who knows, the repeat ascentionists may have warmed up on my old *Chimes of Freedom* or on *Boot Boys*? Unless they're the easiest ways back down now and *Mecca's* the warm-up for Jerry's *Evolution* or Steve McClure's *Mutation*.

Ah! Methinks … I've already relinquished the title of The Dynamo Kid, so perhaps there's now an excuse to finally shed that other old moniker from Tremadog, when Paul told Mel Griffiths I was The Human Clamp under *Bananas*? Moniker duly relinquished and others can crimp over it for all it's worth.

I suppose that makes me a bit of a warm-up man too then? Well, an ex-one anyway.

WALLY AND WILF

I honestly can't remember where I saw these two overly bearded gentlemen, but I know it was on a sea-level traverse across to the base of a cliff somewhere when I was a kid and climbing with Pete Bailey. Gogarth? Doubtful. Probably Pembroke or Cornwall – and they were a right pair!

They looked as old as the planet itself (to me, at sixteen or whatever any-how), one holding the back of the other's moleskin breeches as he made ' … an awfully long stride old bean' between slippery boulders as the sea receded between waves. They made their belay on a small ledge just over to our side. Their gear was ancient! Rope slings, steel screwgate krabs and enormous hexes. One even had mountain boots on and they both wore great big red JB helmets. They did have modern(ish) looking ropes though.

Wally was very cautious – as if it was his first lead in decades – placed his first runner before even stepping off the ledge. I watched him setting off up that hundred-foot slabby fissure as I hung on my runner, pumped out, about twenty feet away on the steeper bit. 'Bumblies,' I thought … and being repelled yet again slumped back on my ropes and looked across to the oldsters.

The leader had made rapid progress and was pulling over the top … I'd gained nothing. After some traditional 'I'm safe … Climb when you're ready' banter, Wilf followed on upwards and reached the top wearing a veritable skirt of removed runners. Back on my harder route I was still resting … albeit on a slightly higher nut …

End of the day, who'd had the better one?

I'd failed miserably on the latest E3 testpiece and 'Wally and Wilf' – in their dotage – had soloed a traverse, climbed a lovely Severe-grade route and safely gotten off.

I've no idea who those two fine gentlemen were, but, with an excess of youthful exuberance and *that* ego, I'd had a giggle at their expense. Wish I'd been a bit more tolerant – not that I was ever outwardly intolerant – I hope not anyway. Who knows, maybe on our seventieth birthdays Jerry and I can swing leads up *Grim Wall* at Tremadog – our quickest way down from the top of the cliff when he was a Crag Rat and I was The Dynamo Kid? He's born March, me October – it'd probably take that long for me to follow … and perhaps we'd hold a few others up for once … or give some young up and comers a chance to smile … or more likely we'd exclaim, 'Oh no, not Douggie Hall again … he must be all of 80!'

So I offer you these last words, not from me but somebody else – a special someone who's made a pretty significant mark upon Welsh climbing, and whom I credit with helping to mould me into the person I became when I lived for climbing …

END GAME
by
John REDHEAD

1980. Who were these two kids arsing around on Mayfair Wall on the Marine Drive? Some local youths drifting out from Parisella's Cafe and pretending to be climbers? What the hell did they think they were doing? One of them had long dark hair and a red bandana around his neck … that's my look! It seems they claimed the first free ascent – tactics or what – cheeky fucks. You must be joking.

I got to know Andy, the bandana lad, and we climbed and laughed as our egos and hearts played with the language of ascent. I was hurt by the *Kleinian Envy* scenario, because Andy, as the 'pretty warrior', was 'goaded' by Perrin, knowing it was a line I was never happy with – *Menopausal Discharge*. But I was happy for Andy with *The Hollow Man*, a superb direct finish up the *Clown/Bells* wall, and a line I should have seen. Damn that man! I did the second ascent with long black hair and a red bandana around my neck, and climbed it like a cheeky fuck. The cheekiness ended when Dave [Towse] set off for the attempted third ascent and serious reality hit when I had to unclip him on the crux, without secure foothold, to throw him a rescue. This sudden 'wreakage' unravels information. It breaks a spell. It dissolves the ego and reveals the hidden strength of the unknown – and in this we all talk to 'The Stranger'.

Andy has profound knowledge of this 'passage', through years of negotiating the old rocks, and through intense moments of raiding his psyche for clues, with a burning passion and hope in the unknown … And yet, I know, I really know the cheeky fuck is all the more something else than a dancer that read the rock, more than the engineer of dealing tower cranes, skyscrapers and concrete. Andy is still in awe, still a playful, cheeky fuck, and without awe we all lack humility to live and to love. I am sure that *Punk in the Gym* is a good dose of what makes life worth living …

John Redhead, 16 April 2015

PART TWO:

THE DOWN UPSIDE BIT

Last day in Nati, trip one, with (L–R) Cec Delaney, Dave Mudie and Trev Smallacoombe. **Photo**: Simon Mentz.

15.

AUSTRALIA: WHAT A 'SHAM

I touch down at Tullamarine, Melbourne, collect my bag, exit the air-conditioned arrivals hall and am almost knocked off my feet. 'Effing 'ell it's hot – no chance of climbing in this!'

I wait and drip until Glenn Robbins rocks up to greet me, Nick White from Devon in tow; it was Nick's first trip too and he was positively buzzing with enthusiasm. We'd not met before but I'd heard he'd been doing some hard stuff in South-West UK.

Glenn took us to his current doss at his mate Rabbit's place in North Melbourne (coincidentally just a few hundred metres from my present place of work). He'd arranged us a lift for later that day to the little town of Natimuk, a major centre for climbing in the state of Victoria. Our chauffeur was to be a young lad called Graham Jones who hailed from up there; apparently he'd been something of a hotshot a few years earlier but had since pretty much dropped out of climbing. So we all piled into young Gray's big car. He pointed it due west and hit the road.

I took on the role of 'nodding dog', jet-lagged to the max and missing a whole chunk of scenery; but perked up en route after a bite to eat (so *this* is a Chiko Roll?) and a 'flat white' coffee in Ballarat. It seemed a long four hours; eventually we pulled up in Natimuk and eased ourselves out – stretching limbs in relief. Gray was off to his folks' place a few doors up, so we dragged our rucksacks from the boot and followed Glenn 'around back' into Louise Shepherd and Chris Peisker's house.

I already knew Louise – we'd climbed together in the Verdon Gorge in France on the FFM (Fédération Française de la Montagne) international meet a few years prior, and she'd also been to North Wales once – and led the first female ascent of *Lord of the Flies*. It was lovely to see Lou again and at least this time she was fully clothed ...

I should explain: I'd led *Tapis Volant*, a stunningly exposed rib of immaculate limestone 900 feet off the valley floor, with Louise holding the rope – when she'd popped over the lip of the gorge having run up the climb, she was topless. 'Ohh, put those things away Lou, for heaven's sake, you'll scratch 'em,' so she duly tucked them back and I wished I'd kept my mouth shut! Heck! I mean, the female climbers I knew always wore tops – but that *was* at Stoney Middleton and somehow I doubted we'd ever see the three J/Gills – Kent, Lawrence and Price free-boobing their way up *Our Father*!

Yeah, it was really nice to see Louise again, and as for her housemate, well ... 'Crispy' was a henna-haired, pony-tailed hippy in a tie-dyed, cheesecloth shirt and baggy pants – dead cool. Terrific fellow. He made Nick and me really welcome at their place: 'Herbal tea anyone?'

'Got any beers Chris?'

'What's your birth date Andy? I'd like to do your astrological chart ... '

No one wore shoes. Sometimes flip-flops, but they're called thongs out here. Nick and I were totally boxed from our flights, so crashed out on the spare-room floor to spend the hot night tossing, turning and being gently savaged by the local mosquitoes. Neither of us was confident we'd be able to handle these conditions, but everyone assured us we'd acclimatise soon enough.

Dawn arose and so did we, eager to enjoy breakfast with Lou, Chris and Glenn. It wasn't bacon and eggs, or the usual 'full set' with fried bread, sausages and baked beans, tomatoes and mushrooms, all drizzled in tomato sauce – but fruit, nuts and 'YO-ghurt'.

Now 'yoggutt' to me was that sugary strawberry Ski stuff from Tesco's in the little plastic tubs, but this enormous jug was apparently home-brewed. Milk left out in the sun till it went all rancid or something. 'Here, have some natural honey, it's from so-and-so's bees.'

'What? Not a jar then?'

'Health freaks. Rabbit food!' Nick lamented. 'How can we climb on this Andy?'

'Definitely no beer then Chris?' I inquired.

Today, Lou was to treat me to a tour of the world-famous Mount Arapiles, but according to my diary Nick didn't join us (or if he did, went and did his own thing).

And Oh My Goodness! What a stunning place. I'd been to many climbing areas but had never clapped eyes on anything quite like this. Mount Arapiles is often, and quite accurately, described as a smaller version of Uluru, aka Ayers Rock. A massive monolith of red and orange quartzose sandstone, rising majestically from the flat earth: scorched wheat plains stretching as far as the eye can see, punctuated only by shimmering salt pans and the impressive hulking mass of the Grampians rearing up to the south-east. The crags were surrounded by an abundance of fine eucalyptus; the wattle trees were in bloom, flaunting their heady honey-laden acacia scent and lovely globular flowers. Kangaroos bounded around in rowdy mobs and I saw stumpy-tailed lizards, a frilly-neck, a million skinks and one day a four-foot-long goanna. There were kookaburras 'laughing' in every other tree and loads of echidnas, plus evidence of the odd wombat or other earth-burrower. No koalas, but I'd soon see plenty when we went to the Gramps – and deadly snakes and terrifyingly enormous spiders too.

'Reckon I could live here,' I thought; but we were here to climb …

Glenn led us up the fine crack of *Electric Warrior* – an Oz grade 20, then I led *Droop Street* and *No Future* – a couple of 21s. I recall chatting to Lou about how weird, balancy and yet pumpy the climbing was on this type of rock – these routes were supposedly the equivalent of UK E1s and E2s, so barely even warm-up fare for me – this place was going to take some getting used to!

Next day Simon 'Barn' Barnaby arrived from Melbourne and with Glenn we did a grade 22 called *Squeakeasy*. 'Right then … day one a grade 20 and two 21s and day two a 22' – at this rate, I reasoned, it should only be another ten days till I could jump on *Punks in the Gym*, then Australia's hardest at grade 32. However, it didn't happen quite like that, and for a month or so I slapped, thrashed and fought my way through a few of the stiffer-grade 'rites of passage'. *Masada* was a good route and I revelled in the on-sight of *Have a Good Flight* – with the pokier direct finish too.

My first-ever day in nearby Horsham – 'The Sham' – wandering around the town to acquaint myself – you know, find the best coffee, the bank, laundromat and sample *every single bar*! Then, who should I clock while passing the sports shop window, staring straight back at me – but me! Stopped me dead in my tracks it did. They had a prominent window display of Grip Masters (the finger exercisers) and I was the full-colour backing-card artwork – up and out there on Gogarth's *Skinhead Moonstomp*.

I smiled (in a somewhat self-congratulatory manner), talking to 'myself' and doubtless appearing rather strange to those country folk around me, and then went to check out the White Hart Hotel, where I'd soon fall head-long for the delightful barmaid. I'm not allowed to give names away but hers did have *Am* and *a* in it! I never fell further in this – or on two more trips. Married though, ugh!

Australia certainly bode well – especially as local journo Keith 'Noddy' Lockwood had given me a terrific and very welcoming pre-arrival write-up – I was splashed all over the front of that week's *Wimmera Mail-Times*. Due to such exposure I was recognised in the bar and even got shouted a few free 'pots', which was super-friendly of the non-climbers. I reciprocated of course, before taking directions to meet the parents' of the Aussie Cousin Ropes importer. They lived on the Natimuk side of town, where two brand-new 50-metre x 8-millimetre, plus two 10.2-millimetre ropes – in the four colours I'd requested – and forty sparkly CAMP 'biners and quickdraws awaited my collection.

I hitch-hiked back to Natimuk laden with a belly-full of 'piss', ferrying new 'kit', feeling rather warm and fuzzy and thinking 'How good is this?,' whilst knowing full well that tomorrow I was to meet someone **unique**.

'H' STOOD FOR HORSHAM

Our introduction was memorable. I'm not really sure what either of us was expecting. We both had 'reputations' that preceded us and were in the climbing magazines and so forth, but this was going to be face to face, and I for one couldn't wait. I'd been told he was a total brute, so expected a genuine monster. 'H' duly arrived at Lou and Crispy's place (he really was all bulging biceps … arms bigger than my legs … OK, I know that's not hard) and gave a proper bloke's handshake – extremely strong fingers evidenced by his welcoming grip – letting go just as I felt my bones crunching. Ouch! But way shorter than me, which was surprising.

I liked H immediately.

And what an unassuming, down to earth, genuinely delightful fellow he was – and still is! I knew he had good form, he'd done 5.13 cracks in the States, even had the car number plate to prove it – HB 513.

To explain – in that Monty Python sketch where all Australian blokes are called Bruce, we were reliably informed that the best way to differentiate Bruce from Bruce from Bruce was to prefix each with their place of birth. Thus my new friend Malcolm Matheson had become 'Horsham Bruce', i.e. 'HB'. Later simply 'H'.

Malcolm, err H, sorry, was the darling of the Australian climbing scene and by all accounts horribly, horribly strong. My generation had only really been fed titbits about Kim Carrigan and Mike Law when we read *Crags* or *Mountain* magazines, but this mythical 'HB' guy was by far the best climber in the country when my plane touched down in Oz.

He kindly offered to show me around the Grampians the next day:

'Try a couple of my 26s, get a feel for the place … Be at mine at 8.27 a.m. – it'll take us 42.3 minutes to get to Hollow Mountain before the sun hits the crag at two degrees. Any later and the friction co-efficient will diminish by .03 per cent a minute. Don't be late.'

'Err, you what?' (Shakes head.) 'OK H, half eight then, I'll be there.'

Severely hung over, I rocked up at H's after ten. 'Sorry mate, slept in. Jet lag.'

He was raring to go, obviously keen to check out my credentials and doubtless eager to display his own. He reached beneath his beloved turbo-charged Torana, spanner in hand … 'I need to lower the suspension a fraction – make up for lost time,' and proceeded to rocket us out via the back roads, 'Midnight Oil' blasting from his supercharged stereo, in precisely 39.25 minutes. Handbrake off till handbrake back on!

H was like that, mathematical to the nth degree, but we chatted easily enough whilst flogging up the path to his new cliff beneath Hollow Mountain.

Graciously handing me the crucial Rock 5 … 'Curved face left,' he pointed me up his latest – *Hamster Roof.*

On-Sight Flash. Great fun, enjoyed that. Then it was over to the fabled Taipan Wall. Been looking forward to this.

'Effin' 'ell!' What a piece of rock! I'd never seen owt like it in all my years of climbing. Huge, seriously steep orange rock, with truly gobsmacking features.

'What's that ramp H?'

'Not done yet.'

'Those scoops?'

'Nothing yet.'

'Surely that arête?'

'Maybe one day, Andy.'

There were only eight routes on the entire cliff and the best was yet to come. A little further along the trail we reached Malcolm's own route *Serpentine*, a fantastic grade 31. 'Fuck me, you're kidding right?'

'Nope, that's it Andy.'

We retraced our steps – I'd *seen it all* now – and began gearing up beneath H's other route, *Sirocco*. Steve Monks (the now Ozzie local from Bristol!) was belaying somebody nearby. He'd recently managed the second ascent of *Sirocco* after a protracted battle, so called over, 'Ha ha ha, bet you don't flash that Andy!' I really don't need to tell you how it went, and moments later gave 'Monksy' a little wink and congratulated Malcolm on a brilliant route.

In actual fact I was pretty lucky, as the crux was a fair old left-hand dyno to an obvious horizontal ripple – about a foot and a half long I suppose – but it had chalk slaps all the way from left to right. H had hinted that there was only one good spot but wouldn't tell me where it was, so this was my 'pass or fail' moment. The dyno itself was a doddle, plus I was good at them, and I hit the sweet spot with three of four fingers, pulling straight through – and that was it, H reckoned I was OK!

Malcolm Matheson (HB) by email, September 2015:

> The thing I remember most about meeting you way back when was that not only was I meeting a British 'rock star' but also that you looked like that other British 'rock star' Mick Jagger! You fitted the bill pretty well too I thought – hard drinking, smoking and partying. Just like good old Mick! The Mick Jagger of rock climbing if you will.
>
> I remember you doing *Sirocco* with a packet of fags stuffed up your shirt-sleeve and getting them out for a puff halfway up. Priceless! And what about the time you discovered that you could imitate the sound of the cicadas on *Serpentine* by tapping two large stoppers together? Not to mention all the stories of the climbing scene in England and wild parties and certain things with the opposite sex which I won't repeat here.
>
> I had great times climbing with you Andy, I will remember them always. What fun times!

Next, H led me to a project he'd had on the back-burner for a while because he'd not been getting anywhere on it. I offered him a belay and egged him on. Now Malcolm wasn't your 'modern' climber by any means. Only did routes ground up and placing all the gear on lead, figured it was a flawed ascent otherwise. Anyway, his project followed an easy ramp which petered out at a horizontal break – maybe four inches bottom to top and quite shallow. The belay ledge was a tad over six feet above with nothing in-between. H had been undercutting the top of the break whilst trying to get both feet in it at the same time (or something equally strange) and at that overhanging angle I didn't think such a contortion was humanly possible (probably not even off a mat on the ground).

I figured from the stance below … 'That'll never work H.' I could obviously spot a good dyno a mile off, so we swapped ends. Even though there's a no-hands rest beneath the break I hung on the bolt and squeaked my boots …

I'd dyno'd further many times before and wasn't going to pinch my new mate's new route. 'Here goes H!' ... B-Doinggg ... almost touched it. Second go, feet up higher, got it – but bodily momentum carried me off. Third attempt and it was 'All Over, Red Rover'. Yey! I let go and shot outwards into total space.

H immediately threw and threw himself up it, eventually latched the hold, and called it *Mirage* (27). He'd actually jumped about 2 inches further than he stood in flat shoes. Awesome. He'd probably correct me with a '2.78 inches actually' but that was H (insert smiley) and I thought how happy I was to be mates and climbing partners with him. We had similar personal morals, ethics and honesty, shared tastes in humour and music – as long as it was Monty Python and Midnight Oil (back then) – and climbing was our joint focus; no surprise we really hit it off immediately. We were both super competitive too of course, but only to spur ourselves and each other on. Neither of us cared who'd do a route first and we'd be urging the other one on, mouthing 'Come on H' or 'Come on And.'

Heading back to the car park he led me off the main trail to show me one of his *two* party pieces: *Daniel Or-tiger* (31) and proceeded to throw rapid laps on it. Gulp! He even timed himself, releading each time ... 3 minutes and 13 seconds flash, 'But that shake-out cost me 14 seconds, won't use it next time.' So he didn't and fired it in 2.59 – a PB. Made his day that! I'd heard he was strong but this was bloody ridiculous, plus we were now in full sun and H's thermometer was showing 45 °C! I *so* nearly flashed it on his draws, but mucked up just past the ever-seeping undercut at half height. With a rest and dry hands I jumped back on and cruised to the top. I reckoned that was by far my best-ever first go on a hard route. Know what? I went back *nine more times* and never even came close! Malcolm and I would climb lots in the Gramps thereafter, but I still reckon that first day together was the most special one.

On the drive back to Natimuk H brought the car almost to a standstill at the start of a long straight section. At the end of this was a *50 ahead* warning sign, just before a serious s-bend in the bitumen. 'Everything OK Malcolm?' I inquired. 'Yeah, yeah, just checking something,' revving the motor and monitoring his dashboard dials. He chuckled to himself and I wondered what was happening, then he dropped the clutch and my head suddenly snapped back as we took off from nought to sixty-something in however few seconds it was. Malcolm's Torana stuck on the road as if connected to a rail – and that s-bend shot past at 130 kph!

'Fuuuuuck H!'

'That was nuthin' Andy, I got pinged in 'Quanny' [Quantong] playing this on the bend and lost my licence for doing 182.' So *that* was H's other party trick then – double the advisory speed limit and add at least thirty kph!

When the G-forces receded from Mach 3 upon re-entry to Natimuk, and I could put the (thankfully unused) sick bag back in the seat pocket, H asked whether I'd like running back out to my caravan at The Mount. 'No thanks mate,' I squeaked. 'Drop us at the pub please, I fancy a beer. Oh, and thanks for today Malcolm … brilliant that.'

The National Hotel was empty but for three locals camped on stools at the bar – all attired in the usual shorts, plaid shirts and sweat-stained blue skivvies.

'Another of them fckn mountain goats are you mate?'

Three sets of glaring, hostile eyes coz climbers really weren't much appreciated at the time, but Trev the publican told 'em, 'Go easy lads, Andy's OK'.

These were big, solid, hardworking Aussie blokes – shearers, and I was a stick-thin plummy-voiced Pom wearing fluoro Lycra tights – in *their* local pub for heaven's sake!

'Poofter too by the looks of you?'

'No I'm not,' (grumpily).

I ended up at the bar going pot for pot with them – no one wanting to back down, and we talked for ages, had 'one for the road', a 'lucky last' and a couple of freebies as Trev ran off the keg prior to laying our glasses on their sides – the Australian sign for 'I'm done.' Mine went down last!

One of them slurred 'Oi mate … ' index finger pointing in my direction – albeit it in that bladdered, one-eyed, figure-of-eight motion, 'You're alright … hic … for a goat!' and promptly spewed up into the ash trough that ran along the base of the bar. Ahh! Acceptance – a beautiful thing and a marvellous way to top off my first day in the Gramps with H.

I probably should've left it at that, but it was only five past eleven and Cec at the Milk Bar always had cans in the cool room and I knew the back door would be open – as was everyone's. But Marion busted me in her dressing gown (*she* was wearing it not me) – rifling around, spilling things and making far too much noise – thought they were being burgled or something. She confiscated the beer and made us a coffee, shaking her head and giggling, 'Andy, Andy, Andy, you idiot … spare room … **now!**'

'Goodnight.'

I was in fckn paradise.

All About Kylie. Road trip to the Red Centre. **Photo:** Simon Barnaby.

16.
FREE-SNAKING THROUGH THE 8TH DIMENSION

Simon Mentz. He's to blame, no question about it! 'Simey' has been a stalwart of the Victorian climbing scene for two decades plus. Been there, done it or fallen off it, and photographed it all *and* written the guidebooks. He knows his stuff!

Allow me to explain: there's a sort of figure-eight-shaped hole passing through the undercut base of Castle Crag – a stand-alone buttress at Arapiles – and Si and a few others (being, err, very silly) reckoned life might be different ' … on the other side … ', although, of course, you only had to nip around the back to find out! The plan was to leave last wills and testaments, hug their loved ones goodbye and head through into the unknown … I tagged along … only been in the country for a few days and was probably jet lagged, stoned enough not to be intimidated, or both!

Glenn was too portly to even consider making an attempt – no matter how much we greased him up (a Robbins' ruse I now know) – so popped round the rear to photograph us slithering out the arse-end: great pic in *Rock* Jan-June '91 having just exited 'smouldering' – according to Chris Baxter's caption.

The 'free-snaking' bit was when the tight squeeze caught on your shorts so that all your tackle fell out as you wriggled through to pop out the other side starkers. Course, I shot through barely touching the sides – being such a skinny bastard. I may've lost a lock of hair that's all.

It was whilst helping Glenn with his tripod (which had become tangled between a nipple ring, his leather chaps and some spikey arrangement strapped to his ankle – or was that the other time?) that I totally failed to notice

Simey and the others had obviously had second thoughts, and gone back through the hole. My point being: *I* never made the return journey ... so have, to all intents and purposes, been living in The 8th Dimension ever since 1990! I guess this may not come as a surprise to many and may explain a lot to some!

Recently, during our five-day odyssey back to Natimuk, I recounted this tale to my old mate Tim Freeman and his daughter Angel – now resident in Queensland – and I got to wondering: is life better 'this side'? 'Should I squirm back out right now Tim, Ange? Or next time I'm up here?' Get back to whatever lies abandoned in (and of) my past? Rope-access work all UK winter? Failed relationships, the dole? As I write, it's almost twenty-five years to the day since I emerged and Glenn's camera went click and Simey was putting his pants back on ...

This trip through the 'hole' was a day or so either side of putting up my first-ever new route outside of the UK – which as it happened was up the stunning profile of the cliff which hung out dramatically above the chortling idiocy occurring directly below on that evening. See, I'd arrived in Australia full of excitement in February 1990 with a bunch of money, six-month visa and the world at my feet. To redpoint the hardest route in Australia was my ultimate ambition, but I'd been drawn to Castle Crag by its stunning profile, so had abb'd and bolted this line which I thought might possibly end up as Arapiles' second climb at the then (almost top) grade of 31.

Vicious jams trashed my hands crossing the initial roof, then powerful layaways led to a series of fingery bulges – the third of which I sidestepped, although it was really the true line. No matter, it was still excellent climbing and finished with an excruciatingly crimpy dyno right where you really didn't want an excruciatingly crimpy dyno![1]

Final decision regarding my dimension? Nah, sod it, reckon I'll stay right here where I am thanks, but *do* wonder if there's a 9th. Simey? Anyone?

We used that name for a somewhat futuristic project Si had bolted through the dossing cave roof at Bundaleer, and he'd said if I could do it (laughing at the thought) it was mine. So I did. Can't recall who was more surprised, Simey or myself! But I gave Si one back by way of something rather special – he takes up the story:

> I don't think I ever did a climb with Andy in the traditional way ... that being
> someone leading a pitch and then the other person seconding. The one time

---

[1] First ascent, *Nati Dread* at grade 30, 6 March 1990. Third bulge included by Nathan Hoette, *17 years later*, at grade 31, just like I thought.

we did almost complete a climb together was a new route on Taipan Wall. It was a line that Andy had spotted on abseil but which he then offered to me, reckoning it would go at grade 24. I was sceptical of a new route up the guts of the wall at such a moderate grade, so I quizzed him as to why he didn't want to do the route. His response was: 'I don't want crediting for the easiest route on Taipan Wall.'

It took a few days of effort, but much to my delight I finally fell up the pitch. Sitting on the clifftop I was pretty chuffed to have a first ascent on one of the best walls on the planet. I was indebted to AP for giving me the chance to do it. After yelling up his congratulations Andy then prepared to second the pitch, which should have been a formality given that he had sent the crux quite easily when having a quick play on the route during my earlier attempts. After a couple of falls it became clear that this wasn't his day. Andy eventually asked to be lowered off and our one chance to success-fully top out on a climb together was never to be. As for a name, we ended up calling it *Father Oblivion* after a sweet, Irish friend of Andy's whose drinking efforts made us look like lightweights. As for the difficulty, the grade eventually settled at 26.

The Grampians were getting – indeed had been for a few years – some seri-ously hard routes; and the landscapes, vistas, quality of rock and sheer purity of lines had gotten me fixated since first acquaintance on that brilliant initial day out with Malcolm.

Over my three long-term Australian visits from the UK I'd get to the Gramps at every opportunity. Problem was that bloody *Punks* epic back at Araps, but we'll get to that later.

One of H's most striking lines was called *Nicaragua*, nowadays renamed *Journey Through* … and it really tested me. Overhanging from the start, pumpy jamming in combination with face climbing on crimps leads towards a slen-der corner system, which has an obvious sharp-looking spike on the right arête to aim for.

A dear and oh-so-cool 'chick' friend Claire Gallagher was holding my twin eight-millimetre ropes on this fantastic trad route. She was a part-time climber and apparently this was her first time belaying on a super-high-grade route – so you should expect some real whippers I warned her, gulping … (the pair of us!). 'Just hold 'em,' I uttered under my breath, 'For Goodness Sake, this looks 'ard.'

Claire held me firm and fast on two short stumbles low down and I thanked her with a 'well caught girl' and probably 'Darl' the second time. Those two 'drops' were typical AP no-warm-up ones, so immediately it was 'pumping stations' and 'power-outages' – I should've known better. I *did* know better, but with the usual over-exuberance and insufficient rest I leapt back on in moments (Ha! Am looking back now twenty-five years later and smiling …).

After the next attempt my body had taken me into new territory beyond that thuggy start. I was well powered out and was carrying that horrible 'first pump', but was on much less steep (though still stupidly overhanging) rock and on positive crimps where power wasn't an issue – so I called my stamina and 'bottle' in for a laugh. I'd have to sprint from here … I slapped for every hold, ignored bomber gear placements – couldn't hang on – and pleaded down to Claire to 'watch us', and only just swung out on to the 'Thank God' spike, by this time facing a virtual seventy-foot ground fall. I was in full sun at about 36 °C, sweating and greasing heavily. Fumbling in a Rock 4 (or something just as chunky) I clawed myself to the top and lay for several minutes, panting and parched in the sun. Brilliant, happy with that! The Second Ascent. Scary as all-fuck, even though you can lace it with pro – if you can stop that is!

'Claire-Bear' opted not to follow, so we went down to Summer Day Valley and swung leads on a few mid-teens. A perfect day in my book that.

But H's other testpiece – *Contra Arms Pump*? Nah, rubbish … couldn't touch it; didn't have the power at the time so left it alone after a few goes.

Trying to get the work/life balance right was always a precarious process – as it still is nowadays with the Vertigo career, these scribblings and my socialising. Back then *Punks in the Gym* had (sadly) almost become my 'day job', and the Grampians became 'life' and an escape from 'work'; so I took every possible opportunity to put my *PITG* ambitions to one side. That route would punish me severely for my lack of attention! Bugger *Punks* – I needed a break – there were new lines aplenty going begging out in the mountains! I wanted and needed something *out there* of my own – so chose my line, abb'd and aided in from above. I'd picked an absolute beauty; albeit spoiled terribly by a stopper move for most on pitch two. Then it has 'that pitch we all dream of finding' – the third and final lead follows a superbly impressive runnel, weathered by rain and wind for thousands of years to provide one of the finest pieces of climbing I've ever done in my life. Way up there in mid-air. Steep, balancy and pumpy combined; and I spaced the bolts for maximum effect – 'sport' climbing à la '90s!

Mid-twenties that pitch and ridiculously good fun; those who've climbed it unequivocally concur. Oh! The route was named after one of my favourite bands at that time who sang about putting a message in some kind of box and driving it around the world until it got heard of or something similar ... That band.

Hilariously, I flashed the whole first ascent having just spilled out of a nightclub at six-something in the morning – was 'rather inebriated', and lucky to have escaped that joint alive, having gotten chatting and a bit too 'up close and personal' with the wrong farmers' girlfriends.[2]

A little crag I named Gondwanaland (that Charlie Creese had discovered) saw me aid-soloing one rest day across a twenty-foot roof crack on perfect Friends as I bolted up a sporty-looking thirty-footer in readiness. Whilst the route got rave reviews in some quarters, I was savaged by many of the locals in Nati. Keith 'Noddy' Lockwood even wrote a letter to *Mountain* magazine back in the UK and my old mate Bernard Newman, incumbent editor, published it. Something along the lines of 'we like Andy P but don't appreciate others coming to our country and shitting in our nests!' Sport climbing European style would have to wait a year or three ... !

HB, Peter Croft and Simey all ticked *Sport Crack* and they seemed pretty OK, understanding fully that it would be just as easy on trad gear and that I wasn't *bringing the route down to my level* – merely testing the water and pushing the boundary somewhat. As far as I know the bolts are still in![3]

The other one I managed to add to that crag later was great fun – hanging high above the olive groves floating into the distance, emus craning their long necks up in bewilderment beneath me as I climbed upwards and outwards ...[4]

On reflection I can see that I was really privileged to be part of this great scene in this wonderful place in the early 1990s – not only were there acres of rock available on which to forge my own new routes and be involved in those of others, but also many opportunities for those coveted second or soonest after ascents:

I was chuffed to flash Nick White's superb *Tyger, Tyger* on Taipan's Lower Tier and then his *Flashing Blade* back at the Mount.

'Good routes them Nick, well done.'

'Aye lad,' he replies, failing to mimic Yorkshire.

On Taipan proper *Mr Joshua* was just in another league altogether and pointed at things to follow. I managed the third ascent of *The Great Divide* and then the second of *The Seventh Banana* – what a pain that slippery fruit was ... fell off repeatedly on the slabby boulder problem moves off the stance but then

---

2 First ascent, *World Party* grade 27, 18 November 1990, with Pete Cresswell.

3 First ascent, *Sport Crack* grade 26, 15 January 1991.

4 First ascent, *Ephemeral Lakes* grade 25, 1 April 1991.

yarded up amazing ground for seventy feet till landing in a spacious nook (or was it a cranny – what's the difference?) just below the final hard bulge and plod (**not!**) to the top. I think it was Paul Riley, my second on that day, who commented somewhere about there being '… a twenty-minute delay in proceedings …' before I popped my head back out and called down I was ready to continue. He'd obviously noticed wisps of smoke drifting out of the hole as I reclined with a couple of ciggies (but no banana) whilst three-quarters of the way up the route … just like HB's *Sirocco*, the pitch went all the way to the top of the crag … I couldn't climb *that* far without a fag if the opportunity arose!

Then it was Kim Carrigan's *Dinosaurs Don't Dyno*, second ascent; plus the three routes either side, followed by *Seventh Pillar* with Ian Anger (aka Ferret) who later became a close colleague at Vertigo for several years before peeing off with another workmate Mark Wood and setting up in competition, as most of our best guys did.

And I clearly recall Pete Cresswell leading me up his new route *Black Adder* – unbeknown to him I struggled up behind like a stuffed pig. A great, ballsy lead from Pete. I told him so at the time – whilst totally faking non-pumped-stupidness!

There was still more and better to come though: Malcolm's magnificent *Serpentine* had been repeated just the once, by an ex-pat fellow Aussie, Geoff Weigand, who'd visited from America. So there I was, staring up at it from the base of the wall wondering: 'If only … Can I?' Then: 'Yeah, 'course I bloody can!' I'd seen the pics in magazines and H's masterpiece was definitely 'the talk of the town' Oz-wise around the world. I made the third ascent on Friday 25 January 1991 with Canada's adorable, humble, free-soloist-extraordinaire Peter Croft holding my rope, and to say it was possibly the best rock climb south of the equator would not, at that time, be stretching the truth.

Launch over the roof to start, sneak across a weird, easily 'slip-offable' traverse, and execute alternate slappy moves up a vague rib to gain good single-joint holds and a blankish section just below a small overlap: the crux. There are two equally obvious yet conflicting ways to proceed: static to the right or a nifty pop dynamically to the left (or is it the other way around)? Either way, I chose the wrong one. Bugger. Off into clean air!

Through that crux after a rest (read *party*) day and I was cruising up and outwards via thirty metres more of truly *the most perfect* holds on immaculate, very overhanging orange-streaked rock; my own choice as to how far I'd run it out between protection placements already predetermined, as I'd left my (very-spaced) gear in overnight. This really was 'me' in my element climbing-wise; suited my strengths to a tee as I made fifteen or twenty brilliant moves between shake-outs and gear – loving every second of life.

Yeah, Australia – Taipan Wall that January and February particularly – was just the 'gift that kept giving', and not for the first time did I lament (as I sat in the shade of 26 °C on a 30+ day) the fact t'lads back home at Sandford Grove Road and Jerry, Basher, Chris, Zippy, the two Bens, Leachy, Hamper, Plantpot and others weren't all there too. Ah well! Cressbrook in the mud and sleet again? -2 degrees. Jerry and Ben (Messrs M and M) will be down there already as usual … probably why those lads all had stronger fingers than me … and much paler skin, drawn, grey faces and sunken eyes and … we're going swimming at Lake Toolondo on the way home again this arvo as it's heading for 37 degrees in an hour.

SEVENTY MILLION POUNDS

That was the budget R.J. Reynolds, the tobacco company, set aside for The Camel Trophy in 1993. From touching down at Tullamarine I only had a day or so to get over my jet lag whilst staying at Barn and Cath's in Melbourne's St Kilda district before I was off again – returning via a ten-hour flight back in the direction I'd just flown in from.

At that time thirty-five Land Rover Discoveries would be shipped out from Britain to no end of amazing places on an annual basis and seventy drivers/co-drivers and a film crew of another twenty-odd would be flown out business class in two halves. It was two halves because the first week or so was the pre-shoot where we did all the scary stunts and the drivers (like overgrown Boy Scouts, really) built makeshift bridges and drove expertly through puddles of muddy water. The second half was the 'event', or rally itself – 1,600 kilometres; but I'd left by then.

The chosen venue in '93 was Sabah, Malaysia – otherwise known as Borneo – and I'd got the 'gig' as safety officer for the week-long pre-shoot. I have to thank my sister Sarah for that, as she was an advertising producer (had just got back from India or somewhere after making a MasterCard commercial with Rowan 'Mr Bean' Atkinson) and she'd recommended me for the job. I had an interview at the agency in London with the producer, Nigel Goldsack, and the director, Harvey Harrison – they offered me ten thousand dollars for the week. Plus six-star accommodation, business-class flights. No expense spared.

They'd sent scouting parties out and had found a huge disused quarry in the jungle. They showed me the stills and said they wanted shots of the drivers scaling the cliff, but I thought it looked loose and chossy, so reserved judgement till I arrived in Kuching to see it for myself. 'Thank God

I'm here,' I thought, as that 'crag' was a landslide waiting to happen – so I grabbed a couple of the Belgian lads and we went looking for safer alternatives in their 'Disco'.

Being the media tart I was, I knew a good photo op or movie vantage point when I saw one, and soon found some perfect examples. One was a little arête that stuck out of the hillside with **the** most stunning backdrop of 'lost-world' jungle. It wasn't more than UK grade Severe, about fifteen feet high and right next to the track – but if cropped or carefully framed looked about a thousand feet off the deck. Back at the Holiday Inn, where we were all booked in for the week, Nigel and Harvey loved watching the drivers scaling it when we checked out the rushes.

One day the teams had to paddle through a stream and cool down under the waterfall and Harvey called out 'Where's the safety officer?' So I was instructed to wire brush all the stepping stones beneath the babbling stream so the lads wouldn't slip in their Camel boots and wet their Camel clothing and Camel watches. 'Product placement' you see, coz R.J. Reynolds couldn't make mention of the 'cancer sticks' could they!

I had a short dalliance too I should confess. A gorgeous young lass who worked in the hotel. She booked us a room in a motel on the outskirts of town for her off-day and it was the classic holiday romance. Lovely restaurant, walk through the town – albeit dripping in moisture in near 100 per cent humidity – a few iced drinks followed by a memorable night beneath a single crisp white sheet. We actually kept in touch via letters and phone calls for a few months, but you know how it goes ...

BIRDS' NEST SOUP

Deep in the jungle we saw orangutans in their natural environment and shot various clips inside enormous caves. Even though the well-worn steps up one slabby route to sunlight were actually polystyrene theatre props, there were genuine lianas, vines and stick ladders rising over a hundred feet up the sides and across the roofs – where locals in the past would risk life and limb by soloing up to claim their precious booty. I saw a shrunken head in the museum too – incredible stuff.

Great experience that I thought, as I flew back from Kuala Lumpur to start my new life as Vertigo's 'safety officer'.

High on Melbourne Central mast in 1993. **Photo:** Andrew Mitchell.

17.

OZ FOR GOOD

And it *was* at first. Definitely …

See, basically, it was another epic … during my visits to Oz I'd become good friends with Geoff Little in Natimuk and he and his partner Maureen threw the best soirées in town, 'cept their little steel bottle opener protruded out of a fluoro-green plastic mould of Geoff's cock, so it was 'Can someone else open the next bottle please?'

They enjoyed the finer things in life, like gourmet food and only the best wines. Anything but ostentatious or snobby, just bloody good taste – for which they both worked hard in high-pressure jobs. My only problem with joining them for evenings at theirs was that they smothered absolutely **everything** in Parmesan cheese, and the smell made me retch. I spent one mealtime out on the veranda chatting through the fly screen until the stench had subsided and dessert came out. Bizarrely, I don't mind the stuff nowadays.

Anyway, Geoff'd had enough of the 'fly-in-fly-out' weld-inspecting game up on the North West Shelf, so had bought into a small outdoor equipment store in Melbourne, but really wasn't cut out to be a shopkeeper – more David Jason's hapless Granville to Ronnie Barker's Arkwright in *Open All Hours*. His interest was piqued when he quizzed me on how I could earn so much money in such a short time and be back at Arapiles again after only a few months away. So I regaled him with tales of the booming industrial rope access industry back in the UK and the money going begging. In actuality, when I'd been back in Britain after my first trip Geoff and the other owners of the business

(Colin Stewart, Phil Carter and Mark Buchanan) had gotten together and, under the company name of Vertigo High Access, had undertaken a lightning protection installation on the VicRoads tower in Carlton – followed shortly thereafter by a detailed rope access inspection of St Patrick's Cathedral, as well as various other rope jobs around town – so this idea wasn't anything totally out of the blue. They certainly had vision and the commitment to succeed, which I thought was admirable and so I really wanted 'in' with these guys.

Having consulted his business partners, Geoff said, 'If we decide to move this up a gear will you come out and help us take it further – we'll sponsor your immigration'.

'Bloody hell, you're on Geoff!' I replied, tripping over my words in the rush to accept. Do you know, I'd always had it in the back of my mind that 'I'll be right' after climbing – don't worry, *something* will come along – *and this was it!*

Not before a few scares though! We'd filled in the forms for 'specialised' permanent residency, but 'dope on a rope' really didn't cut the mustard with the immigration department and, not surprisingly, I was refused entry. I'd scored top points for speaking English ... duh! ... but was two years beyond the preferred age limit (over the hill at twenty-nine was tough to accept) and I only really had my eight UK Ordinary Levels, a (faked) IRATA certificate (Industrial Rope Access Trade Association), a somewhat exaggerated résumé signed by Tim Freeman of Technitube, plus some pretty rock climbing photos to offer.

Furthermore, immigration asked the question, 'If he's that specialised, why are you offering only $27,500 p.a.? Make it $36.5k plus a company car, get some references and re-apply!' My potential new employers agreed and we did all we were asked, but I was knocked back again. Bastards! Nine months later and with the immigration lawyer's $7,000 fee paid (by Vertigo) I was winging my way to Australia on a two year *temporary* visa as 'safety officer'.

Twelve thousand miles away, during that 'fingers crossed' wait for the department's final decision, an odd incident occurred ... one Sunday afternoon I dropped into that cosy little pub out in the Peak District on the way from Stoney to Tideswell – opposite the truck stop – and ran into a fellow rope access worker; ended up spilling my heart out over my immigration woes. The cheeky bugger faxed his résumé to Geoff that very night, with a cover note saying, 'I'm better than Andy Pollitt, sponsor me! Sponsor me!' Geoff faxed it straight back to me going 'Andy, who does this peanut think he is?' Poor form that we both thought.

So Vertigo High Access (pure genius on Col's behalf for the name) was

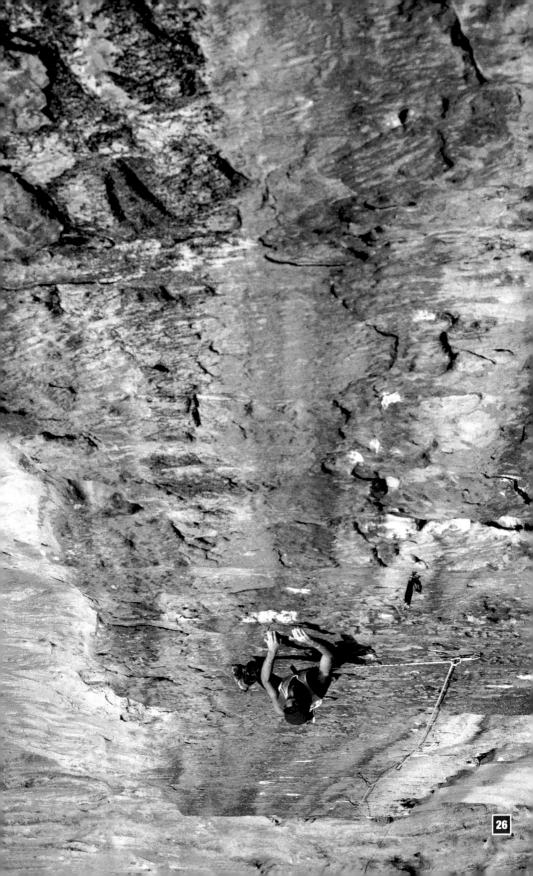

29

30

born in my absence and I rocked up on day one for my first ever 'proper' job. I wasn't yet thirty years old and rock climbing was now behind me. Forever.

We all had little cards with our names and phone numbers on, a facsimile machine, company letterheads and matching analogue Motorola 'bricks' so we could keep in touch. The Vertigo logo was a cool silhouette of Geoff on the cathedral – that image has since been mimicked to death and outright copied; even our early internet presence was hacked and all the writing and numbers changed to somewhere in South America. We each put a ten-cent rope lanyard between our trouser belts and handsets, and to this day I have never misplaced a mobile phone (or dropped it on to some poor old dear's bonce from forty storeys).

They sat me down and we started making plans. 'Oh, by the way,' they advised, 'we can't afford $36.5k and a car – we've just shelled out for the immigration – so you're on $27,500 but you *can* use Geoff's van when it's available – and if you prove yourself we'll cut you in for shares.' Hmm, off to a flying start then!

Geoff's van turned out to be an ancient, rickety, ex-Australia-Post-type Ford Transit – repainted a rather awful poo-brown – with a chair for the driver's seat that wasn't even bolted down. Another exciting feature was a homemade extra-long gear stick – where first gear was in the passenger-side footwell, second was about two feet behind and between the front passenger seat and the chair, and you had to open the driver's side quarter light to shift it into third. I never got to fourth or I would've had to drive standing up! At least it had roof racks – well singular actually – at the front. Some piece of scrap, tek-screwed into the roof so any cargo needed strapping down or gaffer taping on. Things often slid off when I ground the gears and bunny-hopped out of the little yard behind the shop – we soon added a rear rack.

Rope access was still wearing nappies and sucking its thumb back then, and the safety authorities, scaffold industry and Construction, Forestry, Mining and Energy Union (CFMEU) were dead-set against us. They thought we were a bunch of 'spidermen' and 'daredevils' and that we shouldn't be allowed to set foot on their building sites, even when some jobs were a no-brainer for a 'ropie'.

To be fair, the shop stewards, safety committees and decision-makers 'upstairs' at the Victorian WorkCover Authority and in the CFMEU had a point – we were in fact just a bunch of mountain climbers! But, persistence paid off (eventually) and Geoff, Paul Colyvan and myself reapproached the union head honchos with our safety plans and internationally documented procedures and processes – keeping 'everything crossed' they gave us a second look.

About eight of us (the others all far more senior and much longer in the tooth than me) set up a committee – the Australian Rope Access Association (ARAA) – and registered the name. We had fortnightly meetings debating anchorages and breaking strengths ad infinitum. These often went on till well after 10 p.m. We spent months lobbying the head authority – me doing all the physical demos of course – and finally I became Victoria's second-ever authority-accredited rope access assessor.

Now, despite the fact I was 'just a cragger', I'd been well trained in the UK and was very experienced, so this official appointment was actually a blessing in disguise for the abseiling industry in Melbourne (thus also Australia – be it myself or whoever) and not before time! The sole incumbent 'assessor' – a delightful but rather eccentric old Austrian/German chap called Fritz – taught hugely outdated (even then) what he called 'boats-vines-chair' courses at the TAFE College in Holmesglen. A few easy days with Fritz and you were licensed to abseil off anything in the country. Alarming! Well, it was for me – being IRATA schooled, I had every improved technique in the book. One criticism (well two actually) I levelled at the pleasantly bumbling and somewhat nonplussed Fritz, was that he never once showed anyone how to load-share and equalise anchors. It 'voz' … 'Vorking rope here, safety rope over zer … ' stuff. The second blatantly life-threatening bad habit he taught was to lean over a parapet with a loose 'boats-vines-chair', attach it to the first rope (without dropping it), **and then** slide over and slip down into a comfy position **before** clipping in your cow's tail to the main maillon. I once actually witnessed this procedure going tits-up when a chair ('seat' we call 'em nowadays bosun!) and big bucket of soapy water dropped about twelve storeys to land with an almighty explosion in a barricaded off, hence thankfully deserted, courtyard … at least Fritz taught public protection and barricades!

I collected my special, large and laminated assessor ticket from WorkSafe (or whichever name they used back then) at the same time as my mate Darren Holloway was receiving his 'C4 exemption' rigger's ticket. A proud moment for both was temporarily shattered when we noticed our employer details imprinted on the back: Vertiloo High Alless. We got new ID tickets sent out, quick smart!

This was my first personal success of this whole new, well, non-climbing existence, and it was granted by one Mr Les Kriesfeld ('Tough Sarg dar'n the 'thority mate', they said). I had coffee with Les only recently and how we laughed, as we're both still in exactly the same places.

I INHERIT A READY-MADE FAMILY
AND COME FACE TO FACE WITH MY OWN SHADOW

At this juncture, Geoff, Colin, Mark and Phil decided to split the business into three: Phil retained the shop, Mark went off into developing Radwall indoor climbing structures and Geoff and Col (with some external investment) set forth in earnest along the high access route to glory, fame and a hopeful fortune.

My bosses weren't satisfied with just Melbourne though, so I got to fly around the country a fair bit. Brisbane, Sydney and Adelaide – training and assessing all and sundry, and trying to pick up any rope access work. On my first inter-state success I was to supervise a late-middle-aged geotechnical engineer, Mr Andrew Shirley, down the three-hundred-foot undercut Tudibaring Headland at Copacabana Beach north of Sydney. This was because the council was taking permit applications for clifftop homes and it was deemed a requirement that sections of the cliff below be accurately surveyed.

I was staying in a nice hotel in Darlinghurst and blushed at the wolf whistles and purring noises the 'cocks in frocks' and 'chicks with dicks' directed my way (was I 'mincing' along that pavement?). So I headed out to Erskineville to go partying with the tough-as Kerr brothers – Mick and Jason, our franchisees in New South Wales. Erskineville? 'Err-Skin-Full' more like! Lord only knows where we ended up, but I'd been dragged off by the ear by Nicole – one of their younger sisters (up from Melbourne visiting). Completely blotto, the pair of us back at my hotel, Nic stripped off and lay back on the springy queen-size in anticipation – except I was in no state to 'think of England', *and* Mr Shirley the geotech was picking me up downstairs in twenty minutes. In and out of the shower not even getting wet, splash face and exit the door with all the kit. I think the cleaners found her exactly like that four hours later. Still zonked, blissfully unaware and stark naked.

The Kerrs' right-hand man 'Bod' was to be safety officer, manning a retrieval system we'd set up in case Mr S had a heart attack or something. Bar stepping off the edge, Mr S actually took to it like the proverbial duck – loved every minute hanging there taking notes and photos and measuring things with his instruments. All was a great success, and as we arrived safely down on the huge wave-cut platform from the lip of a gigantic cave Bod started pulling up our ropes.

'Call me Andrew please' (by now) led me all the way back beneath the towering cliff and so to the beach and a long slog back up the hill. I was knackered and we found Bod at the top gasping for breath as he hauled up the last of the four long ropes. Mr Shirley thought we were a right pair of lightweights, but when he wasn't looking I took a huge swig of Bod's last can of something-strong-and-Coke and passed it back to him with a wink. Scotch, euww, but phew that's better!

Of course Nic and I got together upon our returns – me to my fancy, top-storey, big, double-bedder in trendy South Yarra; her to a tiny bedsit in St Kilda where she was raising her five-year-old boy Arthur (sans father, deceased, heroin she'd said) as well as two pet rats in a tank that kept eating their own babies and smelt awful. Their cat Mother felt herself lucky that the bedsitter was too small to be swung in.

It wasn't long before Nic and Arty were spending more and more time over at mine – perhaps three or four nights each week. When Nic's lease came up for renewal we agreed that she and Arthur should find a place of their own, 'But of course you can camp here for a bit if you get stuck. Just no rats OK?'

Now, how many love-struck young folk have said *that* only to rue the day?

The next day I got home from work exhausted, parked up the poo-brown van and just made the three flights of stairs to my front door. I was longing for a hot bath and a cold beer. There was noise. **Loud** noise. I entered to find mountains of suitcases filling the hallway, bags and boxes everywhere, everything in my house – *my house* (well 'flat') – had been rearranged. Arty bounced up from a ridiculously blaring television cartoon and leapt into my arms screaming, 'Mummy, Mummy, it's Andy, he's home!' then wriggled when I tickled his skinny ribs and hugged him, spinning around and around till his little legs swung outwards like a 'hecilopter'! He was light as a feather and seemed to me underweight, but then, what would I know? Nic stuck her head around the kitchen door with a welcoming 'Hi babe, how was your day?' and gave me a smacker on the lips as I inhaled both her body spray and her cooking. She looked absolutely stunning in a wild, flowing hippy dress with her 'figure to die for', flames of wild red hair, pale skin and piercing Irish-descent eyes. 'Here hon,' a coldie 'Mmmwwah' on my cheek, 'Arthur, TV off please, quiet!' then 'I'll run your bath'. 'Arty, off. Now I said!' 'Aw Muuuum ... '

'It's OK Art, just keep the sound down, I'm knackered little mate.'

Arty helped me set the table and I let him light the candles, and though I felt Nic had orchestrated the whole thing – and must've rallied a few troops to get all their stuff across – I really wasn't all *that*, well, terrified.

Four and a bit years I think it was before I left and went solo down in Port Melbourne, but as a surrogate dad I'd done my utmost, in every respect, despite Arthur's pyromaniac tendencies ... that night after our first dinner together as a family I'd got up for a pee in the wee small hours (is that why they're called that or is it just more logical than getting up for a wee in the pee small hours?) and seen a flickering beneath the lounge room door. I burst in and there was Arty setting fire to tissues and watching them rise before flaring out. The smoke alarm hadn't gone off and his blanket was alight and I screamed for Nic as the little blighter fled between my legs to hide under his bed – where else? Honestly, no imagination these kids. Lessons about playing with matches, no cartoons for a week, and we were one very content little everyday family.

Very early on in this 'set-up' my days were to become longer still, as I did the 'before' *and* 'after-school care' drop offs and pick ups – five days a week either side of work; but there was kind of a plus to this arrangement as Nic was soon to actually get a job herself and start bringing some money in. She'd had the 'interview,' ahem, and changed her name to 'Ateah'. It went like this: one Sunday morning as we lay in bed screaming, '*TURN THAT FLIPPIN' TELLY DOWN ARTHUR!*' Nic goes, 'That's it! I'm going stripping.' She did too and her first big performance was my birthday present. For about a year and a half she'd get home at all sorts of weird hours – usually well after I'd fed Arthur, run his bath and put him down – and tip a handbag full of fifties on to the bed. Thing was, back in the early days, the girls stripped up close and personal – on one occasion some drunken sod made a grab for Nic's privates and actually ripped her skin with a jagged fingernail. He was dutifully escorted from the premises via the rear door by some big strong men in suits and dickie-bows with security numbers swaying from nametags; and with luck was still lying there next morning – pulverised – in the urine-stinking alleyway next to the industrial bins.

Sure, it was many a lad's dream for a while as my (sorry, our) place became a hangout for her strip-mates – they'd prance around trying on new skimpy outfits and practise their splits and crab-walks in the lounge. 'Legs this wide or this Andy?' Gulp! 'The second one but don't slide the stringy thing down just yet – leave something to the imagination … ' (wiping brow).

Now 'Dearest Beloved' was openly bisexual (as it happened so were the vast majority of the dancing girls), so many 'interesting' three-way Sunday afternoon 'interludes' were enjoyed – providing we could park the boy at one of his chums' places for the day of course. Yes indeed, Nic and I hosted several sleepovers during that period and writing this now I draw parallels with (of all things), North Stack Wall; I mean; 'stuck in the middle … ' *again*, and where we had all the ropes and harnesses we wanted but there really wasn't much protection!

Back then partners of any dancers were expressly forbidden entry on working nights (for obvious reasons) so we kept our relationship under wraps from management and security. Know what? I'd stand in the shadows back from the big, round table with twenty blokes sat around it and two rows standing behind them, as 'Ateah' was led to the stage by a muscle-bound bodybuilder in a loin cloth, their progress accompanied by very loud music, rapturous applause, wolf whistles and cries of encouragement from the baying crowd. I was *ever so proud* of 'my' Nic. A lad's dream? It worked for me!

A rather incredible thing happened late that August: I'd long since booked myself two weeks' holiday to Far North Queensland; it was to be Cairns, Port Douglas, down through the Whitsunday Islands and on to the tacky Gold Coast. My flight was at 6 a.m. but sometime a little after 3 a.m., Mother cat started groaning in the little birthing nest she'd made on some clothes on the floor of our wardrobe next to Nic's head. And very soon out popped the first tiny, moist and blind kitten – right into the palm of my hand. I gave the little creature a kiss, welcomed her to our world and laid her carefully against Mother's engorged nipples whilst she sniffed and licked the tiny thing to life.

On exiting Cairns airport eight hours later I immediately rang Nic to see how many kittens we had, and was crushed by her floods of inconsolable tears. The second one had got stuck and poor Mother was in agony attempting to squeeze it out. It was four in the morning. Nic had little money and no car or credit card, but eventually got the poor thing – wrapped in a towel on the tram, Arty in tow – to the nearest vet. Long story short, the vet was not particularly sympathetic and came out to reception with a 'shoe box' containing one dead Mother – split right down the guts with a scalpel, two dead babies and one small kitten barely clinging to life.

That second one – 'God' Nic christened him – was jet black and beautiful, but had dreadful problems. He was a battler for sure, but as he gulped and gulped at the tiny formula bottle Nic was feeding him and his sister Shadow with, the milk simply spilled back out through his little nostrils – the poor little scrap had a hole in his palate. What did reach his little tum just leaked out into his abdomen through another split and he ballooned.

On my eventual return from hols, Shadow – whilst ridiculously small – was up and about and playful-as. It was quite amazing that within moments she'd switched allegiances and basically stuck her tail up and showed Nic her rear end. *I* was her 'mum', 'dad' or whatever, and Nic the 'imposter', who'd merely raised her on infant formula every three hours for nine straight days and nights. Fickle little girl hey?

When Nicole and I parted it was a no-brainer. She could have everything and anything she wanted but Shadow was mine! Actually it was more a case of *I* was *Shadow's*. For the following fifteen years, unless something out of the ordinary was happening, at precisely 5.14 a.m. every single day she'd wriggle up from the depths of my bedding and start the face tapping and sandpapery licking – to that part of my forehead where we first start to recede. 'Gerroff girl … I know it's time.' 'Meow, waah, waah, miilk.' I swear (and many friends can testify) she could pronounce the word 'milk' and knew where it came from. If she was sat staring at the fridge door I'd ask her what she wanted: 'Miilk.' See, right on cue, I told you.

Shadow never once got sick and was always content. In 2014 she died in my arms at 4.30 a.m. one warm November morning – a tad shy of twenty years old. I was taking her for the 'lethal injection' at 7 a.m. that day anyway, as she'd just become quite unwell; when cats of her age get sick it's usually a very short-lived affair. Her final moments were utterly harrowing – she wailed and wailed in a fit of heinous convulsions (obviously in much distress – as was I) before her life, and a part of mine, ended. My own dear Mum ('They go up to number five don't they?') had passed away three weeks earlier, so for the second time in what felt like moments I plugged in my Gilbert O'Sullivan video for his classic song 'Alone Again (Naturally)', took 'compassionate leave', and spent the entire day bawling my eyes out.

As for hooking up with Nic, 'playing' dad to Arthur, and working hard to provide for our family, no, I never once rued the day. *Ever.*

BACK TO THE GRIND

At Vertigo, from the very beginning, we did the right thing and engaged the services of a fledgling engineering firm, headed by a Mr David Batey along with wife Amanda. They were called Fine Design 'Structual' Engineers (the signmaker had forgotten the 'r' and so Dave had to take the sign back, rather to everyone's embarrassment).

Now Mr B (Dave) was, *is*, a brilliant structural ('r' very much included) engineer. Like most of his ilk, he was dreadfully methodical (read 'bloody slow'), painfully conservative (read 'every steel member went up a size') and he charged like a wounded bull. We became dear friends over the next fifteen-odd years and I was always welcomed warmly into the Batey household. Admittedly, I did have to go there several times a week for work, as FDSE's 'office' was not much more than a couple of tables and a desk lamp in the attic – gained via a tiny stair between innumerable clothes horses, some playpen contraption for their kids, and a yell of 'Mind the puppies.' **Yelp**! Too late. Sorry Fido.

We'd huddle around the desk and pore over hundreds of drawings, working out the best means of providing tactile access to the soon-to-be constructed apartment towers – dozens of them. Historically, tall buildings came equipped with Building Maintenance Units (BMUs) – those crane-type things that carry two window cleaners in a little platform up and down the sides – but shifts in architectural style meant that tall structures were very rarely of the standard square box anymore and many had huge, expansive terraces, soffits (overhangs), ins, outs and 'around corners'. Places the BMUs simply couldn't accommodate or, if they could, would cost millions of dollars.

Of course being a 'ropie' I knew that with the right system our lot could get to every square inch of any building, no matter the shape. I 'invented' and Dave 'comped-up' the now commonplace twin-post, split-balustrade stanchion – basically just that, a double post with a fifty-millimetre gap for the ropes to pass through, with a horizontal pipe welded between the two for the ropes to run over and a second one higher up to prevent ropes sliding up and out of the slot and bearing on the glass infill panels either side.

My other 'invention' – well, adaptation really – was the rope access lateral restraint. This is basically a twisted 'pig tail' of M16 stainless bar fixed to the façade – abseilers could slip their ropes into these little spirals on really long drops so that any side wind wouldn't blow them around high up on the face. Dave Mudie produced, tested, then refined our first prototypes in his workshop in Natimuk, and before long we were producing them by the hundreds – nowadays thousands, literally.

Our 'opposition' (if you could call them that) back in the early nineties was basically the window cleaners themselves – the very people we were making life simpler and safer for – and many of them would cost us jobs by either bunging in a dynabolt or two themselves and calling it an 'access system', or assembling these bloody ridiculous 'mobile suspension rigs' that meant ferrying all the pieces through penthouse apartments to set them up on external terraces. Dave and I agreed that if we'd just forked out $8 million on a forty-eighth-floor penthouse there wasn't a hope in hell that we'd allow a bunch of filthy window cleaners to traipse through our gaff four weeks a year – especially not to clean the windows of the 'inaccessible' plebs below us. No way! Not gonna happen!

On one occasion I was invited to consult to a growing property developer on their next-to-be-released twenty-storey tower. It was stock-standard of the time, with a typical floor plate and no unmanageable ins or outs – just four flat, uninspiring precast concrete sides with 'punched' (cast in) window openings – but the penthouses were set back from the edge in order to provide lengthy outdoor terraces for the big-spenders up top. I recall my price to develop, design, document and certify the entire system was $2,400 ($1,800 going to Fine Design) and I was immediately summoned to their HQ to 'please explain' my 'exorbitant' claim for fees! I'd advised Geoff and Col that I was going to try charging for all my consulting, as up until then it was all pro bono in the hope of picking up the crappy cleaning contracts, which we virtually never did.

One of the founders and owners, Mr B, had assembled his entire immaculately suited team around the 'big' table in their conference room high above Queen Street in the city, and I rocked up bristling with confidence and excitement – a big roll of plans under my arm – in torn jeans and scruffy T-shirt with hair like I'd slept in a hedge. The secretary buzzed me through to the inner sanctum (I'm sure she whispered something on the intercom as she did so) and presented me to the top gentleman, who then introduced me to his 'main man' Vince and project managers and confidants Martin, Silvio and Rocco, and also to the architect Peter from over the road, along with the consulting structural engineer, another Rocco – who'd either studied or worked with Fine Design's Dave Batey – so *he* at least was semi-comfortable!

'You can call me John, Andy,' then proceeded to proudly show me his own concept of little passageways from the lift lobby between the penthouse suites: independent access routes that could get the window cleaners out on to the terraces to set up their rigs.

'I did that, what can *you* give me for *this* much?' whilst swiping my paltry quote with the back of his fingers.

'That's rubbish guys!' I exclaimed rather cheekily and unrolled plans for mine and Dave's scheme:

'Anchors on the roof above, stiffen that gutter up so it doesn't cut the ropes, drop on to the terraces, ropes over the parapet and job's done.'

His face lit up and he immediately whipped out a pocket calculator, went tap, tap, tap, and exclaimed: 'You've just increased my sellable area by Ninety-Seven Thousand Dollars. Sign him up Martin!' and left the room.

As that initial meeting wrapped up I got chatting more informally with Martin and inquired about his noticeable Yorkshire accent:

'Sheffield! Hunters Bar, Andy.'

'Really Martin, whereabouts?'

'Junction Road,' he said.

'Ha. I was Hunter House Road that runs off it – what a coincidence,' said I, and at last I could go 'eh up' or say 'reet waam out tha neet tha noz' to someone without the usual 'yer wot mate' – *and* get a 'double-reet' back.

That was early in 1996 and to this very day I'm delighted to remain their access consultant (and sub-contractor – so far), and whether Andy P works for Vertigo or whoever, it's probable that it's 'my' systems that go in. Not that I rest on any laurels of course. Son Andrew is all grown up now and heavily involved in the high-rise apartments, so I deal more with Jnr than Snr these days. An interest in rock climbing he has too, funnily enough, and when one of his colleagues told him I used to 'do a bit' (I blushed as, during an always-friendly meeting, he unrolled a full-size, laminated poster of me in rainbow tights), pennies dropped and the familiarity of names was a most unexpected surprise – as in, 'What? You're *that* Andy Poll … ?'

'Used to be, yeah.'

OH CHRIST!

Back at Fine Design, Dave's devotion to God and his beloved church was, well, his *life* really – still is and always shall be – and it often overlapped his work commitments, i.e. a commitment to meet *me* at such and such a place at whatever time. Honestly, I could set my watch in the end by Dave's punctuality, it was *always* twenty to twenty-two minutes *late*. And he'd not brought a hard hat or fluoro vest. *Again.*

Never was Dave a 'pusher-on-er' of his faiths, though of course he quoted passages and made reference to all manner of biblical material as often as possible – much of which, amazingly enough, I either knew or was at least familiar with. I wondered where the heck I got that from. Sunday school? RE class? Reading the Bible? But I *did* agree finally, actually promised Dave, that I'd attend a Sunday service.

Some weeks later I slipped in to a church hall as the lights dimmed – all fell silent as a prayer of welcome was read (charmingly to be fair) to the congregation. I honestly can't recall the precise order of events, but this next step I'll never forget. There was a procession of some sorts, but it appeared not everyone was getting up. Wondering what I should do and not wanting to be rude, I caught someone's attention and they nodded me to join in …

'Hey, maybe this is the queue for that wine I heard about?' is what I originally wrote here, but then thought otherwise. Respect, this is church, decorum please. I've changed my mind a few times, so if it doesn't end up in the 'Bureau' (my title remember) you won't be reading it and I've just wasted a few moments of my life. If it does, so have you, sorry 'bout that.

On climbing the few stairs to the 'stage' I was greeted, welcomed and blessed by three rigidly upright elderly men in long white frocks, the third of whom I knew as an engineer through work. I exclaimed, 'Eh up mate!' and gave him a zealous (zealot?) hug which nearly bowled him over – he glowed red in the face before all those fellow parishioners. Apologies were made at our next meeting.

After that though they, well … lost me to be honest (no proper wine and that neither …). I've attended sedate, very solemn C of E churches all my life and witnessed the tears and sympathetic hugs and grim faces first hand (and that's just the weddings), but this 'progressive', American-style 'ministry' was not my cup of tea at all. It most certainly was everyone else's in the building though – the awfully young-looking minister in blue jeans and shirt, pacing around under a trailing spotlight with a radio mic on his head, had them whooping, cheering, punching the air in unison, singing their lungs out and shouting *Hallelujahs*. I couldn't help but be reminded of the 'Jehovah Stoning' and the 'He's not the Messiah, he's a very naughty boy' sketches from the *Life of Brian*, so left them to it with a 'forgive my irreverence, Lord' as I crossed myself, popped $20 into the collection box, stepped out into the sunlight, and almost got taken out by a B-double as I crossed Dandenong Road. If I'd have stayed much longer I figured I'd have ended up like the facially contorted centurion in the 'Biggus Dickus' sketch!

I make light of the above, but I *will say* the amount of genuine, genuine, love and faith inside that building raised the hairs on the back of my neck. I have never said I'd never try again …

Another church-related memory springs to mind: children's Sunday school, up in Cwm church just outside Dyserth, where we'd attend each weekend – and be made to don purple frocks!

'Yeah, OK, so he died right,' I go. 'So we could all live … and play football 'n' stuff. Well, can we please say a quick prayer and well, *go and play football* like he intended then vicar? Christ, he'd be bloody mortified if he knew you were keeping us in on such a lovely day!'

Of course, only a cynical fifty-plus-year-old could *possibly* wish he'd had the foresight as a seven-year-old to say that!

I've digressed; let's get back to …

EARLY DAYS AT VERTIGO

Fine Design were to verify the structural integrity of our anchor points, but before long our quotes were always $500 to $1,000 too much because the other rope access mobs used counterweights and relied on 'up-and-over' friction behind parapets; and building managers always liked cheap.

There was even a father and son team who used to clean the windows of a seven-storey podium building by tying their ropes together and abseiling off in opposite directions, except one day 'Dad' reached the ground first and, forgetting, unclipped and walked off. I don't need to explain the result. Thankfully his lad survived.

Anyway, day one as Vertigo's 'star recruit' and it was difficult access duties at Melbourne Central shopping centre in the 'big city'. I was to change a light bulb and clean a fob watch! 'Yer what Geoff? Is that it?' Didn't sound too glamorous I thought.

The replacement light globe turned out to be atop the north mast of the office tower, a rather spindly and swaying thirty metres above the fifty-second floor. One of those red ones that flash on and off to warn aircraft pilots and that only harness workers can get to. It was mind-blowing and rather daunting. Abseiling over the lip of the thousand-foot Verdon Gorge in France for the first time when I was a teen was one thing, but now – in a busy city-centre environment where the cars and the people below looked positively microscopic – it was truly exhilarating.

As for the fob watch, it turned out to be a ten-foot-diameter, brass-encased promotional Seiko suspended high above the food court. It chimed on the hour and a koala-themed automata dropped from within – but my ropes snagged on the little hand as I was pulling them back up and I advanced the time by three hours. Caused bloody havoc in the morning when hundreds of staff turned up – all thinking they were late.

A great start to my new career!

My second week was pretty much the same – one evening, at around 9 p.m., I took a call from Geoff on my 'brick' when I was at home with my feet up: he was locked in a stairwell in town somewhere with Col and they couldn't get out. It turned out Victoria police had called and advised him the storm had blown out a window high up on the gas and fuel towers, and the fire brigade's longest 'snorkel' lift couldn't quite reach it. The metal window frame was dangling perilously over Flinders Street and needed cutting off and taking down to safety. The whole busy city arterial was cordoned off and the traffic was gridlocked.

I was well over the alcohol limit for driving, but Geoff was insistent: 'We can't Andy, we're stuck. You'll have to do it. You'll have a police escort, no worries … ' so I ran down to the poo-brown van and drove erratically out east to our base to grab two ropes and a kit. About forty-five minutes later I was flying down the tram tracks between the gridlocked inbound and outbound lanes with a cop car ahead under full flashing lights.

The make-safe went OK and I heard applause and was captured by flashing cameras as I brought the window frame down and laid it on the pavement for others to remove. I derigged, jumped in the van and a junior cop waved me into the gridlock. I was stuck in the same bloody traffic I'd just freed up. Ironic or what? I think I billed them $460 for the call-out. It should've been $4,600 or more, but we weren't that business-savvy in the early days. Thankfully I wasn't breathalysed. Now that really would've sucked!

There were two more incidents I'll never forget. Out changing over the vinyl billboard 'skins' with Kelly, Col's then partner, we were atop the big pub at Kew Junction and had removed the old skin and were rolling the new ad along the top of the sign. The skins had pre-sewn sleeves around the edges and we'd use lengths of fifteen-millimetre nominal-bore galvanised water pipe ratcheted back to the structure to tension them up and take out any wrinkles. A pipe fell off the walkway, upended itself and speared straight through the tin roof of the bar, punching out an internal ceiling tile and slamming down on to a small, round table where moments earlier three gentlemen had been drinking – but fortunately for all concerned the strippers had been called on so the guys had just gotten up and left for a quick 'perv'.

'Missed 'em by seconds mate!' the barmaid advised rather ashen-faced, polishing a glass with a tea towel precisely as prescribed in 'the barmaid's manual' whilst three guys were waiting impatiently to be served.

I – most definitely red-facedly – retrieved the six-foot pipe (and copped an eyeful of exposed breast!).

The next one really scared me. Geoff and I had installed the first skin on a new kid's site. Adam was the son of Kelvin, an industry heavyweight, and was following in his father's footsteps – keeping it all in the family so to speak. Unfortunately we'd left an obvious wrinkle along the top coz we were one length of pipe short. Adam, watching proudly, was rapt and it actually all looked fine, but the flippin' wrinkle bothered me on that Saturday night, so super-early on Sunday morning (in my own time BTW) I did a four-hour round trip to tidy it up. Resting our dodgy old aluminium ladder, the one with only one rubber foot, against the third-storey parapet I set off one-handed with the metal pole. Just out behind me on Sydney Road were HV electricity lines, tram wires and phone cables. Aware that these dangers were only feet away I kept close to the metal ladder as I ascended, but it wobbled and slid across the parapet and the water pipe in my hand came to rest on a wire. Thank God it was the Telecom one or I would've been electrocuted there and then. Dead.

☆ ☆ ☆

I can't claim to be quite that conscientious these days, but even after twenty-plus years in the same job (over seventeen now, embarrassingly, with the same car) I'll happily field phone calls every weekend, off-day and evening – often until quite late – and take files home to absorb a hundred shop drawings so I can form a mental 3D image ready to tender on my next forty-storey-plus architectural wonder. My 'issue' these days is partly with my employers and partly with my stubborn self.

A few years ago I was aware the owners were considering selling up to a bigger company and were having numerous meetings about that. The directors and shareholders had all departed from the daily running of the business in any case and were pursuing other interests in their own rights, but tipped in sufficient cash (so they told us) to weather the economic storm around them. Vertigo wasn't exactly top dog in rope access any more as virtually every project manager we'd ever trained had jumped ship and set up against us – and therefore one another – so charge-out rates had/have remained stagnant. But a couple of us and some preciously loyal coal-face employees stuck about to turn things around – forgoing various conditions and accepting no pay rises for the foreseeable future bar the mandatory EBA increases. Insurances, WorkCover premiums, fuel and wage costs rise every year, whilst hourly labour rates in the access industry are being compressed – some firms will 'buy' jobs for no margin just to hold their workers. It's fiercely competitive out there, yet we're in the midst of Melbourne's **biggest ever building boom** and Vertigo's competitors are leaving thousands of dollars on the table by undercutting each other. We can't collude obviously, but rates need to rise – across the board – dramatically and soon. Same, doubtless, for other industries. Australia's new (2015) Free Trade Agreement with China now means, technically, that foreign workers can flood the local market – I see evidence of this daily – and they will work for far less than Aussie award rates; this policy may well end in tears if it really takes off.

Thankfully Vertigo's well back into positive financial territory nowadays and the future looks super promising. The 'access systems' department I have developed and grown over two decades is thriving and healthy, and I have an enviable client base of blue-chip property developers and construction companies. I can't afford to rest on those laurels though as the competition is snapping at my heels and is all too often cheap and nasty. 'Cheap' wins with all but the most responsible firms, so we have taken a few serious hits to our bottom line.

My biggest work gripe (I have a few, don't I?) is that there are Australian (let alone international) *Standards*, local industry *Codes of Practice* and a 'supposed' *Health and Safety Authority* with an *ACT of Parliament* that is inescapable – yet there are **still** mobs of so-called 'experts' out their 'spruiking' their retro-fitted Dynabolts with home-made hangers drilled into a roof or wall for abseilers to descend off! What's even worse is that there are plenty of dumb fucks out there who'll actually use them! Ropes are being laid directly over glass balustrades (not through my twin-post/slotted, **structural** stanchions – they cost an extra grand a pop) and, sad but true, it's gonna take a horrible accident before the 'shonks' are driven out of the industry. Whether I'll be around to witness Vertigo's further success remains to be seen, as I have myriad options to take my skills and knowledge elsewhere for a fresh start: on exceedingly better pay and with a car straight off the showroom floor too. I've been with Vertigo since '93 – not bad in anyone's book – but I can very definitely feel, in the pit of my stomach, those same knots that I'd had eighteen months before I decided that *Punks in the Gym* was going to be my last ever rock climb.

The above sentiments may seem somewhat ungracious towards the guys who put their own money into my sponsorship and have (to be honest) been extremely supportive over the past two decades (I'm a prick to 'manage' by all accounts); then again, as family and friends have pointed out, I don't 'owe' those guys for that initial investment anymore! Forever grateful for sure, but I've certainly done the 'hard yards' over the years and repaid those dues many times over.

SIGNS OF THINGS TO COME

During my early days in Oz, recently single again, with a steady job and real spending money in my pocket for the first time in my life, it was time to explore my new surroundings. I'll always recall an Aussie Rules game at 'The G' (Melbourne Cricket Ground), complete with mandatory piping-hot meat pie that made me squeak the intro to The Bee Gees' 'Stayin' Alive': 'Agh Agh, Agh Agh!' when I took my first bite and lost the skin off the top of my mouth.

But the restaurants – wow! I'd only ever really eaten 'foreign' before (meaning pizzas and Indian curries) in Sheffield, but could now go to Richmond for Vietnamese, Swan Street for Greek or an awesome little African joint in South Yarra where the lion ribs and giraffe neck soup were served in generous portions. That last bit I may have made up, but you get the idea. There really was no end to the variety. Chinese yum chas were my favourite though and still are. I avoided the jellyfish and felt for the poor ducks whose tongues were all piled up in little bowls. I didn't even know ducks had tongues – not something I'd ever considered really and wondered if there were loads of ducks out there that couldn't quack anymore. Or worse, ducks that lisped (actually I've just tried it, a lisp doesn't affect the pronunciation of 'quack' in the slightest).

You just checked too, didn't you?

There were also oddities to life in Melbourne back in the early nineties. I wasn't quite sure about the topless hairdressers, but they were soon banned – apparently boobs got rashes and it became an occ. health and safety issue. Goodness only knows what had happened to the lasses at the topless hardware store when they were forced to cover up as well? Yes, there actually was one such store – but topless was only on Saturday nights from 6 p.m. till closing.

I envisioned hordes of 'home handymen' traipsing up and down the aisles pushing empty trolleys ... 'Err, bag 'o nails please love ... nice tits!'

This was definitely not Dyserth – nor even Sheffield for that matter. I had a lot to learn about Australia. Some streets had *No Standing* signs along them. Why can't I stand here I pondered? I'm not harming anyone. And there were XXX bookshops, adult movie theatres, strip clubs and brothels flippin' everywhere, and the local newspapers ran pages and pages of ads by 'available Asian students' and 'horny housewives'. Even a 'lady' who'd send you her tights for $20. Euww, gross!

I will openly admit to visiting one particular parlour though, one where they promised they could 'correct' your most devious fantasies – 'All pain levels catered for ... ' Gulp!

In the reception area – soft red light and incense wafting – I fidgeted nervously on the comfy red velour settee awaiting the ladies' introductions. In the opposite corner there was a bloke locked in a little cage about the size of a tea chest – thankfully he was totally hooded. I figured he could be that client I'd met this morning, or my neighbour, or even a mate from the pub, I'd never know – but nor would he know who else had entered the establishment. The working girls were meant to spit on him, kick the bars and verbally abuse him in front of the patrons awaiting introductions – and *he* paid *them* for the humiliation!

Well, I soon left that establishment (OK, it was two hours later and several hundred bucks lighter). The best bit was 'Mistress' – a twenty-six-year-old fetish model in magazines and burlesque shows; she was drop-dead gorgeous ... asked me whether I'd like to meet her in a cosy little bar nearby after she'd showered and changed ... reckoned I was gorgeous – not the fat, sweaty businessman type she normally got. We hung out together for three months, but she had modelling assignments in America and ended up marrying a dude over there who had every possible facial piercing; she never came back. Extremely gutted I was!

Work was now seriously picking up as Vertigo had acquired franchises in Brisbane and Adelaide as well as Sydney, so I really had to knuckle down. We'd been awarded the contract to change over all the billboard ads on a monthly basis – hundreds of them. Vinyl banners – or skins – had arrived in earnest and replaced changeable panels and paper paste-ups, and we 'ropies' could do them without the need for expensive cherry pickers or cranes.

When I discovered what the tobacco, motor car companies and banks were paying in rent – per sign, per month – I was staggered. Multi-million dollar campaigns that lasted only thirty days. I knew I had to have a piece of the action, so signed up a couple of landowners, got the necessary planning and building permits, borrowed heavily to build the structures (thanks to my bro Dave) and engaged an agency to sell the space. I was clearing thousands a month – usually between ten and twenty. Pure profit simply for owning the rights – didn't have to lift a finger. In no time I'd repaid Dave my start-up costs and settled with the lawyers and town planning consultants; it was looking like I was financially secure for life, with two 25-year contracts with 5x5 options beyond at my discretion, and rental increases fixed at three per cent for CPI. **Yey**! Happy days.

You can probably guess what's coming, so feel free to skip the next bit.

For the non-skippers:

The 'big boys' in the outdoor advertising industry took umbrage when this Pom (a Welsh one, but we're all Poms to the Aussies. Except for the Jocks. Oh, and the Paddies.) unveiled two of the biggest and best sites in the state, so they convened a meeting at The Cricketers in South Melbourne one Friday afternoon – and promptly decided to black-ban me. They refused to market my signs or take any bookings for the space, wanted it all for themselves, so both signs stood empty – floodlights switched off – for seven long months! Now seven months is over two hundred days. Times that by three or four calls a day to the agency – with the same bullshit excuses – and you get my frustration to a tee!

I still had to pay the monthly ground and wall rent, and for airspace rights for the spotlights above an adjoining building; eventually my cash reserves ran out. I exercised my out-clause on the 180-square-metre (massive) wall sign and sold my 60x15-foot panel atop a 30-foot steel pole on the side of the Westgate Freeway to that young Adam (the lad whose sign I could've been electrocuted on) for a measly few hundred grand. I really should've invested in a house or a unit – I could have afforded to – but went and bought some antique slot machines worth (seriously) thousands of dollars and had them flown out to Australia from Britain and the States (lousy investment) and enjoyed the rest of the cash on booze, cigs and err ... well ... one or three girlfriends (all of sound repute, believe me!).

Oh, and those two mega-structures have never been blank since – I pass them both almost daily and now some other buggers are filthy rich, not me. Permits go with the building or land you see, and I'd left both the structures there, ready to flick on the power supply and good to go.

These days I'll openly admit to still being a bit of a scruff, but neither my hair nor labret piercing have any negative effect whatsoever upon my professional performance. On the contrary actually, they are both sometimes humorous ice-breakers when I walk into meetings full of 'suits' – sometimes I can see two of the ten exchanging sideways glances mouthing 'Who the heck's this?' Usually the other eight are all familiar: 'It's Mr Vertigo. Andeeee, how you going? Thanks for coming,' and being otherwise super-friendly.

Once we get stuck in I can always present a variety of options for any access problem, so the new faces immediately realise I know my stuff. Bloody should do after twenty-plus years. Daft but true, I often point out to my architects and builders when they send me a few hundred drawings that they build **upwards** but I work **down**, for the abseilers, so have to assess everything arse-about! Always cracks 'em up that, but it's 100 per cent logical when you think about it.

Anyway, where were we? None of the four shareholders have any active participation in the daily operations of Vertigo any longer (two never did) though *the little man* Geoff 'consults' and helps with the odd tender occasionally. They've all either retired to play golf or gone on to other things, so I'm truly the **last man standing**. Forgive my apparent bitterness, but I'm the only original 'band member' still here after almost a quarter of a century. Obviously – to Geoff and the others – I've never earned those ' … shares we'll cut you in for if you prove yourself,' that were promised, or that slice of the spoils they waved before my eyes and across my ears on my first day – just after dropping my salary by nine grand and rescinding their offer of company wheels.

More and more these days I'm reminiscing about those first days at Vertigo and thinking how promising my new life in Australia was at the time. How I nearly got electrocuted when I went to straighten out that minor wrinkle on that banner one Sunday morning (unpaid of course), just coz I had pride in myself and 'our' company; and how I risked my own and possibly someone else's life driving pissed behind the cop car to play 'Spiderman' as the papers wrote it up. A stack of other examples too. Who knows? Perhaps there's an inevitable degree of tiredness and frustration with the 'daily grind' within an organisation that (to my way of thinking and twenty-plus years' service) is 'set in its ways' and fearful of change. Like I am.

Ennui. It's a terrible thing – but time will tell.

'NEIGHBOURS, EVERYBODY LOVES GOOD NEIGHBOURS … '

As the theme tune goes.

Kylie Minogue had left the TV show that made her famous and was touring up and down the UK with her singing and dancing act. She was booked to play the big theatre in Sheffield a few weeks before I was hoping to fly out to Oz, so a few of us went along and it was sen-bleeding-sational! I loved it and bought the poster for my loft ceiling.

I had all her albums – on cassette tapes back then of course – and would dance around the house knowing virtually all the lyrics. I'll add that this was in her formative years before she became a gay icon, and it was simply '80s' pop at its best. Within months of my landing she was playing at the Tennis Centre in Melbourne where I now live (the city – I don't live at the Tennis Centre) so Barn and I went along for the show. We fought our way down through a wriggling mass of teenage girls until we arrived near the front, then bopped till we dropped. After purchasing more posters and a tour T-shirt apiece we left the venue and went for a few beers by way of my celebrating seeing her in my 'home' town and then her in hers. Barn and I then went on a road trip to the Red Centre and had our photo taken together on the summit of Ayers Rock/Uluru wearing our Kylie shirts. Typical Poms!

One evening at Melbourne Central, in readiness for yet another out-of-hours work stint, I grabbed my sugar hit from the Doughnut King and sat at a table watching the queue traipse slowly past. I glanced up to see who owned such a fantastic pair of pins: it was none other than 'Charlene's' neighbour 'Jane' – the accomplished Melbourne actress Annie Jones – who I'd always rather fancied. She noticed me splutter into my coffee and blush, so giggled and gave me the nicest smile I think I'd ever received in my life. She mouthed 'Hello' and I wanted to say something but froze. Beamed into a few million households each night, she probably got that reaction all the time, and I felt like a total 'doofus'! I'd see her out and about for several years, walking her little dog around the main cafe and shopping strip; her wedding ring always sparkled so I never said 'Hello' back.

Melbourne city's not that big a place really and our celebrities can, and generally do, mingle amongst us plebs without fear of trouble; over the years I've sat on trams or trains or been in a supermarket, coffee shop or bar with many Aussie soap stars, newsreaders and better-known journalists, and I've never seen or heard a tantrum 'Don't you know who I am?' rant from any of them. Great!

Guitar practice in my own penny arcade in Port Melbourne.

18.

ON BEING 'BI'
and NOT 'ANDY' AT ALL

Well bugger me! Who'd have thought *that*? (Though I'll admit to suspecting it myself years ago.)

See, I'd been clinically diagnosed with 'it' back in 2000 – so it was 'official' – and was dutifully prescribed lots of pills to 'make me better' and correct my 'imperfection'. I must say I questioned the good doctor's judgement at the time with a 'Hey, it's not a disease you know. I can't spread it,' but my 'bi' tendencies certainly eased off for a spell. The wonders of modern medicine hey?

-polar you realise, not the one most will probably think I was about to declare.

Bipolarism is just a modern name for the manic depressive really, and I'm sure the moniker was coined partially in an effort to remove the stigma from such a debilitating condition. I actually think it sounds much worse, so would rarely admit to being an 'afflictee' (albeit it only mildly), but if this is 'mild' I'd hate to know what 'chronic' or 'serious' is.

It was years ago that I realised my head just wasn't quite right (it's now obvious that Mum realised this when I was a small child), so on diagnosis I was prescribed the new wonder drug Prozac, along with an estimated nine per cent of the wider Australian community – a bizarre fact, as we certainly do live in The Lucky Country yet are clearly not all happy with our collective lot. The old Prozac had some nasty side effects though, but thankfully the newer anti-D's worked just fine (although I dropped 'em totally around 2013 – better for it? Reckon so … !)

Bipolarism is a cruel condition and can affect *anyone* – wealthy or poor, hard working or unemployed, man or woman – and is something that's constantly hovering in the back of one's mind. I could literally sit with fifty grand in cash on the coffee table in front of me after a good night at the casino yet next morning be wracked in misery, just coz the chemicals in my brain aren't quite balanced. I assumed those 'happy pills' from the doctor worked, but they cost me a lot of money each week. Money well spent I reckoned, even though I drifted in and out of taking them – which meant life was a bit of a roller coaster for a while.

My last serious episode of utter misery and 'solitude amongst a crowd' was a few years ago, around the time my precious Vertigo turned to shit. This may have been purely coincidental, but certainly doubled my pain as my old friend Geoff walked away and someone with an interest in the business going back to the early billboard days stepped in to take over the reins. One of the first things my new boss did was, well, actually lay me off. For a month! For my own benefit – and that of *their* business.

But it was *excruciating*. I pitied my poor construction sites as he'd confiscated my mobile phone which contained all my personal contacts too. See, I'd been hoodwinked into signing across my personal phone to help Vertigo get a better package from Telstra, so 'lost' the SIM card and number I'd chosen when my then girlfriend Lindy bought me it many years earlier – so I felt particularly isolated … *and* he took my company car off me.

This was after twenty years of utterly loyal service.

Anyway, it was 'We'll run "access," it can't be that hard.'

New 'bossman' saw me as a firebrand – unruly and certainly unkempt (which was fair, to a degree) – so I copped a verbal, the 'My Way or the Highway' speech. I was to leave everything in his 'capable hands' and go away and 'clean up my act' (yes, I agree to some extent – I was run ragged, *but* 'getting the job done' with no complaints from my clients, and I was generating vast sums of revenue – often more than the other departments combined, with just my terrific foreman out there 'doing it tough'). I was to either come back and tow his line as the others all did ('cept they didn't have to sign his little fucking book at seven each morning, spend **all day** on fucking 'spreadsheets' then sign again at four in the arvo as 'proof' I actually did anything) or take his generous alternative to, well, just not come back, whichever the case may be. 'I can sign a cheque for your entitlements right now if you like, I've had it written up already. We'll be just fine … '

'Well fuck me, this guy's not only dead serious here lads – but he's also off his fckn rocker if he thinks *any* of 'em could design, win and run a *single* job, let alone my workload,' I lamented to my mates down at AA (Anonymous Alcoholics – we'd meet every second Thursday, **not** tell each other our names and get plastered) and they agreed. One belched loudly, the other asked what the question was again.

When I was finally 'allowed' back – to the job, career and position I had built up from nothing – there were hundreds and hundreds **and hundreds** of **unread** emails in my inbox and my desk was buried in new tenders, some with closing dates well passed. I spent days whittling the crap out of my inbox and got it down to 257 that required responses.

'We'll run "access",' indeed! They'd not lifted a finger, it was totally un-bloody-believable!

But … not a red cent of my salary was withheld and some surprisingly enlightening counselling sessions were – albeit grudgingly – undertaken to the letter. That, at least, was fair-do's on Vertigo's behalf in my book.

In my book – Ha! So it flippin' is now!

Sometimes I'd wish I had my older brother Dave's temperament. Solid as a rock he is and maintains a constant mental equilibrium. For sure, just like everyone else he has high points and low points in life, but remains unfazed and 'on the level' whereas I'm either flying high or absolutely plumbing the depths. I've grown to love and respect Dave more and more as the years go by, particularly as we get older. Though we fought a bit as kids, that was nothing more than normal sibling rivalry, so no big deal. He went on to be the top sales rep at Pilkington (the glass makers) and headed their military night-sights division. He let me peer through a new long-range telescope one night at Walden Cottage and I could zoom in on the sheep grazing on the hillside over a mile away across our valley. Clear as crystal, albeit with a green tinge – echoes of Chernobyl? I could pick out their individual facial features. 'Now just imagine this is on a long-range rifle Andy, we could take out that woolly back by the hedge without it ever knowing it was in our sights.' Alarming stuff when you consider the intended targets were human beings, hence something David was never really at ease with.

He always 'set his sights high,' so to speak, and was head-hunted (a timely turn of phrase given the above) from 'Pilks' and landed the job of a lifetime with that company who'd developed the secure e-ticketing and security system for the airline industry. A British firm, but he was based in Copenhagen, Denmark, in a luxury company-funded apartment overlooking the canal system. He loved every minute – signed up all the world's biggest airlines and then got tempted away again.

I couldn't quite grasp the concept of the work he was doing with the new mob, a telco, selling what was tantamount to a CD for fifty million quid or whatever, but essentially it was a computer logarithm that broke down every single telephone call – several million per second and each one to the millisecond – so that whatever the mix of primary and sub-carriers, each got their relative share of the call cost. Brilliant, clever stuff eh? Dave signed up the entire European Union (except two of the tiny warring states who preferred to shout across the muddy fields at each other anyway) so was dispatched to glorious Sydney, Australia, to flog it to us Aussies, the Kiwis over the Tasman Sea and onwards into South-East Asia. Signed 'em up one after the other he did, what a legend. Thousands and thousands of pounds of commission per sale – on top of a ridiculous salary and LAHA (Living Away From Home Allowance). The company paid for everything (even food, rent and utilities) and he diligently banked the money, though did splash out on a fancy, powerful speedboat.

Dave stepped off the hamster wheel and opted for the golden handshake aged forty-eight. Along with his delightful wife Val, he now owns and runs a Yoga studio in one of Sydney's classiest suburbs.

We often chat and agree: 'The bros from Dyserth done well.' Dave reckons they'll give it till he's in his sixties at the studio, then he thinks they'll maybe move back to North Wales. 'Why for heaven's sake Dave?' I ask, 'What's wrong with Queensland, Monaco or New York, or anywhere? Take your pick, you can afford it!' I guess he simply misses home, that's all. I wonder sometimes whether I do.

☆ ☆ ☆

Where were we before my bro? Oh yes, *depressed*!

Some days I could not get out of bed in the morning. Given I worked six hard days a week (Saturdays at home and at least one in three Sunday mornings back at head office) and was really pretty autonomous as long as I pulled in the dollars, there was only a one-in-seven chance of it being my off day when Churchill's black dog decided to raise its mongrel head to remind me how completely and utterly pointless my existence was and how I felt I was wasting my own and everyone else's precious time – time we'd never get back. He'd pester and prod at the cracks in my façade and poke fun at the vulnerabilities within, cock his leg, piss down my back and tell me it's raining.

Oh how I wished I was twenty again and back on Gogarth or Pen Trwyn! Life, *everything*, was a total blast back then wasn't it … Wasn't it?

So I'd curl up into as small a ball as possible and hide beneath the covers, gently rocking back and forth in excruciating physical discomfort and mental turmoil; I'd shelter there, wishing I could fall asleep forever, imagining all my old friends back in Britain were thinking that I was living it up in sunny Australia!

Attempting to shake off such thoughts (which I **knew** would soon pass) I'd switch back over to work mode with dread. I'd been blanking it out for a few minutes but I couldn't escape the fact my email inbox would be bursting at the seams and my switched-off mobile chock-a-block with voicemails, so tomorrow will be doubly awful.

Agh, Vertigo! Effing Vertigo office bullshit. Grrrrr. Leave me out here with my clients and site managers … am sick of updating spreadsheets. I don't have time! Just go away people *please*.

Leave me alone today. All of you.

I have faith though, and through years of experience I know it'll only be temporary should it return, and I'll feel better the next day or the day after that … When I eventually would get up during the worst of the 'sads', I'd 'shit, shower and shave' and nip up the pub to see my mates and attempt to drown my sorrows. Problem was, the little buggers had learnt to swim, so it was another 'happy pill' and off to bed before nine. Massive day tomorrow.

Again.

And on it went – for month after month.

Doubtless for many of us.

Oh, the 'Not Andy' thing's pretty self-evident really if you have two Christian names but are called by your second one. Not that there's **that** many of us, I bet.

My siblings are *Sarah* Caroline, *David* James and *Elizabeth* Ann; all called by their *firsts*. How come I got lumbered with Robert *Andrew*?

My parents never even bleedin' used it, I was always Andrew – the 'spare' name. I could've been a *Rob, Robbie* or *Bobby*. Yeah, *Bob Pollitt*, like Marley or Dylan; cool that – but no, it wasn't to be!

The first time I let this private information spill was during the infamous Llandudno Milk Bar raid of 1984, when three police cars screeched up in front of the coffee place where some of us were taking tea (and packets of coffee, sachets of salt, pepper and sugar, anything edible that wasn't bolted down) and five cops burst in. (The blonde cadet in the uniform was very pretty, no ring, wonder if she goes to The Cottage Loaf?). But I copped Sgt Major instead; they were looking for a skinny, scruffy-haired 'youth' who'd out-run a store detective. Wanted him to make a 'statement'. There were about five of us that fitted *that* description (but only young Ben Moon was glowing crimson and somewhat out of breath).

'Name?' 'Flicking notebook open and licking pencil.'

'Robert Andr ... ,' and someone bursts out:

'Who? Since when were you Robert?'

'Robert' played particular havoc when I first immigrated here to Australia, as I had a variety of rental leases, car stuff, trade accounts etc. to set up. The banks were hell. I had a few to choose from and tried to set up accounts in three different ones. One would insist I was Robert, and Robert only. The other only Mr R.A. and the last finally accepted just Andy (and all my life's savings) with a courteous 'G'day'.

Christmas sodding Eve 2011: Before 9 p.m. till almost midnight I spent in the Royal Dental Hospital emergency dept. clutching a rapidly melting ice pack to my horribly swollen jaw. Pain like I've never known – having sheared a tooth off on my still-partially-frozen pre-Christmas 'Lo-Cal Atlantic Salmon in Cheap-Runny-Sauce' meal three days earlier.

'This is ridiculous,' I wept to myself. 'That's at least the third person now that I was here before ... Ohhhhh, the agony!'

I reapproach the counter and join a fresh queue of similar misfortunates – none of us exactly mumbling our 'Mewwy mm Cwrish mm athes' – more doing the eye rolls and mutual head shakes.

'Polite' was called she said. 'Twice! Mr R. Polite then Mr Robert.'

'Mmmmm,' I attempt to acknowledge and wince through teary eyes with legs about to buckle. 'Well they've called you three times Robert, where were you?'

'Oooohhhhh! Fucking Wobert!' I sob, and look for something to punch.

When the young practising dental technician had finally put on all her PPE – she resembled a bomb disposal expert – and had drawn every possible blind across my reclined chair (even wound down the metal roller door to our cubicle!) she went 'boink' on my abscess with a sharp instrument and immediately ducked for cover.

The relief was well, as you'd imagine, and she cleaned me up and sent me on my way with a script for the all-night pharmacy. 'Robert indeed!'

It reminded me of the old 'Bristol goitre' of the eighties. I was in Avon with Basher and had this humungous boil right between my shoulder blades. Basher goes, 'Giz a look,' and squeezed it. Daft bugger, looked like he'd been custard-pied!

What are 'besties' for, huh?

And who'd prefer depression to this nonsense!

Above Gogarth Main Cliff in 1980. **Photo**: Pete Bailey.

19.

THE AFFLUENCE OF INCOHOL

It's summer 1980; I was just sixteen years old, at The Dixieland 'fun pub' by the fairground on Rhyl promenade. 'The Dixie' was merely an enormous hall with a stage at the front, a hundred-odd round tables and long bar running down one side – yet the seven-foot-tall 'goon' on the door had waved me through without even requesting ID, as he knew I was fairground staff. I swaggered in feeling all grown up with my fluffy 'mo' and (illegally) joined the collective throng queuing six deep for drinks.

I was wearing my best new flares and a penny-round shirt, dead stylish-like, and was a veritable time bomb of hormones just waiting to explode. To this day, thirty-plus years later, I have rarely been amongst such a collection of hot girls and women, all of whom competed for the shortest and tightest miniskirt, crop top or cut-down 'Daisy Dukes', and all aiming to out-do one another with the amount of flesh exposed. It was a long, hot summer that year … thank goodness!

So what's this got to do with climbing? Not a lot, you the reader may say! And neither were several other aspects of my life at that time – some crass by today's standards; but the fact is that this was my everyday environment throughout my two years working for Jack the Cake each winter and on the fairground during the summer seasons. 1980 and 1981 – grand years for me looking back. I learnt a lot and did a whole heap of growing up and, despite all these distractions, did still manage to get to Forwyn and the Ormes about twice a week.

However, the most important thing I learnt, or came to realise, was that all I really wanted to do in my life was climb. This work stuff, whilst perfectly enjoyable and paying five times the dole, was just getting in the way and my wages were literally being pissed into the loos of The Dixie every night.

Back at the bar and it was 'Ooooh, there goes that skinny brunette again, I'll have one more … see if I can catch her eye'. The place was absolutely jam-packed and there I was, stranded amongst this sea of tarted-up, oestrogen-oozing femininity, mostly out on the prowl and looking for a good time; table after table of four to six hotties all eyeing up the blokes dressed in their V-neck sweaters and reeking of Brut 33 or Old Spice.

I found a good vantage point, sparked up a ciggie and skulled half of my pint of lager in anticipation, coz the dashingly handsome magician was up next and promised to split his pretty assistant in half – and that's what all the blokes were yacking about and vocalising too, only in an (ahem) *different* way, and oh how the lasses cackled and offered themselves up next at the thought! Crass yes, but that was Rhyl in 1980 and I was earning money and saving up what little didn't go on my new-found vices for a new rope I'd seen in Chris Lyon's Llandudno shop.

Pete Bailey:

> I recall that rope extremely well – the *Luna Bong* abseil in the Verdon Gorge. Andy went first; I followed. Nearing the end of the second abseil (no knots in the rope ends and the deck 800' below) I found myself hanging in mid-air, ten feet out and well above the straggly old tree where Andy was proudly ensconced. It was then I realised Andy's rope was much shorter than mine – it just didn't reach – the Lyons had sold him a dud!
>
> 'How'd you get there Andy?' I croaked.
>
> 'Just swung and jumped Pete!'
>
> So … bollocks … I jumped!

The Dixieland noise was deafening and I couldn't hear myself think, but figured Jerry would be bouldering and traversing at Hyll Drem again all by himself right then, and would have an hour-long walk back to the deserted barn ahead of him all on his own, so weighed all this up in my head and … errrr … decided to buy another pint and stay put.

'Just *one* more won't harm me … there she goes again, look over **this** way girl … please!'

That's one of the reasons why Jez, or anyone else, gets ahead of the pack – in *any* sporting discipline. It's not just the things we *see* them doing, but the training we *don't see* that makes the difference – although I knew darn well what Jerry would be doing as I was sitting there getting slowly rat-arsed!

I hadn't smoked either until about then – had probably struggled to down half a dozen shandies in my life and a warm little can of Double Diamond the previous Christmas – but here I was, mingling with grown-ups in an 'adult venue' with the archetypal working class MC in a cheap, ill-fitting suit and frilly front introducing 'blue' comedic stand-up acts and truly woeful cover bands.

By the way, the magician's assistant required first aid. Again! Second time that week!

The booze and cigs seemed perfectly appropriate in that setting, so I quickly adopted this unhealthy nightly routine. I knew I wasn't going cragging with Pete, Andy or Norm the next day so settled back at the table with a few 'carnies', put my thoughts of climbing the huge blank-looking wall next to *Scalar* at Forwyn to one side, and talked, drank and lusted after all the 'totty' through the smoky haze. Particularly that pretty brunette lass. I swear, I could *smell* those ladies, so sharp were my virgin senses.

Hilariously (at the time, but now cringe-worthy), the staff had placed a full-sized male mannequin in the ladies' toilets, nude except for a small loin cloth covering his particularly prominent 'bulge'. The loin cloth was wired up to a large red light above the stage which started flashing brightly if activated, so whenever a lady went to 'powder her nose' the huge audience would know whether she'd taken a peek or not. Oh, the embarrassment when the women returned to a hall full of applauding and pointing patrons! Cheap gag, but priceless at the time.

I was sitting with the lifeguard (who was utterly 'maggotted' but apparently still on duty!) when someone ran in to grab him – a chap had been swept away from the beach by the tide and there was a really strong current running. We all legged it outside and 'lifey' stripped down to his grots, swam out and saved the 'drowner' – to huge applause from the assembled crowd. Then he dried off, got dressed and we returned to our seats for more pints. His were free for being such a sterling chap and saving another life, mine were paid for (and I've been 'paying for it' ever since) and a life-changing choice too when I come to think about it. He thought nothing of what he'd just done. Today's fellow was number six or seven he'd pulled back to shore already and we were still only early in the season. Incredible chap he was.

It all seemed such enormous fun and pretty harmless at the time – well what little did *I* know? And perhaps inevitably, being a typical Scorpio 'Mr All-or-Nothing', I was to become 'particularly fond' of the, hmm … 'calming effects' shall I say, from then onwards …

Bordering on alcoholism perhaps?

Possibly, yes. *Possibly*? Even 'probably' some say, but I just call that being judgemental and don't take much notice.

But, and this is *my* take on things, nowadays that just means having the cravings going on in the background but *not* acting upon them: I *can't* because I have responsibilities – bloody serious ones in my industry – so *must* remain focussed, on the ball, and if a client says 'Jump' you ask 'How high?' Actually no, I retract that statement (or I'll be swamped with daft requests) so:

Get The Job Done and …

'Be The Best You Can Be Lad' (thanks Brother Dave).

Maybe I'll let my hair down next Friday, if I have the energy … (I rarely do, so generally don't).

Well that's how *I* conduct myself anyway and can live with this (until I win the Lotto anyway …) and by God's grace (or for being too cheap my boss asks!), the amount of new work constantly pouring in suggests I'm doing *something* right out there amongst the piling rigs and Favcos, hammerheads and pin jibs (cranes) and the constant thumping of concrete pumps as they pulse hundreds of cubic metres of the stuff up static lines from rows of trucks on the ground, only to spew out and be 'helicoptered' flat around all the bolt cages that *I'd determined* were necessary and had arranged to be fabricated and delivered for the rock-hard form-workers in time for the next floor pour … Level 49. 'One more to go lads then order the Christmas tree,' being the usual structure top-out ceremony – thank goodness for being busy, it scares me what I could get up to without such a hectic work life!

Should I feel embarrassed for admitting all that, particularly considering my employers and some of my clients, suppliers, site crews and fellow consultants might read these words and take a collection of rather 'dim views'? Well heck no, I'm the exact same Andy P as when I rocked up on day one and am not embarrassed in the slightest, so there you go!

Cigarettes were the obvious next bad health choice – almost everyone smoked back then, and I latched on to that 'hook' around about the same time. Thankfully I was never tempted by the acid, speed, cocaine or heroin that Rhyl was awash with back in those somewhat innocent (for me) but seedy-yet-glorious early 1980s.

Anyway yes, I *did* become 'somewhat partial' to the odd cold one, but hey, that's The Aussie Way isn't it? And I still partake when yet another stressful day is done – OK, 'above average' according to the 'stats', but hey-ho … only sometimes!

These days I don't venture out of an evening much. Crafty planning? No – more 'thinking ahead' and 'being the best I can be' and realising that 'possibly', yes 'probably', I was also a bit daft for a time … back in the day!

Lemon squash anyone?

Cheers!

20.
BERT and HEATHER, FRIENDS OF THE ANIMAL KIND and THE TROOPERS ARMS

Grab the Kleenex, you might need them.

My old climbing mate from Araps (and for the past fifteen-plus years a colleague at Vertigo) Paul Colyvan – 'Animal' or 'Mul' as he was, and still is, generally referred to – came in to work one Monday morning in 2001, buzzing about his weekend away with the then perennial Natimuk 'student' Greg Pritchard.

Bugger the climbing – he hadn't done it for years, even though he'd put up a few new routes on the Sydney sea cliffs that were graded 74 and 125 when the Ozzie system only went up to 28 – but they'd stumbled upon a little oasis on Roses Gap Road, deep in the Northern Grampians, and reckoned the owners were terrific, if somewhat 'off the wall'.

It all seems so long ago now, but is etched in my memory bank and safely filed away under 'never to be forgotten' … **ever**.

For the few of you who went there, as many climbers did, I'm sure you'll share the following sentiments.

New Year's Eve 2001 was going to be a big one, so I booked one of the little cabins and made the four-hour drive up. As I pulled into the car park I couldn't believe my eyes. A stunning two-and-a-half-storey Dutch-style barn set in beautiful surrounds – totally self-built by the owners Bert and Heather. Bloody awesome! Right in the middle of the great Australian bush and scrub. A truly exceptional structure – from the detail in the hand-sawn local timbers and locally quarried stone flooring, to the two 10-metre-tall, planed red gum trunks supporting the triple-faceted Dutch roof; but the centrepiece was Bert's fireplace taking pride of place against the back wall. It was massive and had a huge self-fabricated hood, and a spit roast on a swivel post so he could roast piglets or lambs over the flames.

Each Sunday Bertie would get the fire going and bung on a pig, basting it every twenty minutes or so with his 'secret recipe' of fat, salt and brandy; it made for the best crackling I've ever tasted. Add Heather's bain-marie of veggies, some fresh bread and all the wine you wanted, and it made for the perfect Sunday arvo. People came from Horsham, Stawell and Halls Gap – even Melbourne. It was brilliant! After the dishes were all cleared away, Mul's band would play a set or two for entertainment and the drinks flowed.

Bert was the standout though. The consummate 'mine host' – cigar dangling between his index and big finger and a tumbler of Scotch in hand. Somewhat Lee Van Cleef-esque from the Western movies, he was a brilliant storyteller – especially when it came to **anything** about dearest 'Heady' (Heather). Funnily and rather aptly they referred to each other as 'Basil' and 'Sybil', and many antics up at The Troopers were, indeed, approaching those at *Fawlty Towers*.

It seems that they'd been destined for one another. Bertie had been a helicopter pilot in the Dutch army during the Six-Day War and Heady was a volunteer in a nearby kibbutz. One day Bert copped a bullet in his ankle so had to ditch his chopper, and as the rotor blades slowed to a stop he hopped out – right on to a land mine ... took his 'good' leg clean off just below the knee. His designated carer was one Heather Williams. She spent months nursing him back to health and he was eventually discharged with honours and a lifetime disability pension.

Now I must add a caveat to some of Bert's tales, as we were generally falling around in fits of pissed laughter and he wasn't averse to 'hamming things up' a tad – plus how I even recall some parts is a mystery. Any case, Heady would often correct certain events as Bert told them so please have the salt shaker to hand for this chapter.

Fortuitously, many years later their paths crossed again – in London. Bert had made his way to Britain via Greece and during the journey, having 'run into some trouble' (as he put it), had fled across some mountain pass in the dead of night hauling two enormous sacks of US $100 bills, a home-made prosthetic limb strapped to his stump. I gathered it wasn't **his** money ('technically') and he intimated he was 'dead meat' if he got caught.

Heady was from 'darn sarth' and was spending some time in her native London – they bumped into each other somewhere in the West End. They decided to travel together, so cleared out Heady's bedsit, did a moonlight flit, and shot off in Bertie's wheels. However, they soon parted and went off in opposing directions – so his story went. Yet bizarre things do happen: six or seven years later, with no contact having been maintained, Heady – an avid reader – was browsing her way around a fusty little second-hand bookshop in Parramatta, in Sydney's Western Suburbs of all places, when who else should hobble in but Albertus Gerart Willem Berendsen – Bert. They reunited and moved to Adelaide, South Australia, where Bert plied his trade as a plumber, but fell afoul of the militant construction unions and got black-banned. He was driving home one afternoon and got held up down a back street coz it was packed with people at a property auction. He switched the engine off, got out and observed the proceedings from the back of a large crowd. The hammer was down for the second time but a shrill whistle was heard over everyone's head and Bertie went an extra grand. Ended up owning the joint, did it up, and sold it for a healthy profit. They then came across an interesting place for sale over in the Grampians, Victoria – 120 acres. Unsealed roads and no electricity or piped water, but at least a phone line to the outside world … picked it up for a song and lived off the land for years.

Next they jointly made their first master strokes. Heady was lobbying the state government for funding to seal (Tarmac) the dirt road and it got up – the minister even came across to their place to shake hands for the press photographers, and Roses Gap started to become popular with the tourists.

Meanwhile Bertie was limping around clearing trees, knocking string-line pegs into the ground and digging great big holes. He had a vision and when Bert got something in his head that was it: period! Day after day he dug, laid steel mesh and had concrete mixers turning up from Horsham to pour the foundations and floor slab. Upended his two pre-prepared thirty-foot gum tree support columns then commenced the build in earnest. Three and a half years. That's over *one thousand, two hundred days* he toiled, yet still had no permit from the shire council. 'The Greenies' objected and hired a high-priced lawyer from Melbourne to battle their case. Bertie simply said: 'Fuck 'em, this is MY land, and I'll do what I want with it … ' He was, is, like that – so just plugged away diligently at his project. Drainage, sanitation, plumbing, electrics, fire safety – the works – all 'to code' and to Australian standards, and he had the certificates to prove it, so invited the council out for an inspection and an evening by the fireside.

He was facing not only a compulsory demolition order but a hefty fine as well, but between the pair of them they must've put on a great spread and within days they had retrospective planning and building permits. The nice man from the liquor licensing board signed them off for selling wine too, so The Troopers Arms was able to open at last. The councillors from Horsham became regular patrons and via 'wheels within wheels' Bert and Heady were granted a general liquor licence, which meant they could also sell beers and spirits. And how the crowds came! Heady even registered the barn with the tourist board in Horsham, so they had coaches pulling in for afternoon teas most days.

Needless to say The Greenies acted up again and rehired the lawyer to put a halt to tourism. Thing was, the proponents of that nonsensical and aggrieved legal action all lived in Melbourne and were supposedly wealthy legal or medical practitioners, and their nearby holiday homes were used perhaps three times a year. Thankfully, common sense prevailed.

I became a regular and always had unit 5 reserved for me. Even my own keys to it and to the pub, so I could open up if I got there early. Heady would do the touristy day shift whilst Bert was up the gully chopping firewood or fiddling with the generator, and we'd play endless games of Scrabble and scull wine at the bar. Bert would come into his element at night and keep the whole place buzzing until the last stragglers left. 'Don't drive, here's the key to unit 2. It's empty. No charge.'

Eleven weekends in a row I once made it up there – leaving the big, polluted city mid-morning and doing the pre-dawn drive back at five on a Monday morning. Probably shouldn't have really, but never got pulled over or passed a booze bus once.

Late one particularly debauched evening, in definite *Fawlty Towers* mode with me playing the hapless 'Manuel', Bert and I were slumped in armchairs in front of the fire after everyone had left. It would've been five in the morning or thereabouts. He had a bottle of Scotch and another Amanda (cigar), me Baileys and a Longbeach Fine (fag). Both utterly plastered and one-eyed, he pulled out a thick roll of banknotes from his top pocket – several grands' worth and said: 'Been a huge weekend Andy my boy,' and promptly threw the whole lot in the fire.

'Basil!' I slurred loudly, and dived in head first, taking all the hair off both arms and fishing out a lump of melted 'gloop' (our notes are plastic). Probably saved about four hundred bucks. 'Sybil's gonna kill you for that,' but 'Basil' was emotional and lamented that money was evil, hated it and he only ran the pub for everyone's enjoyment. 'Ya daft old Dutch bugger,' I said and put my arm around his shoulder and gave him a squeeze and a kiss on the forehead and he hit me on mine with a spoon.

The generator ran out of fuel and we were suddenly plunged into what light the dying embers emitted, so decided to call it a night and toddle off. On the drunken starlit stagger back up the track to the house, giggling insanely the whole way, Bert hit the deck seven times, myself three. 'Ah Bertie, you're a one-off my friend, goodnight ... ' splat. Damn! Fourth fall.

Sadly, circumstances conspired against them. Bushfires ravaged the Grampians – luckily not too close to their property – then the global financial crisis hit, and the tourists stopped coming.

They sold what was left of any stock and the bank called in their loan, but with true stoicism and disregard for convention they took it on the chin and hung a *For Sale* sign up on the gate. A fight promoter from Melbourne bought the entire place and turned it into a residential training camp for his stable of boxers, but it didn't last long so apparently was boarded up and abandoned and fell into disrepair. What a shame!

I'll always remember those lovely days spent at The Troopers. Bertie and Heady had Caddie, their trusty Blue Heeler. She was getting on a bit but became a great ball-playing friend. Though I've never been a dog lover (much prefer cats) Caddie was the exception to that rule and we'd play and play then lie in the sun exhausted – her chin on my chest, drooling.

They had Fritz too, a sulphur-crested cockatoo who lived in his cage behind the pub – been there for many, many years. He was apparently quite vicious as a chick and would attack people at random, so was sentenced to life behind bars. Quite a big bird he was too, stood well over a foot tall on his branch inside a cage that was no bigger than the size of your everyday fridge-freezer. Every time I was up there I'd sit next to Fritz's cage and we'd natter away like old chums, often for hours on end. I'd sneak him out treats and would poke my fingers through the mesh and he'd playfully nibble away. 'There's nothing vicious about you is there Fritzy, eh?' One day I broke Heather's golden rule and opened the cage door. Fritzy marched out in almost military fashion and scratched around pecking at the dirt, then to my delight hopped on to my outstretched foot, clawed his way up my leg and torso and nuzzled up close on my shoulder, nibbling away at my earring and chattering away like a mad old fool. Heady came out looking for me and was floored at the sight. She was the only person who could ever get anywhere near Fritz – not even Bert could, so I was indeed honoured.

'Bloody hell, And. How the heck ... ?'

Thankfully she wasn't cross with me. Our man-bird friendship blossomed over the ensuing months; wherever I was on the vast property I was reassured coz Fritz would follow and be perched in a nearby tree watching over me almost protectively. Quite surreal it was. It wasn't long before he was allowed out more often – he had my Friday afternoon arrivals timed to a tee and was always perched on the same branch overhanging the car park when I pulled in. Even before Heather, Bert and I had hugged, he'd swoop down, land at my feet chattering nonsensical but perfectly understandable English whilst doing his little excited 'crouch and wing flap' dance. Once I'd grabbed a beer and sat down we'd catch up on the 'goss'.

Therein lies the rub, though. Fritz had mellowed, was behaving himself exceptionally well, so was allowed to sit in the bar and oversee proceedings, except (inevitably) he got corrupted by too many pissed idiots and picked up the foulest language. He certainly had a pair of lungs on him and would squawk out loudly: 'Fuck off tourists, fucking tourist bastards … Wankers, wankers … ' and similar phrases and one day he just wasn't there to greet me. I wandered around the property and local surrounds for over two hours calling out for him but he simply never came. Heady reckoned he'd probably found a mate and flown off back to bird-world, but Bertie confided later that Fritz wasn't good for business – what with his abusive language – and had to go; so he'd wrung his neck and tossed him into the bush. I was beyond gutted.

RIP Fritz.

Katie and Koo lived on the vast acreage as well.

My younger sister Lizzie and her husband Simon came to Oz to visit Dave and me. They'd had ten days in Sydney and been walking in the Blue Mountains (which is a total misnomer coz they're green for heaven's sake – with orangey cliffs) and were now down in Melbourne with me.

'I'm taking you to the Gramps, I've booked the lodge.' Chinaman's Lodge was another Bertie master-build on the property. Two storeys, overlooking the dam, and like the stunning show homes you'd see in architectural magazines and real estate sales brochures. It slept a dozen in luxury and you could sit on the back veranda and watch as the emus waded into the water and settled down to cool off – just their heads popping out like periscopes.

Incredibly, Liz was yet to see a kangaroo (except for roadkill on the drive up) so I called over to Bert at the bar.

'Is Katie at home Bert?'

'Yeah mate, watching telly as usual.'

'Any chance of introducing her to Liz?'

'Who's Katie, And? Their daughter?'

'Yeah, I suppose so. You'll see in a minute Sis.'

'Come on lass,' Bert said, 'I'll take you up to the house. Andy, can you watch the bar till Heady gets back from Horsham?'

As they entered the kitchen via the rear sliding door Bertie called out and Lizzie heard a sudden loud thud followed by evidence from her own eyes:

boing, boing, and boing as Katie the kangaroo bounced in. Liz leapt out of her skin and jumped behind Bert, terrified. 'Don't worry Liz, she's tame as a pussycat,' and he proceeded to hug and play-wrestle with the five-foot-tall upstanding beast. 'Want some of Caddie's bickies Katie? Here ya go Liz, put some of these in her bowl.'

Liz got back down to the bar and was absolutely buzzing: 'Si, Si, they've got kangaroos – *living in their house!*'

Katie's partner, Koo, was the dominant male of the mob, and when Heather pointed him out to me one day it was fascinating to observe how he protected Katie and kept the young males at bay. Every morning after a chilly night out in the paddock and a bellyful of foraged plants, Koo would lead Katie back to the house, open the sliding door, *close it behind them!* and perambulate through the kitchen using front arms and tail, down the hallway and hop up on to 'their' couch in the living room, to then curl up preening one another whilst watching the ABC on TV. Now caveats aside, I can vouch for this as I was regularly up at the house when the roos were 'in residence'. Remarkable, truly!

Sometimes, Bertie told me, Koo would come in to his room just before dawn and jump up to sleep next to him, 'cept often as not Bert ended up being shoved off on to the floor coz Koo was massive and took up most of the bed. Bert wasn't a big sleeper anyway and could survive on one or two hours' a night as long as he got a 'nanna-nap' every afternoon. He'd explained once that, like so many war veterans, he suffered harrowing recurring nightmares, so sleep was a place he was loathe to go. There is, of course, an extremely deep and far more serious side to Bert and Heather – neither being fools – so whilst 'Basil and Sybil' are both here with us in this light-hearted context, my deep-seated friendships with Bert and Heather were cemented during conversations and observations of 'the world' on far higher planes (even sober once or twice – ha!).

Koo was one bloody fine specimen. About seven feet tall when he lent back on his tail and play-boxed with Bert; had the most vicious claws – a good few inches long, and razor sharp. Rip you clean open right down the guts with one swipe he could, but Bertie never received so much as an accidental scratch.

Neither Katie nor Koo were purposely domesticated as adolescents, nor raised as pets it should be said, rather pulled out of their respective dead mothers' pouches as six-inch-long joeys – the mums having hopped in front of trucks up on the highway. So they'd been hand-reared on formula then let loose into the wild where Bert and Heather knew they belonged, probably not to survive – but 'leave that to nature'. They just came back to the house every night that's all, so what could one do?

A few years ago and just after B and H had moved away, I heard a rumour that the 'new' new owners hadn't bargained on two 'roos living with them, and one day two shotgun blasts were heard ricocheting down the valley.

I was saddened beyond belief.

RIP Katie, RIP Koo.

Even sadder, The Troopers Arms itself was lost in the January 2014 bush fires.

The entire place.

Razed.

Gone.

I struggled to grasp the fact that *it's simply not there anymore* but found the courage in March 2015 to drive out for a 'go see', and there really was *nothing*!

The entire district – all the way up the ridge (which exposes myriad 'hidden' cliffs!) – looked lunar, but for Bert's shattered concrete slab and a few of his rusty old bolts (I took one as a keepsake) which held the roof and wall framing together, and the two steel brackets he made to support the columns that held it all up – deformed and wilted by the extreme heat, lying amongst the charred (and bulldozed to one side) remains of all that effort.

If every bead of Bert and Heather's sweat – and likely the gallons of tears shed with frustration whilst building that amazing property – had been held in a tank, the Country Fire Authority may've been able to save the place; but they weren't, so they couldn't. The bushfires were so bad the fire service didn't even get close.

Yes, all gone … but never the twenty-plus years of memories for Bert and Heather, nor the delightful little book that she'd written about them. I was so hugely privileged to share in their final five years at The Troopers Arms.

Caddie the dog passed away in her sleep one night a few years ago and is buried on their new 400-acre property way out east. Nine hours' drive away and, sadly, too far to visit every weekend.

RIP Caddie.

Another bushfire – over their way, so *another* 400 burnt-out acres (out of thousands I'll add) 'cept this time Bert's five-year, two-storey masterpiece is made from Mount Gambier limestone, and whilst everything around he and Heady became cinders – as far as the eye can see – both they and the house survived. Some neighbours had no chance. Harsh this place! The landscape is sprouting new green buds so will regenerate as Mother Nature dictates. Heather said that on the phone, and added that sadly their little kitten was taken by a snake the other day.

RIP puddy-tat.

With 'Mum' Marion Delaney in Horsham on the last day of my first trip to Australia. **Photo**: Simon Mentz.

21.

NATIMUK REVISITED

Goatfest 2015

I never knew this Natimuk climbers' film night even existed.

There's a hundred and eighty-odd of us packed into the village hall enjoying curry and drinks before the lights dim and a series of six or seven 3- to 12-minute local shorts are shown before an intermission. The film show then culminates in the terrific *Valley Uprising* movie from Yosemite in California, USA.

The next bit – a stand-out short – was a rerun of a recorded 'great debate' from Sydney in 2014, and starred amongst others Nati's own Si Mentz and a hilarious American chap named Crazy John – 'CJ'. It was pants-wetting funny, and afterwards Si introduced me to CJ who was back in Victoria – and now working *Punks in the Gym* ... we compared notes and commiserations!

Goatfest was a resounding success. I met up once again with the two Steves – Monks and Findlay from Bristol, and to top it all I bumped into Charlie Creese whom I'd not spoken to for donkey's years, since being deeply offended by something he'd exaggerated. It was great to make peace with Chaz over coffees on that drizzly, cold morning, beneath umbrellas outside where I could smoke. Charlie mailed me recently reminding me of some slight 'difficulties' we'd en-countered during the early stages of our 'relationship' (if you can call it that!) ...

> I'm still very attached to what you said with regards to dossing at my place on Cardigan St – that after a couple of nights you realised it was either you or me – one of us had to go! Fucken funny!

Time to leave.

Hateful four-and-three-quarter-hours' drive with shocking Easter traffic and wiper blades most of the way. I can't wait for Goatfest 2016.

MANY HAPPY RETURNS

Wow! Nati twice in three weeks, two decades after leaving the place for the last time.

This second time I wandered around for ages amongst the boulders beneath the crag. I was searching for my old problem *Mudie Blues* but couldn't find it – anywhere – so rang Dave Mudie down in Geelong but he couldn't remember its whereabouts either.

So I mooched around the campsite asking various parties whether they had any of the guidebooks and if so could I please briefly check something out. Gosh people are strange! The first lot was a group of three lads dossing around in their own mess watching a coffee pot bubbling on a gas stove; the one who could even be arsed just grunted 'No,' and, barely looking up, flicked a shirt on to his **Arapiles Guidebook** with outstretched foot. 'Precious twit' (or something similar) I thought, so kept walking.

This was **not** the spirit of climbing I once knew and loved and when recounting the event to others later they were equally surprised. Next was better: 'I do, but the girlfriend has it over at the crag I'm afraid. What are you looking for?' He didn't know *The Blues* though. Lastly, a friendly German-accented couple (she was knitting, he was whittling a piece of wood into **the** most amazing skeletal hand) happily passed over their copy of the superb, glossy book that Simon Mentz and Glenn Tempest had produced, but I became so engrossed I totally forgot to check out the bouldering section.

Talk about a 'blast from the past' this trip. Before departing Melbourne I'd fished out a bunch of old cassette tapes – the ones I'd play over and over and over in my caravan, nightly, having failed on *Punks in the Gym* for the twenty-ninth to forty-third day over a period of three weeks, my visa expiry date looming ever nearer. As I write this little piece Talk Talk are blaring out 'Living in Another World'. **I am these days**!

An enormous night in the Natimuk pub (including a three-quarter bottle of port), grogging-on back at some friends' place later, and a very pissed stagger through the dark and deserted town at a quarter to two in the morning wondering where the heck I was staying and bitterly cold in just a loose-fitting cotton shirt, yet happy as the proverbial pig in shit.

It's today proper now – the sun's up and nipping at my alabaster-skinned and somewhat podgy fifty-one-year-old body. Better buy factor 15 when I go to get more ice for my Esky – already crammed full to the brim with the day's refreshments. Wine and eighteen bottles of James Boag's Premium Lager is what'll sustain me between the hours of 7 a.m. and 2 p.m. whence I'll take a nanna-nap, wake up 'sound as a pound' and do it all over again this evening. (Reminder to self: have a piece of toast, or *something* at least.)

Yes! I can drink, though evidently only to excess.

As I often jest, 'No, I can't do 8b+ anymore but I can do 8 **beers** plus, and do so on a regular basis.' Ha!

MOVED TO TEARS (THEN TAKEN FOR DINNER)

It's *Mudie* not *Moody*

Yey! Found it! Well *I* didn't, but old chum and sometimes employee Marlon's young son did – the boulder's location is actually tucked inside the rear fold-in cover flap of the guidebook – so ta Aris.

It was this stand-alone fifteen-foot-high triangular boulder Dave Mudie had shown me back in the early nineties, with an obvious undercut about ten feet up and some crimpy crimps (what did you expect from a crimp?) just below the top on its overhanging side, so I set about bouldering it out. It took a while but soon I could nail it time and time again, even though some of my local friends couldn't quite stick it. I named it *Mudie Blues* in Dave's honour. No idea what V grade it should get as they weren't invented back then, but it was bloody hard (well, *ish*).

Patrick Edlinger repeated it (embarrassingly) almost statically, followed a year or so later by both Jerry Moffatt and Sean Myles – easily, but nobody else ever did to my knowledge. I wonder whether nowadays it's on many people's circuit. Probably not, too easy.

Quite a few years past (but since my day) it appears the old track was shut to vehicular traffic as part of the rotating bush-rejuvenation process, hence I simply couldn't work out how I'd driven right up to it. It isn't a long walk, five minutes tops, but it wasn't chalked. For such an ace problem too. The guide stated that, at the time of publication, the direct version (which I'd christened *Mean 'n' Mudie*) had still not been done (I actually did it once, but with a little push on my lower back from a mate so couldn't claim it). Both problems looked as good and hard as I remember them, though *Mudie Blues* was credited as a very lowly V6 and the name mistakenly recorded as *Moody*.

So, returning to The Pines I parked up next to H's van awaiting his return from the cliff, plunged my hand into the crushed ice and hopped on to my bonnet – beer, notebook and pen in hand – and sat in the sun for about three hours. There I wrote these past few pages – *and myself off in the process.*

I'd stranded myself out at The Mount without a hope in hell of daring to drive back to Nati. Thankfully, a delightful couple were heading in for tea so she (A) drove theirs and he (K) mine. Talk about 'small worlds' – he worked for one of the big architectural firms I occasionally consult to and I suppose I ought to have been somewhat embarrassed as I was half-cut, but nothing of the sort and we had a right old laugh.

Dinner was at The Natimuk Cafe – a wonderful place run by Glenn and Karen Tempest and partners – and it was H's shout. Ta Malcolm. I had the smallest thing on the 'specials' board and Malcolm ate two full-on mains. He still has a voracious appetite – some things never change – though he did have a glass or two of red which he'd never have dreamt of twenty-five years ago, so *that* bit has. It was indescribably good to be back in H's company.

Yeah, my last note in my book the other evening was how I felt Nati was/is simply 'the gift that keeps giving' and for tomorrow I've reserved a table for two at the hotel for a Very Special lunch date. Yep! It's 'Mum' – Marion Delaney's coming over from Nhill and it'll be fourteen years, eight months and three days between hugs!

YESTERDAY

No, not the famous rock climb of the same name here at Araps – I never did that one, I mean the day before today.

'My Mum' (always 'Mrs D' to pretty much everyone else) arrived bang on noon and we had a delightful reunion. I 'lost it' and cried on her shoulder as we hugged, but Marion held it together brilliantly. 'Sorry 'bout the damp shoulder Mum ... '

Bill and Anne – proprietors – put on a lovely feed, then Marion and I went for a drive around the bone-dry lake. 'Dreadful isn't it – remember all the swimmers and water skiers?'

'Yeah, very sad. Look at that child at the end of the jetty – fifteen feet above parched weeds.'

On the run back to town we passed Noddy's place and he was out in the garden with one of his grandchildren and the son-in-law, so Marion pulled over and we got out for a catch-up. I never knew Nod had written the definitive history book of The Mount – *Arapiles: a million mountains* – which covers everything from the Aboriginal Dreamtime, through early white settlers, graziers, the gold rush, fauna and flora, right up to its status as a world-renowned climbing mecca. It's a riveting and engrossing read and brilliantly illustrated, so I bought one on the spot.

We had a post-departure coffee at the cafe and Glenn T kindly took the twenty-four-years-later 'happy snap' of Mum and me. Ta Glenn.

WHAT'S *YOUR* PROBLEM?

I never really got into bouldering at Arapiles, or the Gramps, even though I was surrounded by some of the best areas in the world – not that I ever really did back home either coz it was too much like hard work, hurt a lot and was mainly in winter. Brrr!

That is of course until someone sensible (therefore most likely Simey) suggested on the regular trudge from my caravan towards – you know, work, the 'PiG' thing – that maybe I should 'warm up first this time?'

'Oh, look, there's *Around the World*, Andy.'

The boulder problem christened *A-t-W* has a great little left-to-right maybe eight-move traverse just inches off the ground and it had some ace heel hooks and cross-overs, definitely a good warm-up. Odd thing is I became somewhat besotted with it, and would wander over from my caravan as soon as it was in the shade and chuck laps on it pretty much every other night. This was sober, pissed, stoned or sore from (occasionally) bonk … err, 'training'. No matter, I always bettered my previous record.

So, it was just the low, left-to-right traverse (as the up, left and back down bit was rubbish and a waste of time); eventually I could do this great little traverse totally footless. One early evening, I wandered up there in my sand shoes as usual and saw some lads working it (with 'feet' as was customary). I sat there with a longneck in one hand and a ciggie in the other, watching and giving some encouragement. After a while I was somewhat sarcastically invited to join in with their attempts. My face was shaded from the sun by the wide black brim of my Akubra and whether they recognised 'me' or not was completely immaterial, although I don't believe they did … thank goodness …

Seconds later – having flicked it off footless and getting my beer back from its slightly stunned and muscular holder – I toddled off feeling all smug and smart-as. They weren't to know it was my favourite boulder, a rock I'd played that game on dozens of times … Looking back, that *was* a bit *off* really!

It became a bit of a 'party piece' that problem, and over the ensuing weeks I'd lap it five times, then twelve, then nineteen, twenty-four, thirty-one and finally fifty-five – before getting blasé and mucking it up on my fifty-sixth straight, footless crossing.

Honestly, I was in abject shock, standing upright on the ground within a millisecond, wondering 'what just happened?' So many laps and I'd lost concentration. Fatal to the cause!

Fifty-five footless left-to-rights on the minute would have to do. Damn. I wanted the 'big 6-o'. A hundred even? This was on Saturday 25 January 1991. What were you doing that day? Being born probably some of you … or at least planned?

5 AND ¾ INCHES

Well I hate to brag but that's what I was naturally endowed with. Lucky boy!

I recall from years ago an interesting incident with a near neighbour of mine in Sheffield – a very young, orange-dye-haired Zoe Brown – daughter of the original mythical 'Master' Joe, who, would you believe, I never, ever met. In all those years in North Wales – Llanberis in particular! Nah, maybe he *was* just a myth after all? Anyway, Zoe measured me up one day over at no. 124 – in front of witnesses I might add! And oh! How we fell about in hysterics, particularly as most of us were ridiculously stoned and Zoe scored a minus two inches …

Yeah, the old 'ape index' served me well on many an occasion it did, so of course I used it to maximum effect – wherever possible. HB's *Gilgamesh* on Lower Taipan being the classic example, where for me it felt probably a 31 but for H two grades beyond.[1]

Excuse me while I attempt a funny segue regarding apes and climbing, but on that recent return visit to Natimuk and the Grampians I (very poorly) guided Tim and Angel Freeman out to Hollow Mountain so we could all touch the holds and pay homage to *The Wheel of Life Direct*.

Now *The Wheel Direct* is a horizontal roof problem with probably sixty-plus moves, and goes on and on then on **and on** some more. Bloody amazing stuff and I like to watch the YouTube video of James Kassay, a local Melbourne climber, floating across it to an equally good backing track. I don't think I've had the pleasure of making his acquaintance, but my old boss Geoff hired James for a hilarious job he'd priced and won at Werribee Zoo. The newly constructed ape enclosure was pretty much ready for hand-over by the builder and was by all accounts a massive simian-proof pit with 'inescapable' retaining walls topped by high fences. Geoff had been approached by zoo management to come over and see if this new addition was escape-proof for monkeys, so invited the young Kassay along for a day's work at one of the world's most contemporary ape exhibits. I gather they waved James into the pit, but before the TV news cameraman had focussed the lens this ace climber was metaphorically tapping him on the shoulder going, 'Piece of cake … ' He'd gotten out in literally seconds and the engineers and consultants, I'm sure, would've been thinking 'crikey' or far worse. With somewhat red faces. I know I would!

---

1 *Editor's note*: A neutral ape index is when your outstretched arms, fingertip to fingertip, are equal in measurement to your height. In rock climbing it is most helpful to have a positive, ape-like, index – anything over four inches is a whopper!

With the *Knockin'* peg. **Photo:** Ian Smith.

22.
CAN'T YOU HEAR ME KNOCKIN'?

(Written 27 October 2013.)

So, here I am at Palm Cove in FNQ (Far North Queensland). Fifty years and one day old. My sixty-three-kilogram frame oiled up beneath a palm tree away from the crowds, with nine more days of annual leave still to come, mobile phone *switched off*. Thirty-four degrees in the shade and a mere twenty feet across hot sand to an azure ocean lapping gently against the shore. Exactly as the photos in the brochures depict. Certainly a far cry from Prestatyn's breezy beach back in North Wales.

A dip every ten minutes to cool down, then back to writing the book I hope may be published one day, and to my bag of crisps and freshly made sandwiches I packed this morning.

Between scribbles I'm reading *Life*, the autobiography of Keith Richards, iconic Rolling Stones guitarist … the name of this chapter is taken from one of his songs. His book's a really good read – helped me while away the four-hour flight up here from Melbourne, complete with nicotine patches on both arms, my chest and almost, not quite, one slap-bang in the middle of my forehead – and I'll finish it before the sun goes down and the bronzed beauties wearing nothing but string leave the beach in an hour or so. Some of those bikinis are ridiculous and I think 'Why bother?' But … then again.

Absorbed in 'Keef' … I must get a third electric guitar I muse and set it up as an open-tuned five-string – so that's how he does it! No 'muso' friend of mine ever explained that, and this Richards 'cat' has been doing it for over fifty years! Explains a lot. However, his unique style is complimented by Ronnie Wood who fills in the lead solos. Ronnie's *bloody* brilliant on the old 'leccie' guitar too, and you should check out his paintings – seriously stunning. If you appreciate that style.

I was always a Stones man, never a Beatles one really – although obviously there are many genius Lennon, McCartney and Harrison compositions as exceptions to that rule – but Bob Dylan was my long-time favourite. I think Bob Dylan must've admired some of my new routes too – I mean, who else has so many songs named after their first ascents? OK, apologies, please don't groan like that, it's just my attempted link to this chapter's title.

I'm giving my poor eyes a rest, even though this dappled light beneath my palm tree is perfect for reading in (with my 4x specs) and my mind's drifting (a trifle stoned now) back to the good old days at home – when I was in my twenties … and fifty, let alone 'middle-aged', seemed a *lifetime* away.

There were always – and undoubtedly still are – 'last great problems', particularly on England's gritstone, and one day I chose to have a dip at one of them. I was never really 'that way inclined' as a climber, preferring the endless cranking up steep limestone over the balancy rock-overs and slapping up gritstone arêtes, so this one was a real departure from my norm.

To the left of *Elder Crack* on Curbar is an overhanging prow, so I abbed it and it wasn't that hard. The problem was gaining it, even though the gear was bombproof and overhead in the crack. Its technicalities involved leaning well outwards off a foot jam, pinching the arête, then letting the foot jam go and dragging your toes across the wall to slow down the swing. I couldn't manage it, but have watched Steve McClure's video and that's the precise sequence I was trying – though I noticed on a repeat ascent on video that there's a very precise and lightning-fast hand change by young James Pearson which, if timed perfectly, stops the body's momentum spitting you off. It's a romp from there to the top and no danger of decking out. Except I couldn't hold that desperate swing. Perhaps I would have, given time, but I never bothered putting in any more effort after a few tries on lead. So I turned my attention to the steep, ex-army target-practice slab to the right and, when out with Nick Plishko one day, threw my abseil rope down that instead – as many had previously, each and every one shaking their heads and going, 'Bugger, no way!' Nick and I did a couple of the moves, but it was 'Bugger, no way!' too. 'Or *is* there?'

Hanging there experimenting with my 'Stop' locked off, I discovered that at this particular angle I could just about stay in touch with the rock and in balance on every little indented half- or one-finger bullet scar and smear, as long as the other hand and both feet were exactly where they needed to be

– but the real problems were the links between these positions, which were all extremely balancy and involved critical foot placements. Bloody desperate they were each one – as Scotch Ben agreed the next visit and where I made real progress and top-roped it with just one fall. I really struggled to work these links out, but by day three with Yorick I had a sequence that would take me from bottom to top – slap-bang straight up the middle of the wall – provided it was executed with extreme precision.

As for protection, well, I had two options: fit side-runners by nipping off into *Elder Crack* at half height, or pre-place a tiny blade peg in a little horizontal slot in the centre of the slab and hope for the best. I opted for the latter, placed the peg with two gentle taps of the wooden butt of my hammer, and left a six-inch tearaway quickdraw on it. Years later Graham Hoey and Phil Kelly sought my comments about the first ascent for their soon-to-be stunning *Peak Rock* book: I explained it wasn't a hammered peg, nor was it a good one. You could flick it out from the ground and, in any case, I *wanted* it to be shit coz that's what I was all about at the time – the book came out and the authors had fairly and honestly quoted me verbatim, thanks guys! The little slot was perfectly parallel and the tiny blade I used simply slid inside and sat there. A slightly larger and tapered Lost Arrow could've been used but would have needed bashing in, thus scarring the rock and leaving a difficult but safe-as-houses route against all the traditional protocols about no fixed pegs on natural grit.

Fourth day on the route I top-roped it three times in succession and decided it was 'now or never'. You get that feeling sometimes when psyching up for bold leads and I always went with my gut instinct – no matter whether the conditions were perfect or not, although on this day they were just right, being cold, crisp and with a gentle breeze. If *I'm* 'not right' in my head I'll postpone the day and go elsewhere – that way of thinking has possibly saved my skin on more than one occasion. Sensing when the time's 'wrong' is equally as critical as knowing when it's 'right'.

I set off on lead, clipped the little peg's tearaway lanyard at full stretch, then ballet-danced a technical sequence of foot moves rightwards through the crux to set myself up perfectly for the all-out dyno – Bdoiiiing! Gotcha. I'd caught the big sloper (where it's all over bar about E1 to the top) and was overjoyed, but then slipped at the very finish which I hadn't brushed properly, and was momentarily airborne. My right arm shot out instinctively as I was in mid-air, falling, and I latched on to that big sloper and managed to hold it. A gripping few minutes shaking out and I made it through the finish. I looked back down, gave my rope a little flick and sent the peg tinkling down the rock face to the bottom – saving myself another abseil – and then down-soloed an easy route to the right to get to the deck and a couple of celebratory cigarettes with Yoz.

I figured it was E8 7a for me but gave it E9 for the on-sight and felt it was by far the hardest and neckiest route I'd ever done, let alone perhaps my second proudest contribution to British climbing after *The Hollow Man* back on North Stack Wall – the lack of meaningful protection again only adding to the occasion. This was the late eighties remember and most of today's ascentionists were likely either unborn or just toddling around at the time. I see some of their videos now and there's a top-rope or high side runner in a couple of them. I can't pick where it is but it certainly stops the young lad from decking out and two enormous whippers are taken on to it! What the heck's *that* style called these days? Not that I'd like anyone to get seriously hurt or die, but to me that style simply doesn't count as an E8 lead, let alone E9. Not even a **lead** really. Sorry kids, it just doesn't. Not in *my* book – certainly not in this one anyway! Another 'young un' – Ben Tetler – soloed it in 1999 I believe, so I'll pass the cred to him for that. Having said that though, he only really did precisely what I'd done over a decade earlier with weaker fingers and less sticky rubber – just climbed it. Bottom to top, straight up the middle, and didn't fall off – sure the moves are hard … but *not falling off* is the smartest move anyone can make on this route!

In their respective *Peak Rock Notes* magazine columns, even my housemate Chris Gore and that shrewd observer Neil Foster conceded that the route was a bold and quality outing – yep, gave me a good write up for *Knockin' on Heaven's Door* as I'd named it, so it must've been really something. Yet, along with Basher, Chris continued to wind me up, saying things like, 'Good effort Andy, but yer still not as good as Pete Gomersall!'

'Yes I fckn am, I'd be way higher than him in a top twenty list,' I moaned, but then they reminded me that Mark Edwards had already done an E9 in Cornwall and I was definitely in the lower half of their (imaginary) list. Teasing bastards! 'That's as maybe lads … Christmas Hamper and I are already planning the repeat of Mark's route, but I'm still better than Gommy – and Edwards is fckn dreaming,' I grumbled and slamming the door went off to bed, listening to their hoots of laughter as I climbed the stairs.

Ron Fawcett claimed a quick repeat of *Knockin'* and according to *High* magazine downgraded it – to a mere E7! 'That's bollocks,' I thought, as Ron had been off with a broken wrist for ages – and this was his comeback route? A few nagging doubts plagued me for a while, but it's a pointless exercise and a waste of brain space – Ron had been up there at the top of the sport for nigh on twenty years and I greatly respected him as a climber – and a top bloke too. OK, well done to Ron for the repeat, but someone saying E7 was nothing more than silly one-upmanship – claiming to have a bigger dick basically. Why not acknowledge that one's climbed something beyond that grade? In Ron's defence, the downgrading fiasco had the unmistakable mark of a certain Mr Birtles written all over it!

So, the route has had an interesting history since 1988. It's now a long time ago that I first led it – then led it again *a further four times* for photos with an 'emergency' belayer stationed out of shot at the top by the way – very scary!

From *Peak Rock* (2013):

> Andy's other route in 1988 not surprisingly fell under the radar despite its eye-catching line and lofty position.

Not surprisingly? How come? Didn't the authors actually mean 'surprisingly'? I was certainly a bit mystified – crikey, it was even on the front cover of *High* magazine for heaven's door, err ... sake, complete with classic Birtles photo description. Ah well, there's no accounting for taste.[1]

I was pretty chuffed to get that 'other' route – *Masters of the Universe* – as it was such a gobsmackingly obvious line taking the prominent hanging prow of the Cioch Block at Burbage. I had to abseil in, as the climb commences about fifty feet off the deck at a little cluster of rusty old bolt heads all tied together with thin Perlon. Throwing the abseil rope away and pulling on to the rock it was over in minutes. A truly memorable and very on-off and quite powerful layback-cum-swing/slap sequence and it's in the bag. Those runners way down below would never hold a fall I figured, but I'd arranged the five-milli-metre slings so the bolt heads would pop in quick succession rather than all fall out simultaneously if I took the monster, and I had my tearaway lanyard clipped to the lowest one. I suggested it could be anywhere between E6 and E9 – it all depended on those bits of rust holding, but I'm led to believe it's set-tled at E6 nowadays but on all subsequent ascents those rusty little 'nipples' have been backed up with a rope from above. Probably rather sensible that. No point in dying or – maybe worse for some – living but fucked up and un-able to walk ... just through trying to make a statement.

Obviously, we all adore our own offspring and those two were my gritstone babies. I was a proud father indeed – felt I'd sired a couple of beauties there – and it's comforting as their creator to know that they're still respectable,

---

1 *Editor's note*: It's a great and subtle thing the English language! Maybe they actually meant 'not surprisingly', considering the special and controversial nature of *Knockin'*?

Author's retort: Yes Andy, I see what you mean, and that's why you're the school teacher and the editor (laughs)!

even well into their twenties. One final observation ... [Tongue in cheek of course? *Ed.*] ... as I flick through my first ascent slides there's not a mat to be seen (let alone a whole stack of 'em) coz we woz 'ard back then – not namby-pamby like nowadays!

Ron Fawcett, as usual, has words of wisdom to add:

> Yes, it is a different world on the grit these days with all the rehearsals, side-runners and multiple mats, but hey ho. Today the boys and girls don't have all those first ascent possibilities we had, so all that matters is the post, photo or film on Facebook.

THE YOUNGSTARS

In one of a million emails Andy B and I have sent toing and froing during the assembly of this humble tome he almost, but not quite, took me to task over my perception that perhaps serious trad was a long-forgotten thing back home in Britain. Some laughable relic of the 1980s perhaps? But this is clearly not so ... There are some stunningly bold young climbers who've embraced and extended *silliness* to degrees far beyond the '80s' slateheads, and any contributions that I ever made 'back in the day'. Having said that, it still appears true that 'us lot' did do some pretty necky stuff when we were young and fit – and daft.

That Johnny Dawes E9 on Cloggy deserves a mention I guess! And the 'youngstars' who've now repeated it ... I distinctly remember Johnny explaining to me that there was a tiny patch of grass on the starting ledge – about the size of a tea towel – where if he fell from less than seventy feet he reckoned he could hit it, do a triple somersault, back-flip with pike and land in the 'lush' boulderfield below ... I replied, 'A grassy patch Johnny? Lucky blighter! There are no such luxurious landings beneath North Stack ... '

I need only to scrape the surface and back-track through *UKC* to see what the likes of Dave MacLeod, Pete Whittaker, Hazel Findlay, James Pearson, James McHaffie, Calum Muskett and Ryan Pasquill et al. are doing out there on the sea cliffs, mountain crags and gritstone edges (these names may be outdated when this is read) to be comforted that proper bold stuff is still on the menu – as tough and tasty as ever. As for the deep-water soloing scene – Tim Emmett, Steve McClure, Neil Gresham and their ilk in particular must surely be 'as mad as a bunch of cut snakes'. (That's actually the wrong 'Aussie-ism' as it means really angry, so how's about I rephrase it to 'barking mad'?) ... Oh! And that Ken Palmer chap should listen to his mum Christine on his video and wear earplugs!

I get severely gripped watching deep-water soloing (DWS) on video, but not for the reasons one may think. Long falls – pah! Been there, done 'em; it's just my complete inability to tread water or swim any distance that has me switching back over to watch Natalija Gros on *Le Tango Vertical*. Now, this is more like it, a bit of class. And oh! ... I just watched a clip of Tim Emmett ice climbing ... underground. Magnificent.

These kids on YouTube and Vimeo all appear to climb heel-first these days – who invented that? We mustn't've had decent heels back in the eighties (rarely hooked unless it was on a great big ledge) but they do it on crimps and everything now (shakes head). Maybe we could've done some seriously hard shit using that manoeuvre, coz by gum we were fit and could pull. Well done evolution – and technology for the ability to watch it all at the click of a mouse.

So what – and also to whom – do we look to, particularly as the future of British climbing (comps aside perhaps)? Comparative to 'my day' I can't keep up with progress. A few weeks ago I got the smiles when watching a young lad named Orrin Coley bouldering at Parisella's – I simply had to smile, after all, this cave was my 'bedroom' decades ago ... 'Oi, shove off, I'm trying to get some sleep!'

He seems a particularly pleasant and cool guy with oodles of talent – and maybe the very same youthful expectations for his future that I'd had at that age ... and in *Parisella's* too but over thirty years earlier. But then I almost choked on my Coco Pops watching Tesni and Celt Lloyd-Jones doing first ascents in the slate quarries. The young lass was thirteen, the lad was ten! I hadn't even *discovered* rock climbing at that age! Blimey! I give up ... [You have done AP, remember? Over twenty years ago. *Ed.*]

EXIT STAGE LEFT ...

It's inevitable, of course... those dashing, youthful looks are now gone, and the womanising stopped years ago when middle age arrived with its flippin' Dupuytren's contracture, various other ailments, colonoscopies and prostate checks ... and now false fucking teeth! These *aren't* the best days of *this* life I tells ya but hey ho – at least (they 'say' it's a sign of potential longevity) I still have all that glorious, long, scraggly hair ... ha!

Securely tucked away at home I have my precious collection of antique slot machines – even one 1929 'nickel grinder' from a genuine speakeasy in Nevada, USA. It was placed there when they were constructing the Hoover Dam in 1930 and discovered decades later during demolition of the original building – secreted away behind a false wall. I've another beauty that's **the very first ever** made in Australia, plus a rare Mills Novelty Co. cast iron 1911 stunner from Chicago, and twelve other really special machines ... but I lost interest in the hobby years ago and can't even give 'em away nowadays! Any 'slotties' out there?

So there we have it: I used to do a bit of climbing, not too shoddy in my day; have made a good living ever since here in multi-storey Melbourne; once nearly became a ***seriously wealthy*** 'Ad Man', but blinked and they'd taken it so I promptly lost the lot. I get my ups and downs, continue now and then to drink and smoke rather too much ... looks like it's nearly time to 'exit stage left' as my father would've advised. I'll say cheerio now and leave you with my 'nemesis' ... and a delightful ending from a fine and valued friend.

'Please don't go.' 'Have to, and promised Jerry and Sean … '

23.

'ME SPUNKY THING', ROPE-a-DOPE (AND THE BIRDBATH KERFUFFLE)

Forty-four 'days' to redpoint *Punks in the Gym* over my three UK to Australia trips over two years.

Cost? Well over ten thousand pounds (at 1990s rates), plus my interest in ever climbing rocks again. Any rocks. Anywhere. Ever again! A high price indeed.

It was Martin Scheel who first conceived and attempted the route in the early eighties. We actually exchanged *letters* between Natimuk and Switzerland once (you know, those things we used to write on bits of paper and put a postage stamp on before popping in the red mailbox and hoping to hear back in three or four weeks – hardly email!). I soon got a reply – this was jolly decent of Martin at the time, as *I* felt *he* felt somewhat 'embarrassed' about the whole damned affair. He wrote that there was originally an in-cut, four-finger 'ear' of rock – the crucial hold in the multi-move crux sequence – but that it snapped off during one of his many attempts, leaving a slightly shorter reach but to a barely usable stump of a hold. He never said it was he who resorted to the chisel, but the end result was a perfect first-joint in-cut hold about two inches wide (unfortunately adding to the other two or three already chipped or improved holds en route).

Wolfgang wouldn't have chipped it *of course*, but the manufactured in-cut was there for his yo-yoed ascent. *Punks* was claimed with great fanfare and written up as the hardest route in the world, with no great ethical questions asked. There were scores of chipped holds at Arapiles back then – and let's not even mention the shenanigans going on up in New South Wales, where many routes were entirely 'created'.

Quite early on in the saga of my efforts to lead *Punks* I was standing on that chipped hold, through the crux, in balance and thinking 'Yey! I'm about to make the first clean ascent of one of the world's hardest and most famous routes', and at 32/F8b+ the hardest I'd ever done too – but it all went horribly wrong. Rushing up the headwall, my left foot skidded off a smear – the unexpected shock load to the middle fingers of my right hand led to a snap, and I peeled off backwards in pain. Within those few airborne seconds, as I was rapidly being slowed by the rope, my left hand was already pressing on the palm of my right, desperately trying to comfort my strained tendons.

I was out of action, so conceded defeat and flew back to Britain – bitterly disappointed – back to the rope access industry and game for anything. Day, night, local or away, as long as it paid. There'd been a fire in a chicken feed pellet manufacturing plant down south and the entire facility had been shut down for about three weeks. Paul 'Tut' Braithwaite's firm had won the job to send abseilers into the three 60-foot-high steel silos. The inferno had baked the contents into a foot-thick crust around the vast circumference of each one, and no amount of prodding with long poles up the mouth of the hopper base would make it fall out.

Fish heads, offal, cows' hoofs and no end of rotten animal matter filled the silos to capacity and had to be bucket and spaded out on haul lines dropped in from the little access hatch at the top. The heat, the maggots and the fermentation generated was bad enough, but the **smell**! My goodness. Numerous times a day I'd nip off for a dry retch and to throw down litres and litres of water. We required completely new shorts, vests and paper sperm suits every shift, and for three weeks Leachy and I stank to high heaven. We simply could not scrub away the reek in the showers each evening. Separately, I should add.

It was a 'live', moving, squelching and backbreaking dig to the bottom, and our 'breathing apparatus' (ha!) consisted of spray-painters' face masks which really didn't do much – so twenty minutes in and twenty out was about our limit. Mark Leach was always great to work with, as were Joe Healey and Matt Saunders for the laughs, and Paul Freeman – Tim's younger brother on the Technitube jobs, coz he was the youngest so took a lot of teasing from us older lads.

Leachy and I had clear personal goals to keep us at it – goals which we'd both e.v.e.n.t.u.a.l.l.y. attain. By the end of the first silo I'd earned my next flight to Oz, and Mark (metaphorically speaking) enough for the off-side front wheel for the Porsche he so desperately desired. The remaining two bins later and Mark could afford a full set of custom rims and I had half the required spends for my next six-month trip down under.

A couple of power station jobs for Technitube and I was just about there. I could almost taste Australia and smell those gum trees again, so just kept up my internal mantra – 'Lake Toolondo then *Punks*, Lake Toolondo then *Punks* … that's why I'm doing this,' – over and over in my head.

I think Mark had saved enough for indicators, a steering wheel and maybe one 'go-faster' stripe. Very patient was our Mark!

Next season … and with *Punks* still not redpointed by anyone – or even a third ascent at all despite a fair few attempts – trip number two really should've been it. However, due to all that back-breaking work over winter in rope access and the fact that my fingers were still sore, my training had suffered badly. Climbing fitness gone and reconnecting with friends (girls and drinkers particularly) I was at a severe disadvantage – and then things really turned to shit: the left side of the crux hold snapped clean off as I rocked over on to it and unbeknown to me a mammoth saga was about to unfold. The route was probably still climbable, but what was left of the hold was gravelly and became prone to crumbling. Eventually it started to look more and more like an untenable proposition – for me anyway, back in the early nineties.

Enter the masterful Patrick Edlinger, whom I'd spent two weeks with on his movie-making trip to Australia (we were old chums – went back over a decade). 'Pa-treek' joined me on *Punks* on two occasions and, despite moving with his typical effortless-looking grace, was spat off virtually every move of the entire crux sequence – again and again. Couldn't hold and change on the busted edge, never mind link much of it. 'Huit bee plus? Non, non – huit ceee for sure Andee,' he proclaimed Frenchly.

Frustrated and annoyed that I could no longer hold that broken edge using the dynamic, arcing right hand slap-over, I reverted to my original way of reaching it left hand first (à la classic Wolfgang photo). Patrick had insisted that was the way to go too. (Apologies to those who haven't been there, those who have will know it well.) Making a desperate hand change on this allowed me to run and hop my right big toe on to what was left of the hold, two fingers at its right hand side to allow space for the tip of my shoe, and rock over into semi-balance. Get to here, stand up and basically you've got it in the bag. I fluffed it once, but next try I was again – for the third time – standing on that hold, above all the hard work and eyeing the belay some twenty feet above.

But *again* it wasn't to be.

There was a creak under my right foot and both the last remnants of what was obviously still a good enough hold and I were airborne. It was absolutely excruciating for me, and my patience was wearing as thin as the skin on my tips. Plus the Grampians were calling …

Fingers trashed, tendons and skin in desperate need of rest and recovery, one more attempt, split another tip, so four days off (partying).

It just wasn't going to happen was it?

Having first bust the good edge back on day six or whatever, and with what little was left of the hold rapidly deteriorating (I was up to my twenty-ninth day by this time), when it crumbled some more on day thirty and my foot shot off **again** I threw my hands in the air in complete frustration. Thus the fateful decision was made: shortly before flying back to the UK I managed to source some Sikadur epoxy from my great mate Dave Mudie in Nati and began experimenting – on a small slab of rock I'd picked up – with various mixtures of red, orange and grey sand from around the campsite.

I'd decided to rebuild the hold rather than fruitlessly keep on trying with that ever-crumbling edge, as this classic testpiece was not only slipping away from *me* but from everyone else as well. If it broke any more then … not even a Moffatt, McClure, Sharma or Ondra could pull on just *nothing*. So I moulded the Sika and left it to harden and cure for two days, just like it said on the packet. No going back now!

A couple of paltry attempts in humid conditions – greasing off the easy start and infuriatingly opening up my unhealed fingertip higher up. One thing's for sure, my efforts on that blessed thing were evidenced by myriad bloodstains – generally around the same two holds.

But time was running out and I had a flight to catch in three days, as Simey reminds us:

> Of all the times that I belayed Andy P on *Punks*, the one time that really sticks in my mind was his final effort on his final day during his second trip to Australia. Andy's life up to this point revolved around a three-day cycle … one day spent attempting *Punks* and then two days 'resting' – this involved hanging out in his caravan, chain-smoking and drinking vast quantities of beer. A typical *Punks* day would see Andy attempt the route three times. And a typical attempt would see him cruise to the crux, fall off, pull back on and cruise to the top. Most onlookers (as well as Andy himself) felt that once he was through the crux then the route was in the bag.
>
> Having clocked up a couple of months of this strange lifestyle, Andy's time in Australia was running out. I offered to belay him on his final day at Arapiles. The day rolled along just like every other day that he had attempted *Punks*. Andy gave three strong attempts with exactly the same result. I lowered him from the crux after this third attempt as light rain began to fall.

He dejectedly announced, 'Well that's it, I can't do this route'.

But the rain didn't last. I suggested to Andy that we meet at the base of the route that evening and I would hold his ropes late for one last effort. He had nothing to lose.

With no one else around that evening Andy started up *Punks* for an un-characteristic fourth attempt for the day. Expectations were low as Andy climbed the first half of the route. After launching into the crux he then managed something he had never done previously [whilst Simey had been belaying him. *Ed.*] – *he didn't fall*. Moving past the crux he continued through the well-rehearsed top section. As I fed out the rope I started licking my lips in anticipation of the celebratory beers we would be enjoy-ing that evening, but it soon became apparent that Andy had very little left in the tank. His strength was fading and with only one move to gain the jug that marked the end of the difficult climbing Andy's elbows began to creep outwards as he struggled to maintain contact with the rock. His body sagged, then retensioned, then sagged, before one final lunge … but it wasn't enough.

The fall was silent. There was no screaming, no tantrum, no anything. In fact nothing was said by either of us as I lowered Andy to the ground. Words were pointless. Andy untied and wandered off. He finally returned about fifteen minutes later. He was absolutely devastated.

The next day he was on the plane back to England.

Yeah, another thirty-hour trip home. And another effing fail.

Back in Sheffield I worked out and trained with an intensity that I hadn't ever reached before. I totally rebuilt my board in the garage at Sandford Grove Road (admittedly it had burned down when someone left the electric bar fire on one night: fire engines, sirens, hosepipes and gawping neighbours – the works).

I trained for *Punks* like the proverbial man possessed. Work was appalling, but it simply *had* to happen if I was to get back to Oz. Weeks on end water pressure testing on the outside of the Broadgate development over Liverpool Street Station in London – in the sleet. Aiding around in shopping centre barrel vaults with Leachy again – who'd barely had a shift off work during my entire trip away – dusters in hand on twelve-hour nightshifts, hanging in slings, and taking any other access work going; all the time my driving motivation being the (amazingly still available) First Redpoint Ascent of *PITG* – in sunny Australia some twelve-thousand miles away.

Mark could now afford a chassis, engine and gearbox – even had all the body-work – and was only a couple of jobs off splashing out on his 'dream machine'.

ARRIVALS IN MELBOURNE AND SYDNEY – CHEESY AND CRIMINAL

Annoying at the time but pretty hilarious looking back.

I'd just landed at Melbourne Tullamarine Airport for my third time and joined the queues traipsing along the arrivals wings heading for customs. Every ten feet or so were posters asking whether anyone was carrying a concealed weapon – I patted myself up and down and ticked 'No' on the import card. Explosives? Err, pat, pat, nope, definitely no Semtex ... Cheese? Edible beans and pulses?

Cheese? What-the? 'No, I have definitely not brought any Dairylea cheese triangles or a block of Red Leicester into your country, officer ... Can I pass now please?'

Thing is, despite all the warnings, posters of foodstuffs with big red Xs across them, declaration forms and customs department sniffer-dogs running around, the old Mediterranean-looking couple ahead of me in the green 'Nothing to Declare' queue grunted and groaned when asked to open their suitcase. They heaved it off its trolley and on to the bench, where Mr Customs Man quizzed them one last time: 'Any guns? Dynamite?' Fair enough, then: 'Cheese?'

'We no speak Ingleesh,' quick as a flash. (Ha! They understood alright!)

True as I'm writing this now, their suitcase was crammed to bursting point ... with cheese, beans and pulses! All sorts, different colours, tightly wrapped and labelled – and they got asked to 'Come this way ... ' It was farcical and held me up for ages till I got waved through and went looking for the SkyBus to the city – with 200 grams of Brie they'd dropped stuffed down me right sock! Ha! No, not really ... would've been a pisser that though wouldn't it?

I'd sussed two trips ago that Australian airports and I didn't exactly click, having previously been escorted off my very first domestic flight by the AFP (Feds). Seems some poorly sighted, plain-clothed security dude back down in Melbourne had taken me for a 'master crim' – so he'd phoned ahead to Sydney where I was en route to visit Barn. Well, the Mascot rozzers went 'Ner-ner, Ner-ner' all the way on to the tarmac – passengers who could see from the portholes were totally bemused – then the cops stormed (OK, quietly strolled) down the aisle and stopped at me!

'First name middle name surname?'

'Err … yeah?' (Badge flash.)

'Accompany us, please!'

Marched right off that plane I was – in front of everyone – and I had absolutely no idea what I'd done wrong (other than putting in an extra dole claim back home before I left … Nah, couldn't be that).

Seriously, it was 'good cop/bad cop' when being grilled at the police station as to whom I *claimed* to be, and another few 'Err, you whats?' from me, then: 'It's climbing chalk, honest.'

In a nutshell it came down to a grainy faxed mugshot of a 'wanted man' and his rap sheet: he roughly resembled me – well, he was about my height. He (according to the police facsimile) ' … *displayed a particularly amused facial expression and had fair, albeit very receding, hair'.* I had – well not quite, but approaching – a younger Ben Moon's brown dreadlocks and a particularly grumpy scowl; so when I'd made my one allowed phone call it was to Barn asking him to come around to the cop shop, not to arrivals. To my enormous glee, when Barn was ushered into the interview room to verify my bona fides, he ' … *displayed a particularly amused facial expression and had fair, albeit very receding, hair'.*

'That's him – he's yer man!' I joked, but the 'Jacks' weren't laughing …

BACK TO WORK!

Day one back at Lake Toolondo, sun-baking in thirty-six degrees with Charlie Creese (NZ – a nationality shared with Roland Foster of the Pen Trwyn/Paul Williams belaying episode, and with the delightfully humorous Phil Bigg whose tent I'd dossed in at Stoney when the woodshed was full in 1981) and a few other chums – floating around in the clean, cool water – years before the ten-year drought hit us and it all dried up. My pores were positively shedding mounted-up London pollution and power-station grime as I drifted from shore on a borrowed Li-Lo, staring up at the bluest sky ever and getting torched by the sun: but why worry? I had a third tourist visa, my own car and caravan, and enough money for the next six months – not to mention all the motivation in the world, plus an Aussie girlfriend up in Sydney to boot. (I never kicked her, honest.)

Called me her 'Spunky Thing' she did.

'Me Spunky Thing'!

'As if!' I laughed.

Extremely attractive as well as smart, 'my' Lindy, and I could spot an anagram as easily as an all-out dyno …

A tall, fair lass and ever-so-thin, despite her predilection for constantly eating spicy Promite on crackers or Tandoori leftovers from the fridge – in bed – at three in the morning! It was awfully messy, but I'd snuggle up happy-as. Within a short time I was as fit as I'd ever been, climbing particularly well (those 'press-ups' in Sydney would've kept me fit), where I wanted to be – geographically and in *life*, and had three massive personal goals to achieve: that Arapiles climb and two other routes over in the Grampians. So, I decided to take a break from 'work' and focus on the latter two first.

(Not) funnily enough, as much as I desperately wanted *Punks* out of the way, I was seriously tiring of the whole climbing lifestyle and knew deep down in my heart and head that I was approaching the end of my career. Not ability – far from it – but **desire**. More so though that, with *Punks* out of the way – done and dusted – I would never, ever, have to put the shoes on again. Oh, if only I could just do that route and retire on a high.

See, I'd simply fallen out of love with climbing – but right at the pinnacle of my game at E8. On trajectory for E9 maybe? Australian grade 32 and French 8b+ when that was still generally acknowledged as about the hardest grade in the world.

So why the heck such awful timing?

Believe me, I **did** have questions for myself – many, and asked them. Some were no-brainers (like 'will I miss it?'), others deeply complex, but the final answer I gave myself each time was: 'I'm just over it!' and I knew I'd never let myself do anything half-arsed. Ever.

I found myself reminiscing about Mr Hurst and Mr Boorman at school in Prestatyn, and about leading that *Genesis* slab in my earlier childhood welly-boot playground of a scrappy quarry in Dyserth, with no protection till the very top, on a stiff, hawser-laid rope Mr Carr the RE teacher had given me. And the leader fall off a flippin' Forwyn VS 4c, and all the routes and experiences I've just shared with you. Heck, we're putting the lid on it all now and giving it a tight twist. Now, where's the dustbin?

Scorpios. What are we like eh? Or perhaps it was just me!

Oh, and **press ups** – Ron said he did hundreds at a time. Every day. What a 'stud' (assuming they were 'my' kind of press-ups) and no wonder he was always so flipping fit. ☺

So, the Grampians. A finer place I couldn't envisage – bar the Verdon – to kiss goodbye to my fourteen years of climbing rocks; better get my two projects done then top 'em off with *Punks* – that was the plan.

'So, And,' I tell myself, 'dig deep, apply yourself, the Gramps are now work sites too man!' So I did.

Malcolm's pride and joy *Serpentine* weaves an ahead-of-its-time and imaginative line to the right of a stunning turret, a turret that looks rather like an aircraft carrier tilted up and over vertically, with its take-off ramp leaning severely backwards right at the top, and to my eyes – especially looking straight back down – that turret stood out beyond all others.

Climbing the turret direct and reasonably quickly was a surprise (probably coz it was downgraded a few years later, d'oh!) but certainly another career highlight. Possibly my all-time favourite new route that one, but it had a tiny flaw in that there's a little kink in the middle where I did my old trick and side-stepped another stopper move … and it probably spoils the diagram in the topo! *Nati Dread* Mk2? Nathan? Come on young master Hoette, you're good enough … Get up there and straighten it out lad!

Honestly, that route just keeps on coming at you – move after move after move for the full forty-five metres as you arch ever outwards above the gum trees below. No single move to stop you, just sustained cranking on beautiful holds on perfect rock with spaced bolts low down, then all the protection you can throw into the upper half of *Serpentine*. Four stars on a three-star scale for sure. As is Malcolm's.

As the final twenty-five metres share the top of *Serpentine* I knew them well, and it's an amazing thing when you're absolutely unstoppable (rare that it is) and on form, at your very best and nothing can make you fall off. I didn't often experience that but when I did (other than *having* to on North Stack Wall) I'd be staring at a hold thirty feet above I knew I'd be hanging off moments later. At the top of my turret I did twelve free-hanging pull-ups before rocking over giggling with happiness – yet wishing Lindy was down from Sydney to share in the celebration. Or Jerry, Basher or Chris from back home.[1]

Shortly after *Rage* I returned to *Daniel Or-tiger* – my other nemesis and the second highest number again. This time all went well and, though pumped-as, I clipped the chains and lowered off. 'Out' really – you end up well off into the bush as it's alarmingly steep.

H had been working tirelessly for a year or more on an old aid line on the lower tier called *Gilgamesh* so, often as not, I'd be belay bunny for each attempt. I really felt for Malcolm there, as crossing the initial roof was simply too reachy for anyone of his stature. Big arms and immense core strength can often make up for lack of wingspan – H was savagely well-endowed with

---

1 First ascent, *Rage*, a harder variation on *Serpentine*, 7 March 1992. Originally given a similar grade to *Punks* but, 'I was a bit off, it's now settled down at flippin' 29!'

both of the former attributes – but these were little help in this particular case and he was forced to insert the most preposterous intermediate move into a sequence which I could just out-span.

Directly overhead from where I always stood when belaying Malcolm on *Gilgamesh,* ran a stunning and stupendously overhanging crack-come-groove called *Pegasus,* a Dave Mudie aid route from years ago. I abb'd and bolted it but couldn't find a sequence for the first fifteen feet so needed to stick-clip the first bolt, haul up on that point of aid and then pull on to the rock. The subsequent climbing started with a 'bang', had fifty feet of more bangs, and ended in an explosive leapy bang for the finish. It was pumpy brilliance – if somewhat shades of *The Whore* back home in the Peak. Similarly, and equally annoying, the locals refused to recognise my achievement and insisted the name *Pegasus* remained, but graded 31/M1 (1pt) in the new guidebook.[2]

Mean buggers! I figured it was one of the three hardest routes in the Gramps at the time, along with Scheel's *Daniel* and Malcolm's *Contra* – where's Ben Moon when you need him? He could've done another *Hubble* to my *Whore*! In fact, perhaps he still can? No one else has managed it yet … Ben? Anyone?[3]

I still thought of it as *Sheffield Steal.* I'd left a futuristic problem – just as I did that time back at Raven Tor in the late eighties … for someone better … it was that simple. I sometimes had a brief play on Malcolm's project *Gilgamesh*; I recall one day (from a hang at the start) getting all the way along the lip and making the hard moves into the open corner above (which Malcolm reckoned was only about 'medium') then promptly falling straight out of it. A valiant attempt, but as ever I was never going to pinch H's line, so left it 'in the bag' – awaiting his free ascent. Sadly, that day didn't come, so I was never to return. In 2008, years after H's attempts, the route was eventually freed by Ben Cossey at grade 32. Maybe it really wasn't that desperate for someone with my ape index … who knows? Sensational line though.

So, now that I'd done the best and the hardest I wanted to do in the Grampians, it was time for the *big,* 'big one' – it was back to the *regular* day job, the holiday being nearly over. *Punks* … this time surely? I mean crikey, I'm going well enough and have the darn thing totally wired don't I?

'But we're in the Gramps and I prefer it here with H,' I convince myself, yet again looking for any excuse to avoid that well-worn trudge over to Uncle

---

2 *Editor's note:* 31 is the free-climbing grade – pretty tricky, and M grades in Australia are 'Mechanical' grades i.e. aid climbing grades; thus *Pegasus* was climbed almost totally free by AP, with just one simple grade-1 'M' move to get started.

3 First ascent, *Sheffield Steal* grade 31 – or, failed to free *Pegasus* – depending on your point of aid … err … view!

Charlie's Pinnacle. Thankfully, and in a somewhat timely manner, my epic siege of *Punks* made it back through the local papers and all the way up to the TV execs down in Melbourne. Channel 9 (one of Australia's most popular TV channels – probably coz it's free!) twice approached me to film my 'next go' for *Wide World of Sports*. Now this programme was the Australian equivalent of Britain's *Grandstand* – mass-media telly (except the presenter wasn't busted doing cocaine with a hooker) – but I refused to go anywhere near *Punks* with a camera pointing my way and a director shouting, 'Cut! Now climb again please ... '

No way! I didn't want any more 'cuts' (damn ... wish I *had* filmed it though) so ended up barefoot-soloing *Pilot Error* ... *'One hundred metres above a ragged jagged earth ... and a certain ragged jagged death ... '* They then filmed me leading *Slinkin' Leopard*, playing on my speedball and yarding four times across the fantastic roof of *Savor the Flavor* and generally, err, cutting a bit of a dash. Next it was the ABC (Australian Broadcasting Corporation) for a repeat of my own *Nati Dread* – according to them *'Arapiles' most difficult climb!'* (Woo-Hoo!) And then an abject failure to get the drop-dead gorgeous presenter into my caravan for a ... cuppa. Thence followed more TV commitments including a slot with the French for Patrick's movie *Escalades sur un Monde Précieux*; plus various other bits and pieces – none of which ever went to air. Yes, any old excuse to avoid my 'work' ...

On many a rest day I'd throw a '7-course lunch' (that's a six-pack of 'piss' and a chocolate Cherry Ripe) into my Esky cool box and head off deep into the Southern Gramps to go exploring. Out there – well 'in' to be precise – I came across some amazing 40,000-plus-year-old Aboriginal rock art, miles off-track, generally on overhanging walls or tucked under caves or roofs, and it got me wondering whether the ochre hand prints and pointing fingers were primitive indicators of the hardest boulder problems of pre-white settlement and colonisation. Seriously, think about it; there's no doubt little cliffs would have had 'boulder problems' which surely the then Custodians of the Land would've challenged each other upon – to reach a bird's annual nesting spot or the tasty fruits of a blossoming plant or something? Perhaps thereafter simply for the fun and competition, for one-upmanship or social standing. Choice of women even?

Yes, I passed chunks of beautiful sandstone that today's bouldering community would die for (and have probably now discovered) and around every other corner gasped at unclimbed lines of staggering beauty.

Peter Croft had spotted an amazing face high up on the side of the Victoria Valley down south, a really fine crag that became known as Eureka Wall; but

Monksy beat us all to the routes. *Archimedes Principle* was the stand-out: akin to *Lord of the Flies* in North Wales 'cept on even better rock than Dinas Cromlech. I cannot conjure up in my head a finer climb ... out of all I did over there ... third ascent too.

But ... *Punks* was still waiting. Unredpointed. By *anyone* on the planet!

Then another bombshell – albeit it not an unpleasant one. A letter arrived for me at the Natimuk post office. It was from Jerry in Sheffield. He and Sean Myles would be arriving in a week's time, and could I please pick them up from the airport? Of course I would, and I immediately recalled Jerry jesting around a few weeks earlier during one of our numerous 'board meetings' at Sandford Grove Road with Nick Plishko and the two Bens – Moon and Masterson.

'Andy, do I have to come down there and show you how to do it or what?' says Jerry with his sideways chinny smile and a little wink.

I was clearly under the pump now.

Jerry would run up *Punks*, I knew that, and so did everyone else when news of his imminent arrival spread like a bushfire. Doubtless Sean would too, but how cool would it be I thought – and a dream come true – if Jerry held my ropes as I finally got it, I held his for the flash or second go whatever, then he belayed Sean. All on the same day. Now *that* would be something!

Impatiently throwing myself at it in greasy conditions and unrested I got absolutely bloody nowhere, so steeled myself and dutifully drove the nine-hour round trip to Melbourne to collect my friends. Neither Jez nor Sean had been to Australia before so I was making my best efforts to play Tour Guide:

'Arite lads, brilliant to see you, how was the flight?' and all the usual greetings.

'Done it yet, And?' pretty much in unison.

'Nah lads, pissin' me right off now,' and 'conditions are crap at the moment – way too humid.'

Returning via the Western Highway in 'Tiger', my '70s' Holden Kingswood (bench seats, column gearshift), and passing the Grampians beyond the parched paddocks over to our left, I asked: 'How's Mark going chasing that blessed Porsche, still working hard?'

'No, he finally got there and bought one Andy, over seventeen thousand quid, but it got repossessed and he can't get it back.'

'Yer kidding? But he did all the due diligence and DVLC checks and it came up clean as a whistle, he only needed another few hundred quid – he told me so in The Broadfield just before I left ... ' but then Jerry blurted out 'There's an ostrich!'

'They're emus, Jerry, emus.'

Sean shook his head and giggled.

'Yeah, and there's a giant hopping mouse doofus,' pointing out an eastern grey 'roo bounding across the highway just ahead of us, and the subject changed to climbing.

Criminally unjust (the law certainly *can* be an ass), as Mark had worked for almost three years non-stop for that motor car and I'd had three trips to Australia out of my earnings; but the vehicle he purchased ended up having a dodgy previous (previous, previous) owner who'd apparently defaulted on his finance, and it was towed away from out front of Mark's place one day when he wasn't there. I recall Mark years later recounting that the default amount was bugger-all and he was prepared to pay it just to get the car back with a clean bill of health, but things dragged on and it never happened. Mark threw even more money at the 'legal eagles' but it came to nought. However, possessing such a determined mindset (one that had served him proud on *The Screaming Dream, Mandela* (Kilnsey Main Overhang) and *Bat Route* amongst others) Mark simply said one evening: 'Right Andy, I'll become a lawyer and get the bloody law changed myself.'

Know what? He bloody well became a barrister. What a star!

Specialised in employment law he told me over the phone some years ago, and I'm not sure what he drives as I forgot to ask. Hey, I might have a case for him to look at – mine! Except it wouldn't be considered a 'social call' so I fear I'd detect that tick-tick-ticking of his 'charge-o-meter' in the background. 'Pro bono for an old mate,' mate?

Entering the outskirts of Horsham we got pulled over by highway patrol for a random check. One officer had us empty all our kit from the boot on to the side of the road and rummaged through positively *everything*, whilst the other rifled around inside the vehicle opening gloveboxes and checking under seats. 'We're rock climbers, what's this all about officer?' We certainly weren't drug runners, but lucky thing is, shortly prior to that incident, a 'local' I'd given a lift to had rung – got me at the pub I think – he was in a right old flap. He'd left a bag containing numerous 'quarters' of dope – labelled and price-tagged – 'stashed' beneath a length of old rope under the passenger side of my front bench seat, having unfathomably forgotten to grab his 'shit'' when he got out. I hadn't even known it was there!

'Shit' indeed! That was *close!* E9 or even E10 (maybe Oz grade 33) for an 'On-sight Trad-style Bust'? If that local's 'shit' had still been in my car it would've meant on-the-spot arrests, police cells overnight ('Can I have the padded one please?'), court in the morning, *immediate* visa cancellations and undoubtedly a swift deportation with no chance of a return to Australia for the three of us … **ever**! Just imagine – caught in possession of an undeniably

'commercial quantity' of marijuana – I shudder to this day at the thought …
then shiver once more at the closeness of that call! Now picture how cheery
that flight back to Blighty with Jerry and Sean would've been for *any* of us?
Particularly if I was 'stuck in the middle' yet a-fckn-gain! And *all that way*
between those two poor blighters?

Predictably, Jerry made the first redpoint ascent of *Punks in the Gym* about
second go, second day. Total time? Around three hours on it, tops! Rapt for
Jerry of course, but had inwardly hoped he'd have granted me just a few last
days – he had a whole month ahead of him after all, but he'd been raring to go
– a cool breeze had blown in so *of course* he had to go for it there and then.
I couldn't blame him in the slightest.

I tried again. Nope. Then Sean promptly fired it. Me? Cut tip and another
'excuse'. Then a blow-in Slovenian called Marko Lukic, who I'd never heard
of before, did it in a mere few days – and superbly by some accounts.
'Oh Spare Me, Please!'

Funny isn't it that once the 'first' of something's done the repeats just flow in?

I never got to witness any of those three ascents as I was either in the
Grampians or 'resting' in the White Hart Hotel in 'sham. It was beyond a joke
by this time – well, I felt I was anyway – as I hadn't actually struggled with any
of the moves or links, crux rock-over included, since early the previous year.
Mental approach maybe? So, questions, questions – but **no** answers. I mean,
physically it was a breeze by then, had been for some time, and I easily out-
reached the middle bits that others fell off, had all the stamina in the world
and could probably have run three *Punks* together in a single pitch by then,
were it not for *my head* and *that move* not getting their fucking acts together,
working *with me* – no more cuts – and parting on friendly terms.

My dozens of attempts always drew a crowd of onlookers – equally as eager
as myself for me to knock the darn thing over – they being the witnesses, but
I disappointed them every single time bar once. I was indeed most grateful
for their support and words (and calls) of encouragement, more so that many
still offered to lend a belay as and when required (they probably knew darn well
we'd be back in my 'van in twenty minutes sculling longnecks from the fridge!).

'Hmm' perhaps it's my balance? I'm not eating, maybe light-headedness?
Have another Cherry Ripe. I mean, I get stuck in on *Punks* a few times a day,
do *really* well then stupidly fall off, return to the 'van, 'get stuck in', do *exceedingly*
well and comically fall over!

Know what? If I'd been climbing 1980s' 'Arapiles-style' then my multiple
efforts virtually equated to doing the third right through to the twenty-ninth
ascents! *And* with a certain hold going from good, to poor, to crap, to 'damn

you,' to good again; but I'd wanted that *First Redpoint* and anything less was Xth best.

Jokes aside, girlfriend Lindy from Sydney had come down to Araps to visit and to offer her moral support. She got on famously with Jerry as she had visited me back home in Sheffield over the winter – I'd taken a break from rope access work and had introduced them – but now she was leaving for her long thirteen-hour drive home. Both Jerry and Sean had pretty much 'ticked' Australia and fancied checking out the Opera House, Harbour Bridge and maybe having a night out at the fabled Kings Cross before flying off – missions duly accomplished.

I stood there glumly where the dirt of the camping ground met the bitumen, waving her and my mates off mouthing, 'Goodbye, safe journey, I love you,' (she wouldn't have heard me) as they turned left out of the campsite with a toot-toot of the car horn and Jerry's fist punching the air through the open window as he whooped with joy, 'See ya, And!'

Jerry still recalls our days on *Punks* vividly. By email, May 2015:

> It was so tough seeing Andy repeatedly blowing it at the crux. You could see he was way better and stronger than the route. It looked to me like he had got so used to falling off at the same point (up high on the Sika hold) that his body was almost programmed into doing just that … Andy perhaps started redpointing a little too early in not such great conditions; it was now just clearly a mental battle that he alone had to conquer. For myself I rarely started to redpoint a route until I was sure I was gonna get it. I did nearly all my hardest redpoints first go.

I had never felt more dejected or alone in my life. I just stood there, tears welling then running down my cheeks, until the car was merely a speck on the watery horizon and then finally disappeared from sight.

I was utterly demoralised. My dearest old friend from years ago on *Mayfair* at Pen Trwyn, in the Avon Gorge and the Tremadog barn when we were kids and encountered 'Big Ron' Fawcett and Pete Livesey; my mate who I'd shared a shelf with many times one bitter, bitter winter in the Stoney Middleton woodshed (when he pretty much **lived** there), and our first house at no. 84, plus a million other memories – never a bad one, ever – but he truly had 'shown me how' to do *Punks in the Gym* and had just departed, in *my* seat with *my* girlfriend and *my* two-year, 'First Redpoint' prize.

Horrible day that.

Not wanting to face, speak to, or deal with any other climbers in that state of mind, I drove into Nati to see 'Mum' Marion Delaney at the milk bar. Coffees, cigs, lunch and the best company. I stayed a few hours with her and Cec in the kitchen as they took turns to serve in the store each time the door buzzer buzzed. Cec had allowed me free access to his personal cans of Fosters in the cool room (which was an honour and of course I'd always replace what I drank, plus some) and we punched a fair few in as the sun dipped beyond the horizon and the temperature plummeted to a mere twenty-eight degrees. I felt morose and was probably lousy company, so gave my thanks, declined the usual offer of dinner and the spare room, and drunk-drove back to my caravan in The Gums. My own fridge was well stocked with longnecks of Geoff Little's super-strong homebrew – his 'Little Soldiers' he maniacally called them – so I waded in and skulled two in quick succession, hoping I'd write myself off and get a good night's sleep.

Tomorrow I'll do better – that's what I promised myself (for the umpteenth time) whilst sitting in my stifling caravan with the door closed, listening to Pavlov's Dog and World Party tapes on Simey's old cassette player, doodling on a sketch pad and dwelling on my predicament for the thousandth time, wondering how 'she' and the lads were. Happy-as and having a ball of a road trip no doubt. Be nearing the big city by now I thought. I was all out of ideas. 'What else can I do?' Reaching into the fridge for yet another, my hand dead-set stopped in that 'grab a beer by the throat' position ... the answer hit me ... right between the eyes:

Try it clean and sober Andy!

Well! There's a novel thought – as my hand hovered before my battalion.

'OK, bugger it!' I'll limit myself to just two more, but I can't stay here knowing there's reinforcements backing them up in the fridge. So I threw my swag on to the back seat of the car, seconded two 'corporals', and even more drunkenly drove up the back of The Mount to doss in the scrub at the start of the little nature trail opposite the head of Central Gully. Not the best night. Noisy critters rustling around, plus I'm shit-scared of spiders and was in a dreadful mood. Wished I'd brought four beers too – and that Lindy was still around.

In the wee (pee, whatever) small hours, after downing the second beer and dimping out my fag, I passed out. I woke with a bad head and plenty of bites and scratches, so cleared my site and returned to the caravan for coffees and to see who was around. Robbie LeBreton and a few of his mates were down for a break from Nowra and the Blue Mountains, and Rob was keen to see what all the fuss was about for himself. He had a brief play on *Punks* and I warmed up with my normal all-out attempt. Usual result. Honestly! I could do this thing in my sleep – just never when I was awake.

After twenty minutes rest I said, 'Here we go again,' and Robbie, quite force-fully, replied, 'Come on Andy, nail it!' Seriously encouraging and somehow really striking a chord, these were the last words I can recall for about the eighteen minutes it took for everything to fall perfectly into place. I pulled on to the belay ledge and clipped into Wolfgang's old sun-scorched tat, then lowered off to applause and cheers from the onlookers who'd always gather back then. I left my quickdraws in for Rob – I wouldn't be needing *them* again!

I wasn't even remotely pumped.

Sincerely thanking Robbie, wishing him well on his 'mission' and giving the assembled throng the thumbs up, I returned to my caravan and closed the door behind me.

Sixth Ascent. Fourth Redpoint. I'll settle for that thanks; and I finally got to write it up in the little notebook that Mr Boorman suggested I start 'way, way back in 1978'. And then, for the last time ever, I closed that book ...

Diary entry: 5 May 1992

Today I finally did *Punks* and retired from climbing.

A couple of celebratory (well, more in relief than celebration actually) beers later, all my climbing gear was tossed out on to the dirt: ropes, shoes, hard-ware, the lot – much still unwrapped c/- of my sponsors – and either sold, given away or chucked in the wheelie bin.

Dave Mudie recalls that day with absolute clarity:

> There is something about the way a top climber moves that makes it a joy to watch. The sheer economy, the power and dynamism. As I watched Andy I went back to thinking about the success of the Sika I'd supplied him with, and reminded myself to let him know how pleased I was that it had worked so well. Days of sun, sweat and curses with *Punks* having dominated every second thought for some of us. Andy finally made the move, stretched fully and held the slippery round ...

Dave's commentary continues later that same afternoon [tossing Andy another beer] ...

> ... and laying back into the recliner beneath the old peppercorn I com-mented that the Sika epoxy had done a brilliant job of repairing the delam-ination of Jerry's skateboard as well.

POSTSCRIPT

That Sika hold became somewhat mockingly referred to as The Birdbath, and has become possibly the most controversial, and yet iconic, finger-hold in Australian climbing history. Who coined the phrase I neither know nor care, yet even a quarter of a century later I believe there still exists a degree of unease with some in the climbing community that perhaps Wolfgang's masterpiece was defiled by my actions …

You'll maybe recall that I met an American climber known as CJ at the Easter 2015 Goatfest – he'd been having a real tussle with *Punks*, and that very morning had sheared off part of The Birdbath hold I'd built up some twenty-four years earlier (though he added it had actually been broken and repaired once or twice before). Frustrated as I felt for the guy, I simply **had** to ask: 'and what did you find left underneath it?'

I gathered from CJ's response that there was nothing useable, just a gravelly sloper … He'd obtained some epoxy and hoped to get to stick it back on either that evening or more likely the next morning – I wished him good luck. Yes, I was gutted for the fella, but – inside, kept to myself – felt a degree of vindication because when I first happened upon that *Chockstone* forum of Australia's *UKC*-type interactive website there was a debate raging as to whether my Sika hold ought to be chopped or not. The primary instigator of said action didn't garner sufficient support, and there were humorous replies from others mentioning lynch mobs and baying crowds with placards and pitchforks assembling at the campsite, ready to attack the Defenders of the Glue. I assume the site moderators had toned down many of the published words, but there were likely a few angry PMs exchanged between the warring factions before the thread was closed and locked shut.

Well, by way of a belated reply, I can only clarify and reiterate … when my foot snapped the whole top off that – originally chipped don't forget – crux hold on my 'whatevereth' day, the route immediately became a whole new proposition, and for a further thirty-odd days I persevered whilst the 'hold', or what was left of it, diminished by degrees every few attempts.

Consider this: there were others who were 'working' the route off and on too, plus those darned 'sticky-beaks' who'd ab down it, play around (greasing up all the holds) then often as not leave my 'biners facing the wrong way for the clip. They were all stolen once too, which was most upsetting (mainly as I was forced to trudge *all that way* back to my caravan to grab a fresh set). I wished they wouldn't do that, and fretted every time I saw a 'new' rope hanging down the route. Dozens of people saw that catastrophe of a hold – before, during **and** after – and I was even back in Britain for five months having applied the Sika, so I most certainly wasn't hiding anything from anyone who cared to have a look, or a go, themselves. I couldn't understand the sceptics who refused to believe that the hold had broken, and reckoned it was still there underneath the epoxy. But fuck me, readers! Did those contributors to the old *Chockstone* blog seriously think I'd spend a further **twenty-eight days** trying something just for the fun of it? It wasn't any fun at all. Not one day, believe me now please, even if you didn't back then! If not … well, those ill-informed sceptics can just … well … just … !

I posed this old chestnut of a dilemma to Charlie Creese in May 2015, seeking (I suppose) some warm, cuddly and supportive retro-feedback. His reply, word for word, was this:

> I was thinking … If you write about rebuilding that hold on *Punks*, you should say, yes, of course you've got regrets. I mean, even though it's now visible from The International Space Station, we still have a situation where only two Victorians have managed to do the route in 30 years. So, yes, ahem, I guess you'd have to say to your younger self, do the job properly and put a fucking ledge there, and see if the poor fuckers can do any better!!! *Sent from my iPhone*

My response: 'Harsh, cruel, cunning, cutting, funny-ha-ha!' Honestly, what did I expect from Creese? But, in his own way, I presumed he was being pretty supportive. [Yep, reckon so! *Ed.*]

For better or worse *Punks in the Gym* as we know it *exists*, and has done since 1991 when I Sika'd it back together. For the most part it stands as testament to Wolfgang's world-class talent and its true first re-ascent belongs to Jerry. I think that's fitting – he and Wolfgang were extremely close friends and neither had a hand in any of the route's 'making'.

They just stepped in, tidied up the mess of others, and yet again proved their supremacy.

Me Spunky Thing (anag.). Work it out? Not hard, odd perhaps, but I was pissed-off-bored, missing Lindy, and used to play at making anagrams in my caravan by candlelight back then.

So, goodbye and thanks for sticking with me, here are my parting thoughts on the last route I ever did …

The rock will outlive that Sika by millennia, so it only remains to be seen what happens when it too – inevitably – crumbles into dust.

AFTERWORD:
TRIVIAL PURSUIT
by
LOUISE SHEPHERD

It's summer in the Wimmera.

The fields of wheat stubble are bleached to straw.

At Arapiles, eucalyptus leaves are slowly swivelling on their stems under the relentless sun.

In the middle of a dust bowl is Andy Pollitt's caravan, his old Holden parked next to it. On the little table inside are the breakfast remnants: an ashtray overflowing with cigarette butts and some stubbies. Andy's philosophy is that you can eat or you can drink but you can't do both. Food was the big loser.

It's 1992. This was a time when climbers sent postcards back home; they didn't send routes. There was no such thing as working a route. The term had not been invented.

Andy's battle with *Punks* however, seemed like work. By late summer he had surpassed the Roman siege at Masada. *Punks* was becoming as much a grind as a foot soldier building a giant ramp in the Judaean desert.

Andy looked forward to his downtime with the same anticipation of every wage slave. One of his favourite pastimes was an evening of Trivial Pursuit out the back of the Delaneys' milk bar in Natimuk.

Marion and Cec Delaney and their four kids had played the game so many times they knew half the answers. Andy and a few of the local climbers would be roped in to make up the teams. A closely contested game got more adrenalin flowing than rock climbing.

'Which letter is on the Rwandan flag?'

'It's K,' said Marion with an air of certainty, 'Africans are crazy about K.'

Nobody argued with Mrs D.

'Wrong – it's R! We won!' The table erupted, the last dregs of beer were downed, the last lungful of ciggie smoke exhaled. Andy drove back out to The Mount, ready for another day at work.

2015. In Natimuk, the milk bar is still there but the Delaneys have long gone. Cec died of lung cancer more than a decade ago. The kids grew up and left home, and Marion moved away.

The campground at Arapiles hasn't changed a lot in the last thirty years. The vegetation has thinned, a legacy of thirteen years drought from the mid-nineties to 2009. Half the pine trees in the Pines campground have died from old age and soil compaction.

But one area that has thrived is the copse of native pines, hop bush and eucalypts on your right before you get to the Plaque area. Sometimes you see a goanna wandering through there. Fenced off and replanted decades ago, it has regenerated so well it's hard to remember that it used to be the dust bowl where Andy's caravan was once parked.

Louise Shepherd, May 2015

ACKNOWLEDGEMENTS

So, there we have it – a record of 'Andy P the climber' (well some parts anyway) during those memorable latter years of the twentieth century ... and now I've popped my head above the parapet one last time to share some bits of my life *these days*, and shake it yet again – inwardly tut-tutting, as you (two?) may well be too.

I guess you twigged early on – when I confessed to still wetting the bed in my mid-forties – that this wasn't going to be any old 'ordinary' climbing book?

I owe thanks I can't even begin to convey, to many old friends and incredible people ... hope they enjoy this read once the copies pop out of the big, whirring, crunching machine ...

So, from a not-so-small and skinny little kid anymore, thanks are due to that school in North Wales – the one with a climbing wall and **decent** teachers; and to my early climbing partners; to my mates and landlord Alfie at no. 84 (**the** Sheffield climbing household of all time); to Mr Khan and the lads at Sandford Grove Road; and especially to Yorick's surgeon – even though I never paid the bill! Yep, all brilliant and unbeatable days ...

I'm grateful for the lucky escape in Ambleside when friends shared their 'gear' and put me off hard drugs for life, and I also owe much to my myriad different belayers on *Punks in the Gym*. I was lucky to spend thirteen years travelling Britain, Europe and later Australia, climbing some of the world's best bits of rock – so thanks to my sponsors who paid me to do it – what a gig!

I'm privileged to have helped raise a delightful little boy, and to have a constitution that has coped with stressing constantly for my construction sites, then stressing some more – fearful that I'd over-stressed some anchor stress points. Yep, a middle-aged man now, reflecting upon, and missing, my 'glorious youth' – particularly those friendships, the first ascents (and the fairground excesses) – who wouldn't?

Punk in the Gym was a seed sown out of the blue by Jerry; he had me scribbling for a week or two but my efforts soon got set aside when work, life – everything really – simply overwhelmed me, despite much encouragement from local historian, wit and mate Tony Kelleher. But, in the depths of my tribulations, Andy Boorman and Pete Bailey relit the 'touch paper' during their visit to Australia (before they bleedin' well scarpered back to Blighty). Hodder and Stoughton and Penguin, Mills and Boon (anyone?), and even Geoff Birtles as a come-back publisher – they all knocked me back ... Andy Who?

Expecting more of the same I emailed a couple of thousand words to Vertebrate and – in due, due, due course – received a positive, encouraging and delightful reply (paraphrased) 'Errrr, anything better Andy? That's not a book!' Well, it wasn't an outright rejection ... so later it was, 'Oh, that's much better ... ' and – after further drafts and much assistance from Andy B – I said (in best Crocodile Dundee voice), 'That's not a book? **this** is a book!' ... and it was 'Please sign here'. And they've been here (and there) for me ever since.

Pete and Denise Bailey have been ever supportive – as have my talented siblings Dave, Sarah and Lizzie. Mum Pam wished me well when I started this project, she wasn't quite sure who I was by chapter three, and had departed this earth by part two – a terrible thing is dementia! Thanks dearest Mum for your brilliant support and wisdom ... 'You don't swear like that boy do you Andrew?'

My father Derek? I never really got to know him as he'd been '**ex-term-in-a-ted**' by a Dalek or something when I was at primary school remember, though there were brief moments of sort-of-intimacy later ... I knew little of his many achievements ... didn't realise that as well as TV work he'd toured in innumerable live theatre productions, done lots of radio and appeared in a few films – for virtually thirty-five years non-stop before taking a well-earned breather, and I guess he's due thanks for playing a part in steering my sisters into careers in theatre and TV. Sarah produced TV commercials with the likes of Rowan 'Mr Bean' Atkinson and Lizzie was confidant and personal dresser to famous stars including Vanessa Redgrave and Elaine Paige, and got to mingle with many others such as the late Michael Jackson. Before he finished his stay in this world our father's breather from work was anything but a rest – a train to Scotland's John o'Groats where the land runs out and all signs point back south. On 6 May 1990 he set off on foot with his haversack – and plenty of faith and hope – to do a huge walk for charity (I've just realised this was the same date that I figured out a new sequence of delicate foot changes on *Punks* – my sixteenth 'day' on the route!). The trip from north to south took him a fair while longer than most, as he'd planned a zigzag route to take in seven different long distance walks: The Speyside, West Highland, Southern Uplands and Pennine Ways, Offa's Dyke Path, The Cotswold Way and finally The South West Coast Path ... my sister Sarah met him in the car park on July 28th for the final hundred yards or so to Land's End – for which she graciously suggested she trail five minutes behind. Allow him his 'moment'. So thoughtful that! So yes indeed, thanks for the genes and the siblings Derek, and flippin' well done sir!

As for Andy B – *and* wife Ann – *and* son Ian (who I now share hurried coffees with whenever our Thursdays coincide) – well, how long have you got? Mr Boorman, eh? My schoolmaster when I was fourteen. Mentor, guide – not just to the crags but to life itself back then, and dear friend always! Climbing in his blood – from the Alps at something-teen right up to E5 trad in his prime, and still the occasional F7 sport at sixty-something. A happy cragger is Andy B … and as for being my editor, he's not only done a miraculous job tidying up my words and making sense of them all, but has saved my (and likely many other people's) embarrassment on numerous occasions – not to mention catching some potentially nasty falls … caught my first at Forwyn in '79 and I'm grateful he's still 'watching me' as attentively as ever. He also inspired me when writer's block visited like that foot-and-mouth back in Dyserth, and his gentle prodding from across the ocean caused me to 'burn' a few of my recent ramblings.

Early in this project I invited a select few 'old friends', climbing 'adversaries', contemporaries and peers to pen the odd contribution (one certainly was 'odd' – and unprintable). I shan't do a roll call, but heartfelt thanks to all who so willingly – and cleverly – put pens to paper and fingertips to keyboards … thanks for having the courage to contribute coz, as an old friend pointed out, 'Many people have moved on and lead totally different lives these days Andy … '

Fair enough – it *has been* thirty years! '*Has-been*'? Better that than '*never was*' as the old saying goes!

Special 'thanks' are due to Mike Owen for the foreword; to John Redhead for his 'cheeky' thoughts and that awesome painting *A Touch Too Much*; to Alan James for the use of his masterful Pokketz caricature *Shin-Aid*; and to Louise Shepherd – what a beautifully written sign-off!

Thanks as well Bernard Newman for your kind words and that photo of me – the one that made the cover of *Peak Rock*, and cheers to Phil Kelly and Graham Hoey for picking it, and for a super book! I was thrilled when Graeme Alderson brought over a copy (especially as it had written inside well wishes from literally dozens of climbers – heck, thanks all for those). He also delivered two celebratory bottles of beer … and guess what? I was on the label … yes, a beer label – that's got to be the icing on *my* cake!

Thanks are due to all 'my' construction firms and the fantastic people who also constantly strive for the best; thanks to the architects and engineering companies – past and present – for putting up with me, my irregular hours and sometimes scruffy and unconventional appearance. A particular debt of gratitude is owed to Cole Pritchard, my godsend of a site foreman, without whom none of my 'access systems' bedlam could happen – and we *do* have the most elevated fall arrest anchors in Melbourne – atop the damper tanks around Level 90 of the Eureka Tower – happy with that …

Were it not for my 'nowadays-bestie' Kenn Kelso – not a rock climber, but a proud Mancunian and union man who expertly 'dogged' many a crane lift (including some of those wavey roof panels on to Southern Cross Station here in Melbourne) – I'd likely have gone mad years ago! Yeah … thanks Kenn! We're the local 'odd couple' – coz I'm a 'boss' so therefore 'a twat' by default, but Kenn's humour is infectious – everyone round here agrees; he also has humility and empathy, so constantly reminds me to … 'Stop being weak as piss!' God love 'im!

Oh, and Heather. And Bert of course. Where would I be without friends like these? **Dead** probably! That's where.

I'll now fold up the writing board, having placed my neat, final submission into one of the drawers. Click! There we go, *The Pollitt Bureau* – they've changed the title I know – is firmly locked away, it's in the hands of Vertebrate now and, courtesy of many, we have the photos to prove that *it all really did happen*! Thanks photographers.

So, here's my book. I'd like to think that 'me Dad' Paul Williams would've been proud of this 'first tick' – it took over 600 more 'days' to write than it did to climb *Punks in the Gym* and, unlike all my other ticks, this one will never, ever, be repeated.

Cheers,

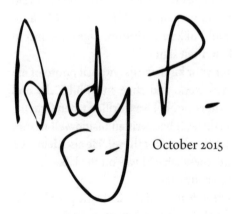

October 2015

PHOTOS and ILLUSTRATIONS

PLATE 1

1 *The Bells, The Bells!*, North Stack Wall, Gogarth. Second ascent, on sight. **Photo:** Bernard Newman.
2 *Masters of the Universe*, Burbage South. First ascent. **Photo:** Neil Foster.
3 *Castellan*, High Tor. **Photo:** Bernard Newman.
4 *Café Libre*, Lower Pen Trwyn. **Photo:** Bernard Newman.
5 *Strawberries*, Tremadog. **Photo:** Glenn Robbins.
6 *Knockin' on Heaven's Door*, Curbar. **Photo:** Richie Brooks.
7 *Manic Strain*, Vivian Quarry. Second ascent.

PLATE 2

8 *Tales of Yankee Power*, High Tor. At the thread Codling grabbed, back when High Tor overhung (ahem, Bernard!). **Photo:** Bernard Newman.
9 *Great Wall*, Craig y Forwyn. Solo. **Photo:** Keith Simpson.
10 Cwm church Sunday school. Back row (L–R): Simon Williams, Bro Dave, Martin Baxter, Peter Williams. Front (L–R): Justin Smart (orphaned shortly after, fairground and lift to Sheff etc.), Joanna Baxter, me.
11 In the *Vector* cave, Tremadog. **Photo:** Jerry Moffatt.
12 La Palud campsite, Verdon Gorge, April 1982. Standing (L–R): Mick Lovatt, Dennis Gleason, me, Andy Boorman, Dave Hollows. Sitting (L–R): John Monks, Mick Quinn, Joe Healey, Gaz Healey. **Photo:** Pete Bailey (who's fed up he's not in it!).
13 *The Cad*, North Stack Wall, Gogarth. **Photo:** Andrew Brazier.
14 *Positron*, Main Cliff, Gogarth. **Photo:** Alan Hinkes.
15 *Wall of the Evening Light*, The Diamond, Llandudno. First free ascent. **Photo:** Bernard Newman.
16 *Surveiller et Punir*, Verdon Gorge, with Georges Perrot. **Photo:** John Kirk.
17 *The Tights, The Tights!* With Chris Gore in the famous (infamous?) Berghaus 'Red Point' advert.

PLATE 3

18 *A Touch Too Much*. **Illustration:** John Redhead.
19 The *Shin-Aid* Pokketz cartoon from *On The Edge* 28, February 1992. Featuring me, Geoff Birtles (then editor of *High* magazine) and Jim Curran (who had recently appeared in *High* with a semi-naked woman on his lap). It also features Sinead O'Connor and Johnny Dawes. **Illustration:** Alan James.
20 *Skinhead Moonstomp*, Main Cliff, Gogarth. Reclimbed for photos. I found that wire by my waist that Joe told me about – it fell out too! **Photo:** Glenn Robbins.
21 *The Spider*, Chee Dale. **Photo:** Neil Foster.
22 *Thormen's Moth*, Thor's Cave, Derbyshire. Yorick belaying. **Photo:** Phil Swainson.
23 *Serpentine*, Taipan Wall, Grampians. Third ascent. **Photo:** Simon Carter.
24 *World Party*, Taipan Wall, Grampians. First ascent. **Photo:** Glenn Robbins.
25 *Archimedes Principle*, Eureka Wall, Grampians. Third ascent. **Photo:** Glenn Robbins.

PLATE 4

26 *Rage*, Taipan Wall, Grampians. First ascent. **Photo:** Glenn Robbins.
27 Between Arapiles and Natimuk. **Photo:** Naomi Guy.
28 This poor fella fell out of a tree right in front of me on the walk in to Taipan and landed on his nose. I picked him up, patted him down and put him in a tree. Gorgeous! **Photo:** Tim Freeman.
29 Beneath the nightly boulders, Arapiles. **Photo:** Glenn Robbins.
30 Doing the dishes outside my caravan at Arapiles. **Photo:** Simon Barnaby.
31 *Nati Dread*, Castle Crag, Arapiles. First ascent. **Photo:** Simon Carter.
32 Me and 'Mum' Marion Delaney in 2015. **Photo:** Glenn Tempest.
33 With Shadow and my slot machines.
34 Me and Pete Bailey at Camel's Hump, Melbourne, in 2011. **Photo:** Andy Boorman.
35 With Andy Boorman in Melbourne, 2011. **Photo:** Ian Boorman.
36 *Punks in the Gym*, Arapiles. There it is, the three-finger gravelly sloper with the left side gone. **Photo:** Glenn Robbins.

Punk in the gym

"WHILE SORTING SLIDES FOR ANDY'S BOOK, I AM REMIND
TOGETHER; OF OUR PERILOUS PURSUITS IN BREATHTAKIN
QUARRIES TO THE MOST REMOTE SEA CLIFF ZAWN. THE IM
★ GLENN ROBBINS ★

"ANDY'S NIGHTS OUT AND CONSUMPTION OF ALE AND CIGGI
CLIMBING; STRONG FINGERS, PRECISE FOOTWORK AND FLUI
WITH A LOVE FOR NEW ROUTEING." ★ CHRIS GORE

"ANDY HAS PROFOUND KNOWLEDGE OF THIS 'PASSAGE', TH
INTENSE MOMENTS OF RAIDING HIS PSYCHE FOR CLUES, WI
I KNOW, I REALLY KNOW THE CHEEKY FUCK IS ALL THE MOR
THAN THE ENGINEER OF DEALING TOWER CRANES, SKYSCRA
CHEEKY FUCK, AND WITHOUT AWE WE ALL LACK HUMILITY

"THE THING I REMEMBER MOST ABOUT MEETING YOU WAY B
STAR' BUT ALSO THAT YOU LOOKED LIKE THAT OTHER BRITISI
TOO I THOUGHT – HARD DRINKING, SMOKING AND PARTYING.
IF YOU WILL." ★ MALCOLM 'HB' MATHESON

"ANDY WAS MORE THAN JUST PHOTO FODDER, HE WAS A MA
HE WAS ALSO ONE OF THE FINEST CLIMBERS OF HIS GENE
SHUNS POSED SHOTS; I LOOK FOR NATURAL BODY SHAPES
ARTIFICIAL AESTHETIC, SO I'D TELL PEOPLE JUST TO CLIMB
ANDY, HOWEVER, NEEDED NO PROMPTING – HE MOVEI
PHOTOGRAPHERS." ★ BERNARD NEWMAN ★

"I WAS TRULY LIVING THE DREAM ... AND HOW LUCKY TO B
ALONE FROM STONEY? ALL MY CLIMBING HEROES WERE THE
WALL BACK IN KINGSTON. I HAD TO PINCH MYSELF TO REA
ANDY POLLITT, TOP BRITISH CLIMBER AND BEST FRIEND TO

"AT SEVENTEEN YEARS OLD WE ARRIVED AT THE SUN-BLE
POLLITT STRUMMING HIS GUITAR FROM UNDER A WILLOV
MOFFATT'S VOICE FILLING THE CAMPGROUND. WE HAD ARR
DOPE PAINTED THE SCENE. THE BIG BOYS WERE THERE, MA
WE HUNG AROUND LIKE FLIES BUT SOMETHING OF THEM SE
AND FOR LONGER." ★ STEVE MCCLURE ★

"GREAT MEMORIES OF THOSE EARLY DAYS DOWN AT TREMA
OF WHICH WERE MEGA FOR SURE), BUT THE CHARACTERS A
IN ERIC'S BARN, YOU AND JERRY. I KNOW IT'S HARD TO BEL

"ANDY, DO I HAVE TO COME DOWN THERE AND SHOW YOU H